Barbara Van Tuyl

THE
HORSEMAN'S
BOOK

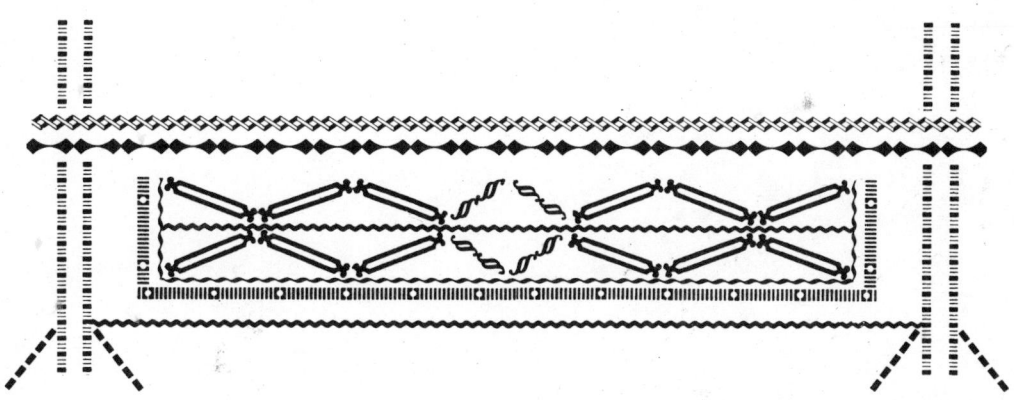

PRENTICE-HALL, INC. ⟞⟞ *Englewood Cliffs, New Jersey*

Prentice-Hall International, Inc., London
Prentice-Hall of Australia, Pty. Ltd., North Sydney
Prentice-Hall of Canada, Ltd., Toronto
Prentice-Hall of India Private Ltd., New Delhi
Prentice-Hall of Japan, Inc., Tokyo
10 9 8 7 6 5 4 3 2 1

Library of Congress Cataloging in Publication Data
Van Tuyl, Barbara.
  The horseman's book.
  1. Horses—Terminology. 2. Horsemanship—Termi-
nology. I. Title.
SF278.V33   798′.2′014   73–9739
ISBN 0–13–394734–3

*This book is for my Mother
with love*

ACKNOWLEDGMENTS

The list of persons and organizations who helped in the preparation of this book appears to be endless, and while I am extremely grateful to them all, I would particularly like to thank the following:

The American Horse Shows Association. Inc., for permission to quote from the A.H.S.A. Rule Book; Mr. Gilmore R. Flautt III, M. F. H.; Mr. Charles E. Herron; Mr. Robert Kelly; Mrs. Joseph Longo; The Maryland Horse; Mr. Ramon A. Molony; Mr. and Mrs. Christopher T. Neale; Mrs. W. D. Osborne; Mrs. Margaret Teller Riggs; The United States Trotting Association; Mr. Theodore F. Wahl; Mr. Alexis Wrangel; Dr. William A. Heffner.

CONTENTS

THOROUGHBRED RACING

ACEY DEUCEY   A riding style wherein the jockey keeps his left (or inside) stirrup longer than the outside (or right) stirrup.

ACROSS THE BOARD   When a horse is bet *across the board*, it means that he is backed to win, place, and show. *Across the board* or combination tickets are valid if a horse finishes first, second, or third.

ADDED MONEY   Money added by the racing association to the amount of money already paid by the owners for nomination, eligibility, and starting fees.

AIRING   When a horse is showing his best speed in a race.

ALL OUT   When a horse has extended himself to the fullest in a race.

ALLOWANCE RACE   A type of race in which the amount of weight carried is determined by the amount of money and/or the number of races which the horse has won over a given period.

ALLOWANCES   Weights and other conditions of a race are called allowances. *See also* CONDITIONS.

ALSO ELIGIBLE   Horses which have been entered in a race but will run only if there are scratches (entrant cancellations) reducing the field below a specified number.

ALSO-RAN   A horse that finishes out of the money in a race—that is, not among the first three on which parimutual betting money is wagered.

APPRENTICE   A novice jockey who receives a weight concession. The amount of weight allowed varies from state to state, but the usual apprentice allowance is five pounds. Therefore, a horse that was assigned 110 pounds would only be required to carry 105 if ridden by an apprentice. *See also* BUG.

ASTERISK (*)   1. When placed before a horse's name (*Royal Vale), it indicates that the horse was imported to the United States.
2. When placed beside the name of a jockey or the assigned weight a horse is to carry in the official program, it indicates an apprentice rider and that the apprentice allowance has been included.

BACK STRETCH The straightaway section of the race track located on the far side between the turns. This term may also refer to the stable area.

BAD ACTOR An unruly or badly behaved horse.

BAD DOER A horse that does not eat well and consequently is difficult to keep in condition.

BARRED *See* RULED OFF.

BARRIER The starting gate or device used to start races is sometimes called the barrier.

BAT *See* WHIP.

BEARING IN or OUT Leaving the straight path and drifting either toward the inside or outside rail. This practice is regarded as a rather bad habit, because in so doing the horse loses ground and risks the possibility of fouling another horse. Also called LUGGING.

BILL DALY, ON THE A horse that breaks and runs his race in front, setting the pace from start to finish is said to be "on the Bill Daly." In this expression reference is made to old-time trainer "Father" Bill Daly, who frequently ordered his jockeys to ride according to this plan.

BLANKET FINISH A finish of a race in which the horses are closely bunched together, with only heads or noses of separation, so that a blanket would cover them.

BLEEDER A horse that suffers a nasal hemorrhage during or after a race or workout as a result of a ruptured vein in the throat. Horses which become chronic bleeders (bleeding two or more times in a single racing season) are prohibited from any further racing that year.

BLIND SWITCH (POCKET) When during the course of a race a horse is trapped behind and between other horses so as to make it impossible for him to improve his position or get clear of the pack.

BLINKERS A common piece of racing equipment consisting of a hood with complete or partial eyecups (depending upon the reason for which they are being used), designed to limit the horse's vision to the side and/or rear in one or both eyes and prevent him from shying from other horses or objects. Blinkers were once referred to as the "Rogue's Badge." Their use or discontinuence must be approved by the stewards, and a change of such equipment must be entered on the official program or announced prior to a race.

BLOW OUT   A fast workout over a short distance (three to four furlongs), which is generally used to sharpen a horse a day or two before a race.

BOLT   A sudden swerving from a straight course, usually in the direction of the outside rail. If he finishes the race, a horse that has bolted is not disqualified, but he does not stand much chance of staying with the leaders. In steeplechasing a horse is disqualified if he fails to stay on the course.

BOOKIE   Slang for Bookmaker.

BOOKMAKER   (Illegal in the U.S.A.) A person who makes his own odds, takes bets, and pays off his clients himself. Bookmakers usually have a limit on the payoff odds, i.e., they will pay off at track odds up to a point, 20 to 1 for example; thus no matter how great the track odds on a winner, they will still only pay off at the rate of 20 to 1.

BOTTOM   A term used to denote the amount of endurance in a horse. Also the underlying surface of the racetrack.

BOTTOM LINE   In Thoroughbred breeding *bottom line* refers to the dam's (female's) side in the genealogy of a horse.

BREAK   1.   The initial handling and training of a young horse to carry weight on his back, become familiar with a track, and working with other horses. Thus a person who is going to *break* a young horse is beginning the animal's education.
　　　　2.   The start of a race is also called the *break;* horses are said to *break* from the starting gate.

BREAKAGE   Depending on individual state statutes, the parimutuel payoff is calculated regressively to the nearest nickel or dime. If breakage is to the nickel and the actual division of the pool comes to $5.78, a bettor receives $5.75. If breakage is to the dime, the

4

official payoff on $5.78 would be $5.70. In most instances the breakage is divided between the racetrack and the state in varying proportions.

BREAK DOWN   When a horse sustains a serious injury or becomes sufficiently lame as to prevent him from finishing a race or continuing his training, he is said to *break down*.

BREAK MAIDEN   When a horse or rider wins the first race of his career, he is said to *break his maiden*—graduate.

BREATHER   Holding a horse slightly off the pace of a race for a short distance to save his speed or stamina for the finish drive.

BRED   1.   A horse is said to be bred in the place where he is born. Since more states are now offering breeding incentive programs the actual birthplace of a foal has become increasingly important. Under such a plan there are two outstanding benefits. First, a horse foaled in that state is automatically eligible for special races open to homebreds only. Second, the breeder (*see* BREEDER) registers any foal out of his mare at the time of birth. Then, despite subsequent sale or change of hands of the mare or offspring, any races won by that foal in his birth state render the breeder eligible for an award (usually equal to a percentage of the purse), which is presented by the state breeder's association.

   2.   Also the mating of horses.

BREEDER   The owner of a mare at the time of foaling is considered the *breeder*. See BRED.

BREEZING   A workout in which the horse is asked to demonstrate speed but not extend itself to the fullest.

BROODMARE   A female horse when she becomes a mother.

BRUCE LOWE SYSTEM   A method of tracing the bottom line (female) of a horse's pedigree back to the earliest known ancestresses; the system was developed by English expert Bruce Lowe.

BUG, also BUG BOY   A slang term for an apprentice rider or the apprentice allowance, which stems from the *bug* or asterisk placed beside his name or the horse's weight in the program to indicate that the apprentice allowance is included in the weight carried. *See also* APPRENTICE and ASTERISK.

BULL RING   A slang term for a small racetrack.

BUSH TRACK   *See* LEAKY ROOF CIRCUIT.

CALK or CAULK   A projection on the bottom of a horse's shoe designed to give him greater gripping power in bad going such as mud.

CALL   The call is the announcement of the running positions of the field during a race, usually at such major points as the start, quarter pole, and top of the stretch.

CALLER   The person who gives the *call* of the positions of the horses during a race. *See* CALL.

CARD   The schedule of races for a day is called the *card.* For example: "There are six flat races and two over jumps on today's *card.*"

CATCH WEIGHTS   The term catch weights refers to a jumping race in which there are no specifications as to weight.

CHALK HORSE   A term stemming from the bookmaker days, when racing odds were chalked on slates. It refers to the favorite or most heavily backed horse in a race.

CHART   The newspaper résumé of a race. In the racing paper it is an extensive and comprehensive account of a race specifying the number of the race, the date of the running, the distance (or length) run, the track record for that distance, the *conditions* (or requirements) for entering the race, the division of the purse, the mutual handle, the type of equipment (i.e., blinkers) if any on the horses, the age of the horses, the weight assigned to each horse, the *post positions* from which they started, the running positions of the horses at various points during the race, the jockey on each horse, the amount of *claiming price* (in case of claiming races), the owners of the horses, the odds to the dollar in the mutual win pool, the *fractional times* of the leading horse at various points during the race, the condition of the surface of the *track,* the number of each horse as listed in the racetrack program, the pari-mutuel prices paid, the pedigree of the winner, the *post time* and the actual time the horses were off, *footnotes* on the race, any scratches in the race, any horses that were overweights, any horses that were claimed, waiving of an apprentice allowance, and—when necessary—disqualifications and dead heats. *See* CONDITION BOOK, POST POSITIONS, FRACTIONAL TIMES, CLAIMING RACE, TRACK CONDITIONS, POST TIME, SCRATCHES, OVERWEIGHTS, DEAD HEATS, FOOTNOTES.

CHUTE   A straightaway extension of the homestretch or the backstretch leading on to the main course. Its purpose is to eliminate an extra turn, and it is used to allow a straight run at the start for distances that would otherwise have to begin on a turn.

CLAIMING RACE   A race in which the horses are subject to purchase for the entered price by any owner who has started a horse at that meeting. The claims must be presented in writing and deposited in a box provided for that purpose by the Clerk of the Course at a designated time before the running of the race. When there is more than one claim for a particular horse, the new owner is determined by drawing. The stewards approve all claims, and the new owner takes possession of the horse at the completion of the race regardless of the horse's condition, i.e., sound or unsound, dead or alive. The previous owner is entitled to any winnings earned by the horse in the race.

CLERK OF SCALE   A racetrack official whose primary duty is weighing the jockeys before and after a race to make certain that the assigned weights are carried.

CLIMBING   A break in a horse's stride wherein his action is unusually upward instead of outward. Climbing frequently occurs at the start, when a horse may have trouble getting a foothold, possibly because of the ground breaking away beneath his feet.

CLOCKER   A person who is paid a fee to record and report the times of the horse's morning works, usually for a racing publication.

CLUBHOUSE TURN   The turn on the racetrack in front of the Clubhouse; it is usually located to the right of the grandstand.

COLORS   The colorful silk (or nylon) jacket and cap a jockey wears. Colors are provided by the horse's owner to identify his stable—a practice dating back to 1762 in Newmarket, England. The colors, distinctive in design, combination, and possible emblem, are registered by the owner with the Jockey Club (subject to its approval) and the state racing authority.

COMEBACK MONEY   The money telegraphed by out-of-town book-makers to the track just before betting is closed to cover bets placed with them earlier in the day.

CONDITION BOOK   A book listing all the requirements for entering each race (the *conditions*), the purses, and qualifications at a given race meeting. The book is reissued at stated intervals (usually covering ten to fifteen days of the meeting at a time) by the racing secretary of a particular track.

CONTRACT RIDER   A jockey who is under contract to ride for a specific stable. A rider may hold more than one contract provided that any agreements made subsequent to the first one are contingent upon the priority of the first contract holder.

COOLING OUT   Walking a horse after the exertion of a race or morning workout until his pulse, blood pressure, body temperature, and the like are restored to normal.

COUPLED   *See* ENTRY.

CROPPER   A slang term used most frequently to refer to steeple-chasing, meaning the fall of a horse or rider: "He came a *cropper.*"

CUPPY TRACK   The condition of a track's surface being loose and tending to break away from beneath the horses' feet.

CUSHION   The loose, superficial layer of the racetrack.

CUT DOWN   When a horse sustains an injury from being struck by his own shod feet or those of another horse, he is said to have been *cut down.*

DAILY DOUBLE   A separate wagering pool involving the first two races of the day in which, with a single try the bettor attempts to select the winner of those two races. To qualify for a payoff, both horses must win, and there is no place or show betting in a *Daily Double.* A Daily Double's payoff is unaffected by regular betting pools, and the entire amount in the *Daily Double* pool is distributed to the holders of winning tickets after the deduction of state and track commissions.

DAM   Mother of a Thoroughbred.

DARK HORSE   A winning horse that was thought to have a slim chance of winning.

DEAD HEAT   A tie: A finish in which the photo-finish camera reveals that two or more horses simultaneously reached the wire.

DEAD TRACK   When the surface of a racetrack has little or no spring or elasticity, it is called a *dead track*.

DECLARED   A horse entered in a stakes race that is withdrawn prior to scratch time on the day of the race.

DIRECTION   On U.S. tracks, horses run only counterclockwise. At most European and English racecourses, horses traditionally run clockwise; at some, counterclockwise.

DOGS   Temporary barricades placed on the racetrack during the morning work hours to indicate that horses are not to be galloped over that part of the course. Most frequently set out during inclement weather, *dogs* are designed to save the best part of the track from being cut up to insure the best possible footing for the day's racing.

DRIVING   1.   Said of a horse that is extended to the utmost at the end of a race or workout: "He won *driving*."
2.   Strong urging or pressure from the jockey, usually with whip and/or spurs, at the finish of a race.

DWELT   A horse that is slow to break from the gate or get away at the start of a race is said to have *dwelt*.

EARLY FOOT   A show of speed in the first part of a race.

EASILY   A horse that is working or racing without pressure, either from the jockey or his competition, is said to be running *easily*.

ENTRANCE FEE   The amount of money paid to start a horse in a race. Entrance fees are not usually required for races other than stakes or special events.

ENTRY or COUPLED   When two or more horses that either belong to the same owner or are trained by the same individual run together as a single betting unit, they are said to be coupled and are called an *entry*. No matter what actual post positions they

9

draw, the first *entry* in a race is officially numbered 1 and 1A in the program. If there is a second *entry* in the same race, it is listed as 2 and 2B despite post position. A bet on either horse in an *entry* constitutes a bet on both.

EVEN MONEY   Odds of 1 for 1.

EXACTA   A method of betting which, in order to win, requires selection of the first two horses and their order of finish.

EXCUSED   In order for a horse to be withdrawn from a race after the designated time for all cancellations, permission must be granted by the Stewards for it to be *excused*.

EXERCISE BOY   A rider who gallops or works racehorses in the morning.

EXTENDED   *See* DRIVING.

FAMILY   The maternal side of a Thoroughbred's lineage is referred to as the *family*.

FARRIER   In bygone days a *farrier* was a veterinarian/smith, who specialized in the shoeing of horses. The term now simply refers to a horseshoer—the man who fits the horse's shoes or *plates,* hence a *plater. See also* PLATER.

FIELD   1.   All the horses starting in a race are grouped together and referred to as the *field.*
2.   When there are more horses starting in a race than there are betting units supplied by the pari-mutuel equipment, the racing secretary designates a number of horses (usually the ones thought to have the smallest chance of winning) to run as a single betting unit known as the *field* (or correctly, the pari-mutuel field). Example: There are sixteen horses entered in a race at a track where there are twelve betting units on the pari-mutuel equipment. Ten of the horses start as single betting units, while one trainer has a two-horse entry, thus accounting for twelve horses and eleven betting units. The remaining four horses thus run as a single betting unit—the field.

FLAG MAN   The official timing of a race begins at a point located a short distance in front of the starting gate. It is at this spot that the *flag man* is stationed, and he designates a race's proper start by dropping the flag.

FLAT RACE   Originally used to designate a race on level ground without obstacles such as hurdles or fences. The term is used colloquially today to differentiate between Thoroughbred racing and harness racing, despite the fact that trotters and pacers also race on the *flat*.

FLATTEN OUT   When a horse that is running in a race stops trying and drops his head so that it is almost parallel with the rest of his body, he is said to *flatten out*. Such an occurrence is generally indicative of the horse being overtired or exhausted and unfit.

FOOTNOTES   It refers to the chart of a race as published in the racing newspaper: Footnotes are a professional description of the actual running of the race and is a supplement to the chart itself. *Footnotes* tell where and how most of the field was running at various points during the race and provide comments on any occurrence that might have influenced the contestants' performance such as interferences.

FORCE THE PACE   It means running just behind the leader in a race, pressuring that horse into a consistent effort while front running, and giving him no chance to let up for a breather. *See* BREATHER.

FOUL CLAIM   *See* OBJECTION.

FRACTIONAL TIME   The running time of the leading horse at different positions between the race's start and finish. Depending upon the distance of the race, the number of points where time is taken will vary, but most often the locations are at the quarter-mile, half-mile, three-quarters, and so forth.

FRESHENED   When a horse becomes sour or jaded from racing or training, he is often *freshened* by a trip to a farm or some other program that is completely apart from the racetrack routing.

FURLONG   One eighth of a mile—220 yards. A corruption of a furrow long, which was the length of a plowed field.

FUTURITY   A stakes race for two-year-olds for which they are nominated as foals.

GAD *See* WHIP.

GALLOP 1. In racetrack terminology *galloping* usually refers to an easy workout pace in which the horse is simply exercised and conditioned, as opposed to breezing or being sharpened for an upcoming race. Used in this sense, it means to ride a horse at that gait: He *galloped* three horses this morning.
2. A type of gait. *See* GALLOP in Conformation and Way of Going section.

GARRISON FINISH A breathtaking, late bid run for the wire resulting in a triumph by the narrowest of margins. This type of finish was a specialty with Edward "Snapper" Garrison, a turn-of-the-century jockey for whom it was named.

GET A stallion's collective offspring is referred to as his get.

GETAWAY DAY The final day of the meeting at a racetrack.

GOING The conditions underfoot at a racecourse are referred to as the *Going*. *See* TRACK CONDITIONS.

GOING AWAY A horse is said to have won *going away* when the margin of victory between him and the second horse was increasing at the finish.

GROOM *See* GUINEA.

GUINEA or GINNEY A groom: A distortion of the English word *guinea,* which in olden times was traditionally awarded to the groom of a winner. Racetrack grooms are commonly called Swipes.

GYP or GYPSY A slang term denoting a horseman who only has a few horses at the track. It is neither a derogatory word nor does it carry any connotation of dishonesty.

HALTERMAN When a horse is claimed (*see* CLAIMING RACE), the new owner must provide a halter to lead him from the track. An owner or trainer who often claims horses is thus referred to as a *halterman.*

HANDICAP RACE A race in which the weights are assigned by the Racing Secretary according to his estimation of each horse's potential ability. Hypothetically, if the evaluations were perfect, the entire field would finish in a tie.

HANDICAPPER   1.   The person assigning the weights to be carried in a handicap race. *See* RACING SECRETARY.
2.   A person who makes his choice of winners for a race on the basis of his study of all factors of each horse's past performance and works. Such a study entails track conditions, distances, jockeys, certain horses' peculiarities, and so forth.
3.   An expert who studies the horses' past performances and makes selections for publication.

HANDILY   A horse that is racing or working with a fair amount of effort but without urging or under the whip of the rider is said to be running *handily*.

HANDLE (MUTUEL)   The total amount of pari-mutuel money paid in and out of the machines for one race, the daily card, one meeting, or the entire season.

HAND RIDE   A method of urging a horse to give his best running effort by use of the *hands* on the reins rather than by employing spurs or whip.

HARD BOOT   A slang term meaning a Kentucky horseman.

HEAD   *See* MARGINS OF FINISH.

HEAD OF THE STRETCH   The point at which the horses in a race begin the straight run home to the wire.

HOMESTRETCH   The final straightaway on the racetrack running from the last turn to the finish.

HORSE   A blanket racing term referring to any Thoroughbred regardless of sex. However, among most horsemen, especially those associated with the track, it specifically denotes an entire male horse over five years of age.

HOTS   A slang term referring to horses that have just finished a workout or race and must be cooled out: "He was walking *hots* all morning."

HOT WALKER   Usually the first duty given an apprentice stable-

13

hand, *hot walking* consists of leading a horse around the walking ring or shed row after a workout or race until he is cooled out. *See* COOLING OUT.

HUNG   A horse that is tiring towards the finish of a race but manages to retain his position is said to be *hung*.

HURDLE RACE   A jumping race run over obstacles other than those found in a steeplechase. *See* STEEPLECHASE.

IMPOST   The amount of weight assigned to a horse for a race.

INFIELD   The part of the racing grounds completely encircled by the inside rail of the actual track is called the *infield*.

INGERSOLL WILLIE   A clocker at morning workouts.

IN HAND   When a horse is not running at his fullest extent and has speed to spare if asked by his rider, he is said to be going *in hand*. A horse that is ridden in hand is most probably being rated—that is, placed in a certain position in the field and held there by the skill of the jockey, awaiting an opportunity to make a bid for the lead, or going to the front and then setting a slower pace to keep some reserve speed.

INQUIRY   *See* OBJECTION.

IRONS   The stirrups are called *irons*. See also the saddle diagram in Equipment section.

JOCKEY   A professional male or female racehorse rider.

JOCKEY CLUB   The Jockey Club, located at 300 Park Avenue, New York City 10022, is the keeper of the American Thoroughbred Stud Book. In the offices of the club's Registrar, thousands of North American Thoroughbreds are annually identified, numbered, recorded, and assigned their approved names (from a list of choices submitted by the owners). It was the Jockey Club that set forth the bases and code on which the rules and regulations of the State Racing Commissions were established.

JUMPER, also TIMBER TOPPER or STEEPLECHASER   A horse that runs over hurdles, timber, or in steeplechases.

JUVENILE   A racing term meaning a two-year-old horse of either sex.

LEAD PAD   A pad which is equipped with pockets for strips of lead and is placed under the saddle in order to make up the weight difference when a rider's poundage is below that which was assigned.

LEAD PONY   1.   The horse (not an actual pony as defined by height) that leads the starters from the paddock to the starting gate.
2.   A horse (again, not a true pony) which is used by many trainers to accompany young or unruly horses to keep them quiet.

LEAKY ROOF CIRCUIT   A slang term referring to the small or minor racetracks which are also called bush tracks.

LEFT AT THE POST   A horse that was slow to break from the gate or for some other reason did not get away with the rest of the field is said to have been *left at the post*.

LEG UP   1.   Refers to the conditioning or strengthening of a horse's legs or more broadly, of his whole body, by means of regular and increasing amounts of exercise.
2.   The act of assisting a rider to mount a horse by grasping his bent left leg at the knee and ankle and lifting him up as he springs to the saddle.

LENGTH   The distance between horses during the call of a race or at the finish is measured in *lengths*. The term originates from the actual nose-to-tail length of a horse—approximately eight feet.

LINE   *See* TOP LINE.

LUGGING   *See* BEARING IN or OUT.

MAIDEN   A horse of either sex that has never won a race in any country. Also a rider who has not won a race at any time.

MAIDEN RACE   A type of race open to horses that have never won.

MARGINS OF FINISH   The terminology for horses finishing a race separated by distances that are not measurable in lengths are:

15

Neck—about a quarter of a length; Head—about an eighth of a length; Nose—the narrowest *margin. See also* LENGTH, NOSE.

MIDDLE DISTANCE   A racing distance that is more than seven furlongs but not more than a mile and a quarter is considered to be at *middle distance.*

MINUS POOL   An infrequent occurrence in pari-mutuel betting, wherein one horse is played so heavily as the outstanding favorite there is not sufficient money in the remainder of the pool, after the deduction of state tax and commission, to pay off the minimum as required by law. In such instances, it is referred to as a *minus pool,* and the deficit is made up by the racing association.

MORNING GLORY   A horse that trains well and shows speed in his morning workouts but either has insufficient talent or refuses to extend himself in the actual races in the afternoon.

MORNING LINE   A forecast of the approximate odds on the horses in a race. More accurately, it is an educated, professional guess made by the track handicapper or his associates, after learning the day's scratches and the condition of the track in the morning. This conjecture is then printed in the official program and posted on the totalizator board before the betting windows open for each race.

MUDDER or MUDLARK   A horse that prefers a muddy or soft track and runs his best under such conditions.

NAMES OF HORSES   In order to race on the flat or over jumps, all Thoroughbred horses must be registered with the Jockey Club. There are specific rules governing Thoroughbred names, all of which must be approved and then officially assigned. Originally a name could not exceed sixteen letters and spaces, however the limitation has recently been increased to eighteen.

NECK   *See* MARGINS OF FINISH.

NINE OF HEARTS   A horse that is thought to have little or no chance of winning a race.

NOM DE COURSE   A fictitious name that an owner assumes for the purpose of a racing partnership.

NOMINATOR   The owner of a horse when it is named as a starter in a future race.

NOSE   A term of measurement for the slight edge or advantage that one horse may have over another during the course of a race or at the finish. When a horse wins by a nose, the margin of victory is so small that the results are usually not deemed official until the photographs of the finish have been examined. *See also* MARGINS OF FINISH.

NUMBER CLOTH   Every horse running in a race must wear a number cloth beneath his saddle. This cloth shows in large figures on both sides, the horse's racing card number, which is also his post position.

OAKS   A stakes race which derives its name from the English ancestral estate of Lord Derby; it is open only to three-year-old fillies.

OBJECTION—FOUL CLAIM, INQUIRY, PROTEST   A complaint of the commission of a foul during a race; it may be lodged by a jockey, patrol judge, or other racetrack official. When such a protest is made, the word objection or inquiry is flashed on the board. The results of the race are not official until filmed studies of the running have been reviewed, after which the foul claim is either upheld or denied. In cases in which the claim of foul is allowed, the nature of the offense determines the penalty—disqualified and placed last or disqualified and placed third—and a rider may be suspended for a number of days. *See* SET DOWN.

ODDS-ON   When the pari-mutuel payoff is less than dollar for dollar (even money), it is known as *odds-on*. An odds-on favorite that won would pay less than four dollars on a two-dollar wager.

OFF TRACK   Any track that is not fast. *See* TRACK CONDITIONS.

ORDER OF FINISH   *See* PLACINGS.

OUTRIDER   A horseman employed by the racetrack whose duty it is to lead the starters to the post, catch any loose race horses in the event that a jockey is thrown, aid a rider with a fractious horse if the stable has not sent a pony with him, and generally maintain order in the field of horses while they are on the track.

OVERLAND   When a horse is running in a blind switch (*see* BLIND SWITCH) or locked in behind other horses in the field with no opening through which he can make a move, the jockey may take him to the outside around the horses in his way. Such a move is called going *overland,* meaning the longest route to the finish.

OVERNIGHT   1.   A daily printed sheet made available to trainers through the racing secretary's office that lists the entries made for the following day's races.
2.   A race in which entries will be accepted as late as seventy-two hours or less prior to the post time of the first scheduled race on that day.

OVER THE STICKS   A horse that runs *over the sticks* is one that races over brush or hurdles.

OVERWEIGHT   The amount of weight a horse carries is determined by the conditions of the race. If a jockey cannot reduce to the assigned poundage, the horse may carry the added weight, but not more than five pounds is allowed.

PADDOCK   1.   At the racetrack area where the horses are saddled and walked prior to a race.
2.   A fenced-off field on a farm, where horses may be turned out.

PADDOCK JUDGE   The racetrack official whose duty is to supervise the saddling of the horses before a race and the general paddock routine.

PARI-MUTUELS   The method of betting employed at most racetracks today. Originating in France, this system works by taking the monies wagered on the win, place, and show pools, deducting the commissions, and then distributing the remainder among the holders of first-, second-, and third-place horses. In this way the odds against each horse and the eventual payoff figure are actually determined by the public.

PARLAY   Applying an original bet and its proceeds to another bet on a subsequent race is called *parlaying.* It is possible to *parlay* any number of bets—as long as one keeps on winning.

PASTEBOARD TRACK When the surface of the racing strip is in superlative condition and lightning fast, it is referred to as a *pasteboard track. See also* TRACK CONDITIONS.

PATROL JUDGES Racetrack officials placed at strategic points around the racing strip to observe the progress of a race and watch for possible fouls or interferences within the field.

PENALTIES The extra weight assigned to a horse in accordance with the conditions of a race.

PHOTO FINISH The finish of a race in which the horses are so closely grouped at the wire and the margin of victory is so minute that the placing judges cannot determine the winner without first consulting a photograph.

PINCHED BACK When a horse is running in such close quarters that he is forced to "take back" or "back off" he is said to have been *pinched back.*

PIPE OPENER A workout without excessive speed—a breeze. *See* BREEZING.

PLACE *See* PLACINGS.

PLACING JUDGE A racetrack official whose duty is to ascertain the order of the first four horses to reach the finish wire.

PLACINGS The first three horses to finish in a race are said to Win (first place), Place (second place), and Show (third place), respectively.

PLATER 1. A horse that runs in claiming races rather than stakes, allowances, or handicaps—a cheap racehorse.
2. Another term for farrier. *See* FARRIER.

PLATES or RACING PLATES Another term for the lightweight shoes worn by racehorses.

POCKET *See* BLIND SWITCH.

POINT TO POINT A jumping race held over a flagged course through natural terrain.

POLE   Poles placed around the racetrack at measured distances as markers. Usually the major points are denoted by different colors or heights: quarter pole, half, and three-quarters are different from the eighth poles, which in turn are distinguished from the sixteenth poles.

POOL   The total money wagered on the entire field to win, place, and show in a given race is called the pool.

POST   The actual starting point for a given race is called the post.

POST PARADE   The parade of horses from the paddock past the grandstands to the starting gate before a race.

POST POSITION   When the entries close on the day before a given race, a drawing is held to decide the positions in the starting gate from which each horse will break. The stalls are numbered from the inside rail of the racetrack (post position No. 1) outward, and the positions closest to the inner rail are generally considered the better starting points.

POST TIME   The time at which the race is scheduled to start and at which all entrants are required to be at the post and ready to break.

PREFERRED LIST   A list of horses which for one of several reasons have priority in starting in a specific race, if that event draws more entrants than can be accepted.

PREP or PREP RACE   An event of lesser importance which is used as a tightener or final training phase prior to a major engagement.

PRODUCE   The collective offspring of a mare is referred to as her *produce.*

PRODUCER   A broodmare is referred to as a *producer* after one of her offspring has won a race.

PRODUCE RACE   A race in which the contestants are the produce of horses named when the nominations for the race were closed.

PROP   *See* REFUSE.

PROTEST   *See* OBJECTION.

PUBLIC TRAINER   A person who is not under contract to any one particular stable and accepts horses to train from several individuals, usually on a per diem basis.

PULL UP   Taking back or pulling on the reins so that a horse reduces his speed and/or stops completely—*i.e.* to *pull up* after a race.

PURSE   The term purse originates from the days when prize money for a race was placed in a *purse* suspended from the finish line wire. In that time, sayings such as "going under the wire" and "taking down a *purse*" were expressions of fact. *Purse* refers today to an amount of prize money offered by the track, to which the owners have not contributed.

QUARTER POLE   Usually found at the turn leading into the stretch, it is the pole marking the distance a quarter mile from the finish line on a one-mile track.

QUINELLA   A form of multiple betting in which horses are chosen to finish first and second, without stipulating the order. Therefore, if the horses selected were numbers two and six and as long as they were the first two horses to cross the finish line, the player would be eligible for a payoff.

RACING PLATES   *See* PLATES.

RACING SECRETARY   The racetrack official who draws up the conditions for the races offered at the meeting and assigns the weight to be carried in handicap races. *See* HANDICAPPER.

RAIL RUNNER   A horse that runs best and prefers to run close to the inside rail.

RATE   *See* IN HAND.

RECEIVING BARN   1.   Found at most major racetracks, the receiving barn is an isolated building where the horses for a given race are required to report at a prescribed time prior to appearing at the paddock. Such procedure is designed to minimize the opportunity to tamper with a horse before he runs.

2.   An arrival barn at a track or breeding farm used to accommodate horses newly shipped in until they are assigned appropriate stabling.

21

REFUSE or PROP   1.   When a horse stands flat-footed and refuses to break from the starting gate he is said to refuse or prop. 2.   In steeplechasing it also refers to balking at an obstacle.

RIDDEN OUT   A horse that has been well rated throughout a race and then extended completely in the drive for the finish is said to have been *ridden out.*

RINGER   A *ringer* is a horse that because of similarity in size, color, and particularly markings (or lack of same) is substituted for the horse named as the starter in a race. Running a *ringer* is a dishonest act; if detected, the practice carries severe penalties for all parties concerned.

ROGUE   A fractious, unmanageable horse.

ROGUE'S BADGE   *See* BLINKERS.

ROMP   A horse that either runs or wins without extending himself at all is said to *romp.*

ROUTE   Any race that is run over a distance longer than a mile and an eighth is referred to as a *route.* The expression "go the *route*" thus carries the connotation of an arduous task.

RULED OFF or BARRED   1.   An extremely unmanageable horse may be *ruled off* or *barred* from competing in races at a given racetrack. 2.   Any person whose conduct or practices while at the racetrack are in violation of the rules and regulations of that track may be *ruled off* for varying lengths of time or indefinitely, depending upon the offense and the discretion of the racetrack officials.

SADDLE CLOTH   *See* NUMBER CLOTH.

SALIVA TEST   A laboratory test usually performed on all winners (in some states the first three horses are tested) to detect the possible presence of drugs in the horse's system.

SARATOGA   The racecourse at Saratoga, New York, which was inaugurated in 1864, is the oldest racetrack in the United States in continual use.

SAVAGE   In the language of racing savage is a verb meaning a horse that tries to bite (or *savage*) another horse or man. In an account of a race or a chart footnote, it might be mentioned that one horse tried to *savage* another.

SCALE OF WEIGHTS   A fixed set of weights for horses to carry, contingent upon the horse's age, sex, and the time of year and distance of the race.

SCHOOLING   Acquainting a young horse with the practices and requirements of racing: Running with other horses, working in close quarters, being jostled by horses around him, and so forth, as well as introducing him to the starting gate. When referring to steeplechase or hurdle horses, *schooling* means teaching a horse to jump.

SCHOOLING LIST   A list of horses that have misbehaved in the starting gate and are required by the starter to further their education at the barrier before being allowed to run in a race.

SCRATCH   Withdrawing a horse from an engagement. When a horse is to be *scratched,* the owner or his authorized agent must notify the Racing Secretary, usually in writing, before the designated closing prior to post time established by the Racing Secretary. Such a declaration is irrevocable. If it becomes necessary to scratch a horse after the deadline, permission must be obtained from the Stewards.

SECOND CALL   Employing a jockey when permitted by the conditions of his original contract. *See* CONTRACT RIDER.

SELLING RACE   A term loosely but incorrectly used to refer to claiming races. Actual *selling races* are now practically nonexistent.

SET DOWN   1.   Suspending of a jockey for a definite period because of a foul or misdemeanor is known as being *set down.*
2.   When a horse is given a particularly strenuous workout or is called upon to extend himself completely towards the finish of a race, he is said to have been *set down.*

SEX ALLOWANCE   In all nonhandicap races or races in which the conditions specify otherwise, fillies and mares are allowed to carry slightly lesser weights than those provided for on the scale. (*See* SCALE OF WEIGHTS.) Usually the allowance is three pounds for two-year-old fillies and five pounds for fillies and mares over three before September 1 and three pounds after that date.

SHED ROW   The rows of barns at a racetrack.

SHORT   When a horse that was running well in a race lacks the endurance to maintain or improve his position, particularly in the stretch or very close to the wire, he is said to be *short*. Used thusly, the term implies that the horse was entered too soon and that, with more work or preparation prior to starting, he might have had sufficient bottom (*see* BOTTOM) to last to the finish and possibly have won the race.

SHOW   *See* PLACINGS.

SILKS   The jacket and cap worn by the jockey. *See* COLORS.

SIRE   1.   A stallion is referred to as a *sire* after one of his offspring has won a race.
2.   The father of a Thoroughbred is referred to as his *sire*.

SKINNED TRACK   Refers to a racing strip made of dirt rather than turf or grass.

SKULL CAP   The protective leather or composition helmet worn by jockeys beneath racing caps.

SNUG   A light hold taken by a rider to restrain a horse.

SOLID HORSE   A horse that is thought to have a fairly good chance of winning.

SOPHOMORE   Refers to a three-year-old and indicates that the horse is in the second season of racing.

SPIT BOX   The containers into which the horses' saliva is deposited for laboratory testing. *See* SALIVA TEST. Also the place where horses have to go after a race to have the samples taken.

SPRINT   Any race run over a distance up to seven furlongs is considered a sprint.

SPRINTER   A horse that is at his best running over distances under a mile.

STAKES RACE   Originally called a "Sweepstakes" because the fees put up by the owners for nominations, entries and starting all went to the winner, stakes now have money added to the fees by the track. (*See* ADDED MONEY.) And the total sum is distributed among the first four horses to place, and sometimes horses finishing further back. Naturally, the lion's share goes to the winner—in most cases all the original fees and a major portion of the added money.

STALE   A horse that is not training up to his previous form may be referred to as *stale*.

STALL WALKER or STALL WORKER   A nervous, fitful horse that apparently cannot stand still for any length of time and is constantly moving around in his stall. Such a horse is difficult to keep in condition because it receives improper rest.

STARTING GATE   The mechanical barrier from which the horses break at the start of a race. This device is divided into sections (stalls) for each horse. While the horses walk into the stalls, the doors in front of them are held closed by an electrical current. When the official starter is satisfied that the horses are well settled into position, he breaks the current thus allowing the doors to fly open and the race begins.

STATE RACING COMMISSION   The governing body of racing in a particular state. A *state racing commission* is responsible for defining and upholding the rules, regulations, and conditions of racing as well as licensing owners, trainers, and jockeys in the state.

STAYER   A horse with a great deal of stamina that does particularly well in races over a long distance.

STAYER DISTANCE   Any race that is more than a mile and a half in length is said to be run at stayer distance.

STEEPLECHASE   A race run over two specific types of obstacles. First, a bank topped with a brush or hedge; second, a liverpool fence, which is the same type of obstacle except that there is also a ditch filled with water either in front or behind it (also referred to as the water jump). The term *steeplechase* is a carry-over from the 18th century cross-country races that were popular with the sporting gentry. The average distance was about four miles, and frequently the only visible marker on the horizon was the church steeple, which was designated the finish. The term steeplechase was coined and since the shortest route to the steeple often required jumping over obstacles, a steeplechase became a race over jumps.

STEEPLECHASER *See* JUMPER.

STEWARDS The judicial body of Thoroughbred racing usually consisting of three appointed members who represent the Racing Commission and the Thoroughbred Racing Association. All objections or foul claims lodged by owners, trainers, or jockeys are reviewed and ruled upon by the *Stewards* who can also initiate an inquiry. The *Stewards* are assisted in their ruling on interference or unfair riding in a race by the patrol films, the report of the patrol judges, and interviews with the persons involved.

STICK *See* WHIP.

STICKERS A type of shoe with calks designed to give a horse better grip and footing when the condition of the track is muddy or otherwise poor.

STOOPER A racetrack scavenger who searches through the pari-mutuel tickets that have been thrown away in hopes of finding a valid one.

STRAIGHT AS A STRING A horse that is extended to the utmost and therefore stretched out and close to the ground is said to be running *straight as a string*.

STRETCH Short for homestretch. *See* HOMESTRETCH.

STUD 1. A stallion used for breeding.
2. A breeding farm is frequently referred to as a *stud*.

STUDBOOK The registry maintained by the Jockey Club (or comparable organization in other countries) showing the genealogical breeding record of Thoroughbreds. Only those horses whose lineage is traceable through horses already in the studbook to one of the three foundation sires are eligible for admission.

SUBSCRIPTION   The nomination fee paid by an owner to name a horse for a stake event or to maintain eligibility for it.

SUBSTITUTE RACE   In the event that a scheduled race is either cancelled or does not have enough entries, a race with different conditions may be offered in its place.

SUCKLING   A foal that is still nursing, so called until he is weaned.

SULK   A horse that will not try to run and refuses to extend himself is said to *sulk*.

SWIPE   *See* GUINEA.

TAKE—MUTUEL   The portion of money deducted from the mutuel pool and then shared by the racetrack and the state. The amount of this commission is fixed by the state.

TB   Common abbreviation for Thoroughbred.

THOROUGHBRED RACING ASSOCIATION (TRA)   An organization of racetrack management whose primary function is to uphold a high level of eithics at member tracks. Founded in 1942, the association consists of fifty-four racetracks of which seven are located in Canada. All members of the TRA are subject to its Code of Standards and, as a group, maintain the Thoroughbred Racing Protective Bureau.

THOROUGHBRED RACING PROTECTIVE BUREAU (TRPB)   A national investigative organization established in 1945 by the Thoroughbred Racing Association. The Bureau's central headquarters are in New York City with field officers at every member track during its meeting. The vital data maintained by the TRPB is unequaled in racing or in any other sport; it includes case files, fingerprints, and the lip tattoo identification records of more than 155,000 Thoroughbreds.

TIGHT   A horse that is fit and in condition to race is called *tight*.

TIMBER TOPPER   *See* JUMPER.

TOP LINE or LINE   The paternal lineage of a Thoroughbred.

TOTALIZATOR   The electronic machine that individually records the wagers in each of the three betting pools—win, place, and show—as the tickets are sold by a manually operated vending machine. This equipment simultaneously calculates the odds on each horse as the result of the monies wagered and determines the payoff after the race's finish.

TOTALIZATOR BOARD   A large board placed in the infield of the racetrack within easy view of the spectators on which information necessary to the racegoer is posted electronically. Such data usually includes the approximate odds on each horse, the total amount wagered in each pool (on some boards), the track condition, post time, the actual time of day, the race results, the length of time it took to run the race, any official sign such as *Inquiry* (if there has been an objection) or *Photo* (if there is a question as to the order of finish), and the amount of the payoffs when the race is declared official.

TOTE BOARD   *See* TOTALIZATOR BOARD.

TRACK CONDITIONS   The condition of the racing surface of a dirt track is classified as follows: Fast—even and dry, with the best possible footing; Sloppy—usually after a heavy rainfall and often with puddles on the surface, but before the base is affected so the running time remains fast; Muddy—footing is wet and soft; Heavy—as the track begins to dry, between muddy and good; Slow—the track is still wet, but the footing is between heavy and good; Good—the rating between slow and fast; Off—any condition other than fast is called off; Good Bottom—the track is said to have a good bottom when, despite light mud or sloppy going on the surface, the base remains firm; Frozen—in unusual extremes of weather the surface may become frozen.

TRACK RECORD   The fastest time that a horse has ever run over a certain distance at a given track. If, during the course of a race, a horse should better the existing fastest time for that distance, a new track record is established.

TRAIN OFF   When a horse becomes bored or jaded after reaching a condition of racing fitness, he may be said to *train off*.

TRIPLE CROWN   The Kentucky Derby, the Preakness, and the Belmont Stakes comprise the triple crown of racing in the United States.

TURF COURSE   A racing course on grass.

TWIN DOUBLE   A type of multiple betting involving four races. A person who has correctly selected the winners of the first two races of the twin double exchanges his ticket for his choices in the remaining two races. In some states persons holding valid tickets on the first half of the twin double may cash them instead of exchanging them for the second half of the "twin."

TWO-YEAR-OLD   A Thoroughbred becomes a two-year-old and eligible to race on his second New Year's Day after being foaled.

UNDER WRAPS   A horse being restrained and not allowed to put forth his best effort in either a race or a workout is running *under wraps.*

UNTRIED   1.   A horse that has never been tested for speed or raced is said to be *untried.*
2.   A stallion that has not been bred.

VALET   A person whose duty is to attend to the jockey's equipment, making sure that he has the correct silks at his locker prior to a race, the proper amount of weight is in his lead pad (if necessary), and so forth. He also carries the saddle and any other equipment to the paddock, aids the trainer in saddling the horse, and then meets the jockey after the race and returns the saddle and equipment to the Jockey's Room.

WALKOVER   An unusual occurrence wherein the number of starters scratches down to only one entrant. This horse is then simply required to gallop the required distance as a necessary formality under the rules of racing to be declared the winner and collect the purse or winner's portion thereof.

WARMING UP   Galloping a horse on the way to the post to loosen him up for the race.

WASHY   A horse that breaks out into a heavy nervous sweat prior to a race is said to be *washy.*

WATERING OFF   Allowing a horse to take periodic sips of water while cooling out to prevent him from drinking a great quantity when he returns to his stall. *See* COOLING OUT.

WEANLING   A Thoroughbred in the fall of his first year after being weaned from his mother until he becomes a yearling on his first New Year's Day.

WEIGHT-FOR-AGE   A certain type of race in which the horses carry weights according to a fixed scale depending upon their age and sex, the distance of the race, and the time of the year. *See* SCALE OF WEIGHTS.

WHIP (also **BAT, GAD, STICK**)   An implement, usually made of leather, with which a rider hits a horse to induce him to extend himself or put forth a better effort.

WIN   *See* PLACINGS.

WINDED   A horse having difficulty breathing after a workout or race is winded.

WINNER-TAKE-ALL   A type of race in which the winner receives the entire purse or stakes.

WORK HORSE   A horse used to provide company and/or competition during workouts for a horse of better quality.

YEARLING   To avoid confusion, all Thoroughbreds are considered to be one year old on the first New Year's Day after being foaled; they are referred to as yearlings until the following New Year's Day, when they become two-year-olds. *See* TWO-YEAR-OLD.

HARNESS
RACING

AGE   The age of all Standardbred horses is reckoned from the first day of January of the year in which they are born. For example, a foal dropped on March third is considered to be one-year-old on the *following* January first. Recently a new rule has been put into effect specifying that foals born in November and December will also be reckoned with foals dropped during the next twelve months; such foals become yearlings on the following January first. In other words, it is now possible for a Standardbred foal actually to be 14 months old when his first birthday occurs. This new rule is calculated to allow an expanded breeding season and make many of the two-year-old racing colts and fillies much stronger and sounder when they go to the races.

BLOWOUT   The last workout prior to a race; in most instances, it occurs on the day before the race.

BREAKING   When Standardbred horses race it is essential that they maintain either the trotting or pacing gait. Should a racing horse leave the required gait and *break* into a gallop, the driver is charged with the responsibility of returning him at once to the racing gait. Failure to do so may result in having the horse placed last, and a penalty may be levied on the driver. Where circumstances permit and there is room, the driver of a horse who has broken gait must take the horse to the outside and immediately pull it in its gait. All punishments are subject to the discretion of the judges who rule on the gravity of the break. For example, if a horse breaks gait and his driver complies with all the requirements, it is up to the judges to decide whether the animal gained by the break. If they decide the animal has gained, then they set him back accordingly.

CHECK REIN   The check rein is an important part of the equipment worn by most trotters and pacers. In order for these horses to race in their best form—that is, with the most rhythmic, well-balanced, longest reaching stride—they must maintain a high head carriage. This is the function of the check rein, which runs from the bit in the horse's mouth, up over the top of his head, and then back to the saddle hook on the harness.

CLAIMING RACE   A race in which any of the entrants may be claimed for a specified amount of money in accordance with the rules of the USTA.

CLASSIFIED RACE   A race in which the contestants are selected on the basis of their performance or ability, regardless of eligibility.

CONDITIONED RACE   A race whose entrants must meet certain requirements in order to start. The qualifications for eligibility are set forth by the track and may be based on any one or more combinations of the following factors: Sex; age; monies won over a specified period of time or in a stated number of races; and number of starts or finishing positions over a specified period of time.

DASH   A type of race in which the victor is decided as the result of a single trial. A series of two or three dashes governed by the payment of one entry fee may also be offered, but it is an entrance condition that a horse must start in all dashes.

DECLARATION   A *declaration* is actually a statement of intent to start a specific horse in a given race. The driver of the horse and his colors must be included in the statement. A horse may be declared as a starter in only one race per day. A declaration may be rejected if the eligibility certificate was not in the possession of the Racing Secretary at the time the condition book was published, or if the Secretary feels that the nominee for the race is not up to the competitive level of the other participants.

DISQUALIFICATION   In the case of a horse being disqualified, the animal is not allowed to start in a race. Disqualification of a person means that the individual cannot start, drive a horse in a race, or officiate at the track in any capacity.

EARLY CLOSING RACE   A race in which the purse is a fixed amount and which has a closing date for entries at least six weeks prior to the race. The form of payment of entries may be the installment plan or otherwise, but regardless of the method, all payments are forfeits.

ELBOW BOOTS   Protective boots (usually sheepskin lined) worn by some trotters at the points of the elbow, high on the horse's front legs at the joint located at the rear and bottom of the shoulders. Their purpose is to prevent the horse from doing himself injury by grazing the elbow with his shoe when the foot is folded back in the height of his racing stride. Particularly high-gaited trotters are most prone to this problem.

ELIGIBILITY CERTIFICATE   An eligibility certificate must accompany a horse at all race meetings and be presented in proper order before he may start. The information contained therein must be accurate, stating the name and address of the owner, the color, sex, and breeding of the horse, as well as a declaration of the gait at which the animal races and a listing of all the starts for the current year including monies won and numbers of times placing first, second, and third. The normal calendar year coincides with the time-span of the racing season. If a horse increases his earnings between the closing date for entry in a specific race and the actual race itself, his subsequent earnings do not affect his eligibility as long as he met the eligibility requirements on closing date. In addition to all the necessary information pertaining to the horse, a valid eligibility certificate must name an owner who is a member of the USTA in good standing.

ENTRY   Any two or more horses that start in a race under the same ownership, management, or trainer constitute an entry.

FREE-LEGGED PACER   A pacer that is able to race in the pacing gait without the aid of hopples. *See* HOPPLES.

FUTURITY   A stake race in which nominations are made for the dam of the starter either during the time she is in foal or in the year she foals.

GAITING STRAP   A strap strung inside the shafts of a sulky for the purpose of keeping the horse traveling in a straight line. Without a gaiting strap, some horses tend to swing their hind ends either to the right or left and thus wind up moving sideways instead of directly forward.

GREEN HORSE   An inexperienced trotter or pacer that has never raced in public or against the clock.

HEAD POLE   A stick or pole (usually a billiard cue with a hole drilled in the handle for a leather thong), which is fastened alongside a horse's head and neck. Its purpose is to keep the animal's head straight and prevent him from turning his head to the side, particularly when racing in the turns.

HEAT   A single trip in a race which requires the winning of two or more trials to determine the victor.

HOPPLES or HOBBLES   Leather (sometimes plastic) fittings extending between the lateral legs on both sides of a pacer. At each end of this connecting strap is a loop which encircles the right rear and fore leg (or left rear and fore leg) above the knee and hock to synchronize the strides and ensure that both pairs of side legs move in unison. The fittings are suspended from straps across the pacer's back which are called simply hopple hangers.

KNEE BOOTS   Most frequently used on pacers, knee boots are a protective covering worn on the inside of the knees and held in place by suspenders which fit over the horse's withers. When making a turn it is not unusual for a horse to brush his knees—that is, hit the inside of his knee with the opposite foot. When a horse feels the blows on his knees, he may attempt to break his gait and knee boots lessen this tendency.

LAPPED ON   When the nose of an oncoming horse is at least opposite the hindquarters of the horse ahead, he is said to be *lapped on.* Should the leading horse break his gait at the finish wire, he is automatically placed behind the horse(s) lapped on him in the official standing.

LATE CLOSING RACE   A race for a fixed purse in which entries must be made less than six weeks and more than three days prior to the actual contest.

MAIDEN   A horse of any sex which has never won either a heat or a race at the gait at which it is entered to start. For example, a horse which has never won any race or heat is naturally eligible for a maiden race at either gait. However, a pacer which has won at the pacing gait is still eligible as a maiden at the trotting gait provided he has never raced and won at the trot.

MARK   Every horse may have a *mark,* which simply means his best winning time for a mile. However, it is not unusual for a horse to be faster than his mark. For example, it is quite possible that his fastest winning time might have been 2:04, but he might have finished a close or photo second with a horse winning in 2:02.

MARTINGALE   A strap which attaches to the girth and passes between the horse's front legs after which it forks into two pieces with a ring at the end of each. The bridle reins are threaded through the rings (one rein to each ring) and then held by the driver. If the horse throws his head, he is met with a downward pull on his mouth due to the stationary position of the rings, and the driver need not raise or change his hands.

MATINEE RACE   A race which requires no entry fee to start and offers premiums other than money, if any.

ON THE LIMB   When several horses are so bunched into position at a given pole or on the rail so as to prevent another horse from getting in, the only route to the front is around the entire pack. Such a move requires an outstanding horse to remain even in contention, because he must travel a greater distance and gain ground at the same time. A horse that is faced with such a situation in a race is said to be out *on the limb.*

OVERNIGHT EVENT   A race for which the closing date for entries does not exceed three days prior to the date named for the contest.

PACER   A Standardbred horse that races with a lateral gait moving the front and hind legs on the same side in unison: right front and right hind step forward simultaneously, then left front and left hind. In order to maintain this type of motion roughly nine out of ten pacers wear hopples. *See* HOPPLES.

PARKED OUT   When a horse winds up in a situation where he is forced to race on the outside (and therefore the longer distance) because another horse is between him and the rail, he is said to have been parked out. This occurs enough times and has sufficient bearing upon the horse's time for the race to warrant noting it upon the horse's past performance chart. In such an instance the performance line might read 3-4-2°-2, with the circle indicating the point at which the horse was in a parked out situation.

POST POSITIONS—*Heat Racing*   The winner of a heat is automatically assigned the inside (or pole) position for the following heat, unless other provisions have been made and are published in the conditions of the race. The remaining contestants determine their post positions according to the order in which they finished in the first heat.

PULLED OUT   A horse that leaves the path directly in front of him in favor of a line towards the center of the track to pass another horse ahead of him is said to have been *pulled out.*

RACING COLORS   Unlike Thoroughbred racing in which the jockeys wear the silks of the farm or owner for whom they are riding, the colors worn by the drivers of harness horses are registered by the U.S. Trotting Association and belong solely to that driver. Each pattern and combination of colors become the personal hallmark of a driver, and he is readily identified by the colors of his jacket and cap. It is possible for a driver to submit a request for a change of colors any time during his career; if his new choice does not duplicate another already registered, then his request may be granted. However, such requests are seldom made, and the drivers race year after year in the same colors so that a true harness fan needs little more than a quick glance at a blur of color to know who is at the reins.

RATED MILE　　When a harness horse races, not only is he affected by the pace set by the other horses in the race, but he is also rated by his driver in accordance with a stopwatch carried in his left hand. This is called a *rated mile*. Each driver is familiar with the peculiarities and abilities of his particular horse and has a pretty good idea just how fast that horse can go per quarter mile. The final quarter is usually the fastest quarter. Using this knowledge each driver rates his horse and positions him accordingly. If he feels that the pace is too fast in the early stages of the race, he will keep his horse slightly off the pace until it is time for him to make a move. If he finds the pace too slow, he will move his horse into a position where he can race at a faster speed.

RECALL　　Once the horses have formed the parade to the post, they are under the control of the Starter. After allowing them to score (*see* SCORE), he then has them brought to the starting gate. There is a definite progression of speed of the gate until the starting point is reached and the word *go* is given. After reaching a speed in the course of a start, there is never a decrease except in the case of a recall. The decision, concerning a recall lies solely with the Starter who is himself limited as to the conditions under which he may turn the field. These conditions are interference; a horse having broken equipment; fall of a horse before go has been given; a horse scoring ahead of the gate; and a horse refusing to come to the gate before the gate reaches the pole an eighth of a mile before the starting point.

RECORD　　A horse's record is the fastest time made by him in winning a heat or a dash.

REGISTRATION—*Nonstandard Bred*　　In order to register a horse as nonstandard bred the application must show satisfactory identification of the animal for racing purposes—name, age, color

and markings, sire, dam, and a history of previous owners—
and be accompanied by a mating certificate which indicates
that the sire is some type of a registered horse.

REGISTRATION—*Standard Bred Horses*   In order for a horse to be
registered as Standard bred, he must meet one of the following
qualifications:

1. The offspring of a registered Standard stallion and a registered Standard mare;
2. A stallion whose sire is a registered Standard horse, provided
   his dam and granddam were sired by registered Standard
   horses and he himself has a Standard record and is the sire
   of three performers with Standard records from different
   mares;
3. A mare whose sire is a registered Standard horse, and whose
   dam and granddam were sired by a registered Standard horse,
   provided she herself has a Standard record;
4. A mare whose sire is a registered Standard horse provided she
   is the dam of two performers with Standard records;
5. A mare or horse whose sire is a registered Standard horse,
   provided its first, second, and third dams are each sired by a
   registered Standard horse;
6. No horse more than four years of age is eligible for registration.

If a horse fails to fulfill any of the necessary qualifications
for registration, he still may be registered if, in the opinion
of the Standing Committee on Registration, the animal should
be registered as Standard.

SCALPERS   Close fitting boots covering the coronet and hoof of the
hind feet to protect against cuts and bruises from the front feet.
Scalpers are worn primarily by trotters.

SCORE   Just prior to the beginning of a race, a preliminary limber-
ing up which the Starter allows the entrants. Once the horses
come onto the track for a given race, they are in the control of
the Starter. He may permit two preliminary scores before notify-
ing the drivers to assemble at the gate. The distance of a score is
arbitrary, but it usually includes the length of the homestretch
and the first turn.

SHADOW ROLL   A large roll of sheepskin or similar material worn
across the horse's face just below his eyes. It is meant to cut off
the animal's view of the track and thus lessen the possibility of
his shying from shadows, paper, or other objects suddenly ap-

pearing in his path. While a shadow roll is not a piece of equipment confined to horses racing in harness, it is particularly popular in this field of racing, and many horses wear one when racing.

SIDEWHEELER   A slang term for a pacer.

STANDING HALTER   A device used on a horse that has a tendency to throw his head up and then break his gait. It consists of a tight halter on the horse's head with a strap running from it to the girth. The resulting action is similar to that of a martingale.

STAKE   A race in which the track offers a specified amount as the purse. To this is added all monies received in nomination fees. The entries for stakes races close in the year prior to the actual start, but all nominating, sustaining, and starting payments must be paid to the winner with the minor exception of certain permissible deductions.

START   A race is under way once the Starter has given the word *go*. This is done at the starting point, which is a spot marked on the inside rail and must be at least 200 feet from the first turn. Once the word *go* has been given, there can be no recall; any horse is considered a starter regardless of his position. *See also* RECALL.

STARTING GATE   The mobile starting gate was first introduced to harness racing in 1946. Prior to that time, lining up horses for a fair and legal start was no small task, and horses in a race more often than not were recalled several times before they got the final *go*. The mobile gate was born somewhat by accident when a movie director was filming a harness racing sequence and was unable to get what he wanted with his cameras in a stationary position. The solution to his problem was simple. He attached his equipment to a truck and directed the drivers of the horses to follow him. The results were exactly what the director wanted, but, more important, an idea was born.

Steve Phillips, a knowledgeable horseman as well as trainer, driver, and Starter, witnessed the filming. He noticed how quietly the horses followed the truck as well as the large percentage of good starts they were able to get. It was his thought that if such good starts could be produced behind a moving barrier for a camera, they could be duplicated for a race. Phillips got his brainstorm in 1931, but it was not until 1946, with the financial aid of the young Roosevelt Raceway, that the first gate was built at a cost of $53,000 and introduced. Its success was immediate, and a giant step was taken in the already popular sport of harness racing.

Present mobile starting gates, most of which are direct descendants of the Phillips Barrier, consist of a pair of wings with an approximate span of eighty feet. This mechanism is mounted on a specially built automobile that has an acceleration capability of fifty miles per hour in a distance of fifty yards, a speed unequaled by any horse.

SULKY or BIKE   The vehicle used in actual harness races. It is a light racing rig, weighing between twenty-seven and thirty-five pounds, with bicycle-type wheels. The shafts are usually made of hardwood, but aluminum and steel may also be used. When a driver is in proper position in a sulky, his legs are parallel with the shafts. Seated in such a manner, the driver's weight is of little or no importance, because the sulky and its wheels are in almost perfect balance resulting in an extremely freewheeling action.

TOE WEIGHTS   Two to four ounce brass or lead weights that are clipped on to the horse's front hoofs at the edge to lengthen a trotter's stride. Toe weights are rarely used on pacers.

TRAILING   Racing in the most advantageous position—the number "two-hole" or sometimes called the "win-hole." This particularly desirable spot is just behind the leading horse in a race. It is so favored because the leader—the pacesetter—breaks the force of the wind for the horse racing behind him.

TRAINING or JOGGING CART   A cart used to train harness horses and for the early warm-ups before a race. Generally heavier and longer than the racing sulky, it allows the driver to sit with his feet in a normal "down" position rather than parallel with the shafts, as with the sulky. For these reasons, a training cart is a more comfortable perch for the driver of a harness horse.

TROTTER   A Standardbred horse that races with a diagonally gaited motion, moving his opposite front and rear legs forward at the same time. His left front and right rear legs move forward almost simultaneously, then the right fore and left hind. Trotters frequently display a pronounced high knee action as well as a definite swaying of the head from side to side.

TWO IN THREE   In a *two in three* race in order for a horse to earn first place money he must win two heats. In the event that no winner is decided out of three heats, a fourth and final trial is held that is open only to the winners of the first three heats.

USTA   The United States Trotting Association is the governing body responsible for the registration of Standardbred horses and the conduct of all racing by members and upon member tracks. The rules and regulations set forth by this organization must be ad-hered to by member tracks, and all race conditions and pro-grams must operate in accordance with them. Violation of any of the rules or regulations of this association is punish-able upon conviction by a fine and/or suspension or expul-sion from the association. USTA's main offices are located at 750 Michigan Avenue, Columbus, Ohio 43215.

WALK OVER   A race in which all the contestants represent the same interest. To claim the purse, the entry (*see* ENTRY) must start and complete the course once.

WARM-UP   Several hours before a harness horse is scheduled to race, he begins his warm-up routine. This usually consists of jogging slowly for several miles around the track hitched to a training cart. Then he is brought back to the track at half hour inter-vals for increasingly faster workouts until the last one, which is roughly thirty minutes before he races. During this last work-out, he is asked to work about a mile with a sulky just seconds off the pace the driver intends to set during the race. Between each of these workouts, he is scraped with a sweat scraper and cooled out as much as possible. Most racetracks have some means of identifying the races in which each horse will compete; con-sequently patrons can tell which race horses are preparing for as they warm up between races.

BARBARA VAN TUYL

HORSE SHOWS

AGED   For purposes of describing a horse for entry in a show, any horse that is more than nine years of age is called aged.

AMATEUR   For purposes of competing under AHSA rules, an amateur is:

1. Anyone under eighteen years of age;
2. Anyone more than eighteen years of age who does not engage in any aspect of the horse business as a principal means of his livelihood and might thereby be considered a professional. (*See* PROFESSIONAL.)

Competitors more than eighteen years of age in amateur classes must have an AHSA amateur card.

AMATEUR CARD   A card issued by AHSA upon submission of the required forms, stating that the holder is an amateur and therefore eligible to compete in classes restricting its entrants to amateurs.

AMATEUR CLASS   A class in which all entries are required to be ridden or driven by an amateur.

AMATEUR OWNER CLASS   In order to compete in an Amateur Owner Class under AHSA rules, all entrants must be ridden by amateur owners or an amateur member of the owner's immediate family. In either case, classes are restricted to riders who are no longer eligible to compete as a Junior Exhibitor. Leased horses are ineligible, and multiple ownership is not permitted unless all owners are members of the same immediate family.

AMERICAN HORSE SHOWS ASSOCIATION (AHSA)   This association is the governing body of all member horse shows in the United States. Its rules and format are set forth in the association's annual publication the *AHSA Rule Book,* which is available to all members.

ASHA STEWARD   The AHSA steward is the association's representative at a horse show. His duties are numerous and widespread, but he is mainly concerned with seeing that AHSA rules are upheld throughout all classes in all divisions. He is responsible for clarifying any rule on which there is a question; he should be available at all times to judges, exhibitors, and the horse show management. The steward is required to submit a written report to AHSA as to the conduct of the show (including any offense or rule violation) within three days after its completion. In this way the interests of both the exhibitors and the horse show management are protected. The requirements for becoming an AHSA steward are clearly defined in the *AHSA Rule Book*.

APPALOOSA HORSE DIVISION   To exhibit a horse in the Appaloosa Horse Division at a member show, an animal must first be registered with the Appaloosa Horse Club, Inc., or the Appaloosa Horse Club of Canada and then shown under his full registered name. Appaloosas may be shown with either a natural or roached mane, and the tail should be trimmed to fall near or slightly above the hocks.

Appaloosas are shown under both English and Western tack as pleasure horses and trail horses as well as in a variety of Western events, including Calf Roping, Reining, Cutting, and Stock Horse. There are also specialty classes for Appaloosa Buckboard Pleasure Driving, Open Jumping, and an unusual classification of competitions called Appaloosa Horse Individual Competitive and Racing Events, which are conducted in the age-old custom of the Nez Perce Indians. In these competitions the contestants run horse against horse until the eliminations have been completed. The individual and competitive racing events are held under the auspices of the Appaloosa Horse Club, Inc., and copies of the rules are available from the Appaloosa Horse Club, Inc., Box 403, Moscow, Idaho 83843.

APPOINTMENTS—*Rider*   When competing in any horse show, it is generally understood that, out of courtesy to both the show management and the other exhibitors, all contestants should appear in clothes that are clean and neat as well as fitting for the division in which they are exhibiting be in English or Western. There are some classes, such as a Working Hunter Appointments class in which the dress of the rider counts a certain percentage in the judging of the class itself; in such instances, the dress requirements are specifically described in the *AHSA Rule Book*.

APPOINTMENTS—*Tack*   Clean, well-cared for tack in good repair is not only a rule to be followed for the sake of competition, but also one of the most important safety considerations. It does follow that the better the tack, the better the overall picture presented for judging, but cleanliness and neatness are the main requirements. Certain types of classes may demand that the horse be shown in a specific piece of equipment or without a particular device (e.g., martingales are prohibited in Hunter Under

Saddle classes); however, such classes are clearly indicated in the horse show prize list and the rules governing them are set forth in the *AHSA Rule Book.*

ARABIAN DIVISION   To be shown in this division, horses must be registered with the Arabian Horse Club Registry of America. These horses are exhibited with a long natural mane and unset tail. Arabians may be shown in three ways: pleasure horse under English tack, pleasure horse under Western tack, and park or "showy" horses under English tack. They may also be driven in Pleasure and Formal Driving classes as well as in Roadster classes. Specialty classes may also be offered within the division for Arabian dressage horses, hunters, jumpers, and parade horses, the requirements for which are defined in the *AHSA Rule Book.*

Each section has its own qualifying gaits that have been set forth by AHSA. In pleasure classes, manners and suitability are emphasized, whereas in the park horse classes, brilliance is emphasized by showing off the horse to the utmost.

BREEDING CLASS, also IN HAND CLASS   A nonperformance class in which the horse is judged solely upon type, conformation, substance, and quality. Any transmissible weaknesses and/or unsoundnesses count heavily against breeding stock. Such classes may limit their entries to stallions or mares, with or without get or foal at foot. There may also be restrictions as to age such as "Arabian Division—Mares, Four Years Old." In breeding classes the entry is led in by the exhibitor and stands on the line for judging. In some classes the exhibitor may be asked to jog the horse a short distance so that the judge may evaluate his way of going: Does the animal wing or paddle; does he break a lot at the knee or move close to the ground.

In all breeding classes each entrant must be registered in the studbook of his particular breed and is shown under his registered name and number.

CHALLENGE TROPHY   A trophy which has been donated to or offered by a show for a specific purpose. The donor sets forth the conditions of competition for the trophy and specifies the number of times it must be won for permanent possession.

CHAMPIONSHIP   Under AHSA rules, there are two ways to earn a championship. In the Hunter and Jumper divisions, championships are awarded on points. In the Morgan division, championships *may* be awarded on points. When championships are awarded on points, all competitors must be given an equal chance to obtain points. In all other divisions, championships are awarded in a championship performance class.

CHAMPIONSHIP CLASS   A performance class in which the winner is adjudged the champion of the division. To be eligible for entry in a performance championship class, AHSA rules require that a horse must be properly entered, shown, and judged in one qualifying class in the same division or section.

CHILD   For purposes of showing in the equitation or Junior Horse divisions, a child is defined as a rider who has not reached his eighteenth birthday. For uniformity, the *AHSA Rule Book* maintains that the rider's age on January first of a given year is kept throughout that year, despite the fact that perhaps the next day, he might actually be a year older.

COMBINATION CLASS   A class in which the entrants are shown both in harness and under saddle.

CONFORMATION HUNTER   A conformation hunter is judged on his appearance and physical build as well as on his performance. Conformation can count anywhere from twenty-five to fifty percent depending upon the section (Regular Conformation or Green Conformation Hunter) and the specific class, the other fifty to seventy-five percent being on the performance over fences. Each horse in the class jumps the course, and then the top eight to twelve are asked to line up without saddles to be judged on conformation. It is possible to be called out on top on performance and to be moved back as many as four places (or more, in unusual circumstances) on conformation, depending upon the quality of the horses behind you. It is also possible to be rated second, third—even fourth on performance and be moved up to first, again depending upon the quality of your horse in comparison with the horses called out in front of you. *See also* HUNTER.

CORINTHIAN HUNTER CLASS   Under AHSA rules, a Corinthian Hunter is a horse ridden, in hunting attire, by an amateur who is a member of (or in case of subscription pack, fully accredited subscriber to) a Recognized or Registered Hunt.

COSTUME CLASS   A class within a division in which the entrants compete in and are judged on costumes befitting their breed. For example, Arabian Mounted Native Costume Class.

ELIMINATIONS   Sometimes there are such a large number of entries in a given class, it becomes necessary to hold eliminations or qualifying rounds before the class itself is held. In some cases the horses carry their scores from the eliminations into the final competition with them, other times they are simply qualified to compete in the class that is then judged as a new class, or, as is the case with the year end finals for the AHSA medals, all qualified entrants perform in the eliminations and then the judges select approximately fifteen riders for the actual finals.

ENTRY BLANK   The form provided by the horse show on which an exhibitor lists the classes in which he and/or his horse will be competing. Entry blanks for AHSA-member shows are a little more elaborate than those for a nonmember show and must meet AHSA's requirements.

ENTRY FEE   The fee required by the horse show to exhibit an entry in a class. The amounts are variable and must be stated on the prize list for each class or division.

EQUITATION DIVISIONS   The word *equitation* refers to the act and/or art of riding horses. It follows that an equitation class is one in which the rider is judged on the position and use of his hands, seat, legs, and overall coordination, while the horse's performance is considered only in so much as it is a direct result of the rider's direction. This means that the horse's way of going on the flat or jumping style over fences does not influence the judge's decision unless, for example, a poor jump on the horse's part occurs as a result of the rider's bad hands or faulty judgment.

Equitation is synonymous with *horsemanship,* and in a horse show prize list or catalogue the division might be called Equitation Division or Horsemanship Division and could offer as many or as few classes as the show committee wished. There are three possible types of equitation divisions: Saddle Seat, Stock Seat, and Hunter Seat. Within these divisions there are three types of classes: 1. Those restricting the participants with regard to previous winnings—Maiden, Novice, Limit; 2. Those without restriction—Open; 3. Specialty classes—Saddle Seat "Good Hands" class or Hunter Seat "Medal" class. In the Saddle Seat and Stock Seat divisions, the classes are all held on the flat. In the Hunter Seat division, there are classes on the flat, classes over fences, and —in a few instances—combination classes wherein the riders perform either on the flat or over fences and are then recalled to jump or work out on the flat.

The recognized equitation divisions are open only to children under eighteen years of age (*see* CHILD); however, some shows may offer Adult equitation classes or divisions where local interest demands and, in such cases, the show committee determines the qualifications for eligibility and the age limit.

EXCUSED
1. Once a class is in progress, a rider may be excused from the ring before the completion of the class by asking the judge's permission to do so.
2. Should a horse prove to be fractious and unruly in a class and the judge considers it a safety threat to the other exhibitors, he may have the animal excused and either called to the center of the ring for the duration of the class or temporarily halt the class and put the horse out of the ring.
3. A horse that has committed too many faults in a jumping class to be eligible for an award may be excused and asked to leave the ring without finishing the course. (Most shows try to give each exhibitor a fair opportunity to perform; however, when there are large numbers of entries and time is an important factor, the considerate exhibitor will voluntarily withdraw, if he realizes he has no chance.)

FALL OF HORSE According to AHSA, a horse is considered to have fallen when the shoulder and haunch on the same side have touched the ground or an obstacle and the ground.

FALL OF HORSE AND/OR RIDER Under AHSA rules, in all classes, except Hunter, Jumper, Western, and Equitation (in which specific rules prevail), the fall of horse and/or rider does not disqualify the entry, unless due to bad manners of the horse.

FALL OF RIDER A rider is considered to have fallen when he is separated from his horse that has not fallen, in such a way as to necessitate remounting or vaulting into the saddle, according to the rules of the AHSA.

FEI The *Federation Equestre Internationale,* which is the governing body of International Jumping competitions.

FINALS The last or ultimate judging of a class for which there have been one or more qualifying rounds or eliminations.

FINE HARNESS HORSE SECTION A part of the Saddle Horse Division as outlined in the *AHSA Rule Book.* These horses are shown with full mane and undocked tail at the park trot—an animated park gait in which extreme speed is penalized—and the walk, which is to be animated and graceful. Light harness with snaffle bit and overcheck is required, and these horses should be shown with an appropriate vehicle—preferably a small buggy with four wire wheels but without a top.

FIVE-GAITED SADDLE HORSE—*Qualifying Gaits*   According to AHSA rules, a five-gaited Saddle Horse is judged on the performance of the following gaits:

1. Walk—animated and graceful;
2. Trot—square, collected, and balanced with hocks well under;
3. Canter—smooth, slow, and straight on both leads;
4. Slow gait—a slow, high, animated gait and not a slow rack;
5. Rack—a four-beat gait done at speed and in form.

FLAT CLASS   Any class at a horse show in which the entrants perform at the walk, trot, canter, slow gait, or rack (and sometimes hand gallop or gallop)—or *on the flat* only and are not required to jump.

GAITED HORSE or CLASS   Refers primarily to either a three- or five-gaited American Saddle Horse or a class for these horses. It may also be used to describe any horse which has been schooled to artificial gaits such as the running walk of the Tennessee Walking Horse. *See also* THREE-GAITED SADDLE HORSE and FIVE-GAITED SADDLE HORSE.

GO CLEAN   An open jumper that negotiated a course without touching any of the fences is said to have gone *clean.*

GO-ROUND   The Western equivalent of eliminations. *See* ELIMINATIONS.

GREEN HUNTER   For purposes of showing under AHSA rules, a *green hunter* is any horse, regardless of age, that is in his first or second year of showing in jumping classes at recognized, rated horse shows. Going on the premise that the more experienced a horse is, the more difficult the course ought to be, first-year horses are shown over fences no less than three feet, six inches high, and second-year horses are shown over fences no less than three feet, nine inches high. Thus green refers to a sort of "beginner" state of the horse; it may be applied to classes in the Working and Conformation Hunter sections of the Hunter Division—Green Conformation Hunter Section or Green Working Hunter Section. Once a horse has completed two years of showing at recognized, rated shows in the green divisions, he is no longer eligible for this classification and must be shown in the Regular Working Hunter or Conformation Hunter sections over fences four feet in height. *See also* HUNTER, CONFORMATION HUNTER, WORKING HUNTER, REGULAR HUNTER.

GREEN STOCK HORSE   AHSA defines a green stock horse as one that has not been shown in any stock horse, reining, or cow horse class prior to December first of the previous year.

HACK CLASS or HUNTER HACKS   A hunter class in which the entries work both directions of the ring at the walk, trot, and canter and at the gallop (with the exception of Green and Young Hunters, which are not required to gallop) in only one direction of the ring. Then at least eight horses, if available, are required to jump two fences three feet, six inches high.

HACKNEY AND HARNESS PONY DIVISION   AHSA requires that entries in Hackney Classes must be registered with the American or Canadian Hackney Horse Societies and must be entered under their full registered name. A Harness pony in performance classes may be any breed or combination of breeds.

For horse show purposes, the maximum height of Hackney ponies is 14.2 hands and of Harness ponies is 12.2 hands.

Hackney ponies are exhibited with a short mane braided and short tail, while Harness ponies are shown with a long mane and undocked tail. Ponies may be shown in either the Hackney pony section or the Harness pony section, but not in both. Requirements as to the types of vehicles and equipment permitted are described in the *AHSA Rule Book*.

HACK OFF   In the Hunter Division in which the championship is awarded on points earned throughout the show, it is possible for two or more horses to be tied with an equal number of points. In such an instance, the qualified horses are worked before the judges under the rules governing an under saddle class and the top two horses are awarded the Championship and Reserve Championship, respectively. This workout on the flat is called a *hack off*.

HEAVYWEIGHT HUNTER   *See* HUNTER CLASSIFICATIONS.

HIGH SCORE AWARDS   For the purpose of encouraging exhibitors to participate in recognized shows, AHSA offers over thirty High

Score Awards. These awards are presented to the horses accumulating the highest number of points in their respective divisions or sections at regular member shows throughout the show season (December 1 through November 30). In order to be eligible to receive an award, the horse must be registered with AHSA, and the owner must be a member in good standing.

HOLD HARD   A command borrowed from the hunt field which may be issued during the hand gallop or gallop in an under saddle, hack, or occasionally a hunter seat equitation class on the flat. It means that the exhibitors are to halt and stand in place as promptly as they are able.

HORSE   The term *horse* when used for horse showing purposes designates animals over 14.2 hands, with the exception of Registered Appaloosas, Arabians, Half-Arabs, Morgans, Palominos, Pintos, and Quarter Horses. AHSA maintains that if an animal that is 14.2 hands or under is eligible to compete as a horse in any one of these divisions, it may also compete as a horse in other appropriate classes. It may not, however, compete as a horse in one class and a pony in another class at the same show. A mature horse is one that is more than four years of age.

HORSE SHOW CATALOGUE or PROGRAM   The horse show catalogue is prepared as a result of entries made from a prize list (*see* PRIZE LIST). In addition to the order of events, specifications for each class, and names of committees, judges and officials, there is also a listing of entries for each class, which includes a description of each horse, indicating its name, color, sex, height, AHSA registration number (if any), and the owner's name.

HUNTER   A hunter is shown over a course of fences simulating those which a horse might encounter while following a pack of hounds fox hunting across country. He is judged on his performance, manners, and way of going if he is a Working Hunter, and on these points plus his physical beauty, build, and appearance if he is a Conformation Hunter. He should gallop over the course at an even hunting pace with long, easy strides, and without excessive motions. He should approach every fence in a straight line and jump in stride without hesitation, land, and move on all in one motion. He should exhibit good manners, be easy to control, and present a smooth performance from the first fence to the last. He is not charged with "faults" of specific value as are open jumpers, but his round will be penalized for uneven hunter pace; refusing or ducking by a fence; knockdowns; swerving; jumping in bad form or dangerously; excessive speed; and, in cases where there are a number of outstanding performances, the way he moves—long and low to the ground or short and high stepping—can make the difference between being first and being out of the ribbons.

All horses competing in the Hunter Division must be service-ably sound and will be refused an award if there is any evidence of lameness, broken wind, or impairment of vision. *See also* WORKING HUNTER, CONFORMATION HUNTER, GREEN HUNTER.

HUNTER CLASSIFICATIONS   Under AHSA rules, the Green and Regular Sections of the Hunter Division may be further divided into the following classifications:

1.   Small—not to exceed 15.2½ hands;
2.   Lightweight—up to carrying 165 pounds;
3.   Middleweight—up to carrying 185 pounds;
4.   Heavyweight—up to carrying 205 pounds;
5.   Thoroughbred—registered in any studbook recognized by the Jockey Club;
6.   Non-Thoroughbred—not registered as a Thoroughbred;
7.   Qualified—A Qualified Hunter is a horse that has been hunted regularly and satisfactorily for one or more seasons with a pack of hounds recognized by the Masters of Foxhounds Association of America or England. A letter or certificate from the Master to this effect must be filed with AHSA and is good for a period of two years.

IN GATE and OUT GATE   The opening through which the show committee has requested that all entries go into the ring is called the *in gate*, while the designated ring exit is the *out gate*. In and out gates are an important safety feature of most shows, and it is in the interest of keeping the show moving along (by facilitating the emptying of a ring after a class and the entrance of the riders for the following one), as well as avoiding collisions that exhibitors should use the gates to which they are directed.

IN HAND CLASS   *See* BREEDING CLASS.

IN THE RIBBONS   A horse that receives an award in a class is said to have been *in the ribbons*. There are customarily four or six placings in each class, although the larger shows sometimes give out as many as eight or ten. *See also* RIBBONS.

53

JOG FOR SOUNDNESS   In all hunter classes over fences, the horses selected by the judge to receive awards on the basis of performance must be jogged before him prior to being pinned. Should one (or more) of the animals chosen appear to be lame, broken in wind, or defective in vision, he will be eliminated, and the horse with the next highest performance score will move into the vacant position for the final pinning of ribbons.

JUDGE'S CARD   The card on which the judge scores the performance of the participants in a class. Each class requires a separate card on which the exact specifications for that class are listed. Once a class is completed and pinned, the judge's card becomes the property of the horse show. No exhibitor is permitted to inspect the card without first obtaining the judge's permission, and the judge has the option of refusal.

The license of a "recognized" judge is also called a Judge's Card.

JUMPER   A jumper, which may be of any breed or type, is required to negotiate a course of obstacles that he may clear in any manner. He is scored mathematically by faults, which he commits by either touching or knocking down any part of a fence with any part of his body. Refusing to jump a given obstacle on the first attempt is a disobedience, which also costs the entry faults. A second refusal in a round contributes further cumulative faults; a third causes elimination from the event. Jumpers are shown under FEI (*see* FEI) rules as well as AHSA rules, which differ on only two points:

1. Only knockdowns are scored under FEI, touches do not count as under AHSA;
2. Fall of horse and/or rider does not require elimination under FEI rules as it does under AHSA's; instead an entry is penalized eight faults for a fall.

Time is also a factor in many open jumper classes, which literally makes it a contest to see which horse can jump the highest, widest fences with the least number of faults in the shortest time.

There are no requirements as to soundness (as in the Hunter Division), unless the unsoundness is sufficiently severe as to be considered an act of cruelty. In such instances, the horse show management is responsible for barring the entry from further participation.

Jumpers may be divided into three sections based upon their cash winnings—Preliminary, Intermediate, and Open—in addition to the Amateur/Owner section, which requires that the horse be ridden by an Amateur-Owner irrespective of cash winnings. *See* AMATEUR/OWNER.

JUMPS   Horse shows are encouraged to use the largest variety of obstacles available to them as long as any "unusual" jumps presented can still be considered a fair, "jumpable" test of the horse's ability. Since hunter courses are comprised of obstacles that might conceivably be encountered in the hunt field, there is some limitation as to the types of employable fences. However, there are no restrictions (except those pertaining to safety) on the obstacles that may be offered in the jumper division. *See* diagrams on pages 56 and 57.

JUMPOFF   In the open jumper division in which rounds are scored mathematically by faults, if two or more contestants perform over the course without incurring any faults, or with an equal number of faults, they are tied. Depending upon the conditions of a specific class, one or more rounds will be jumped again with the fences raised and/or spread. Time also becomes a factor in many instances, and frequently the course is shortened by eliminating one or more fences from the original. This practice gives the riders a greater opportunity to make "time turns" and take short cuts and chances in an effort to jump the course in the fastest possible time with the least number of faults. Such additional rounds are called *jumpoffs.*

JUNIOR HUNTER DIVISION   The Junior Hunter Division is basically the same as the Hunter Division with the following exceptions:

1. All exhibitors must be children as defined by the AHSA. (*See* CHILD);
2. The entries must be handled by Junior Exhibitors in all phases of a class. This means that an adult may not jog a horse for soundness or stand him up in a model class, despite the fact that he has been ridden by and is owned by a child;
3. Stallions are barred from all classes limited to Junior Exhibitors; and
4. The height of fences should never exceed three feet, six inches.

JUNIOR JUMPER DIVISION   The format of the Junior Jumper Division is the same as that of the Jumper Division, with the exceptions that all entries must be exhibited by children as defined by AHSA (*see* CHILD) and that at no time may the fences be raised or spread more than five feet (except in

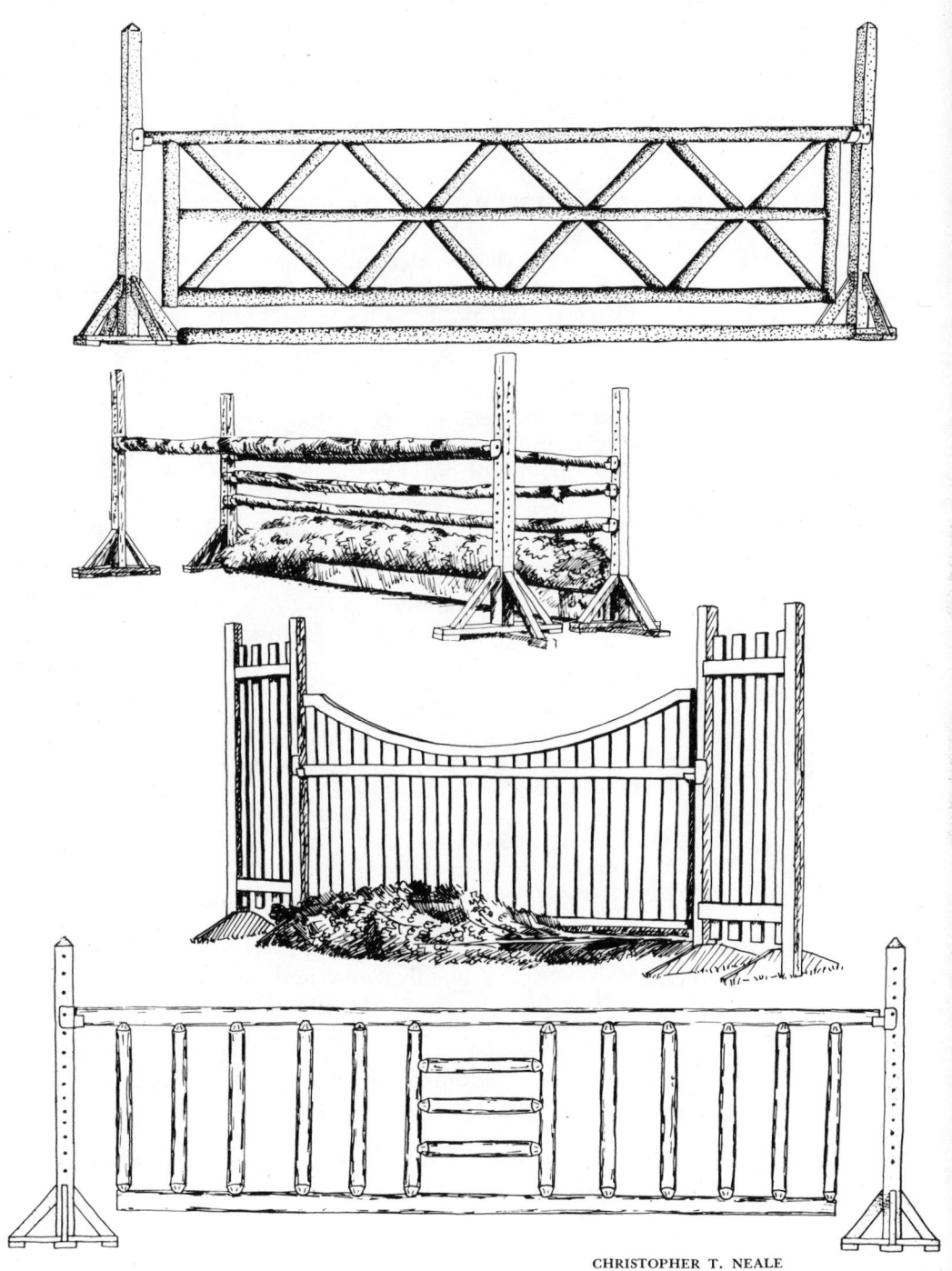

CHRISTOPHER T. NEALE

Puissance Classes at an "A" rated show, in which they may be raised to five feet, six inches).

LADIES CLASS   A class requiring that all entries be either ridden or driven by a lady.

LIGHTWEIGHT HUNTER   *See* HUNTER CLASSIFICATIONS.

LIMIT CLASS   A class that is open only to horses or riders who have not won six first ribbons at Regular Member Shows of AHSA— Limit Three-Gaited Saddle Horses or Limit Hunter Seat Equitation.

LINE UP   After all entries in a flat class have been worked both ways of the ring at the required gaits, they are usually asked to *line up* in the center of the ring, either for further individual testing or for the purpose of pinning the ribbons.

LOCAL CLASS   A class in which all exhibitors must live within a certain area specified by the horse show as a condition of the class in the prize list.

LOCAL HORSE SHOW   A Local Show Member is one in which the divisions and sections offered have no AHSA rating. Ribbons won at such shows thus do not count towards AHSA Annual High Score Awards. Maiden, Novice, Limit, and Green status of horses are not affected by winnings at Local Show Members. However, ribbons won in the Equitation divisions are applicable to the rider's maiden, novice, and limit qualifications.

MAIDEN CLASS   A class open only to horses or riders who have not won one first ribbon at a Regular Member Show of AHSA— Maiden Hunters or Maiden Hunter Seat Equitation.

MANNERS   When the judging of a class is to include a score for manners, the judge is mainly concerned with the horse's overall attitude. He is looking for a horse that does not fuss and throw his head around; maintains an even, steady pace; and does not pull at the bridle, kick at other horses, or move at a high rate of speed. The animal should display a docile yet alert temperament and give the appearance of being easily controlled.

MEASUREMENT CARD   Under AHSA rules, in classes restricted to ponies, no animal may be shown in a performance class, unless the owner possesses a measurement card issued by AHSA or by an affiliate or possesses a duplicate copy of a measurement form. The duplicate copy of the measurement form is valid until the end of the year for ponies five years old or under. It is only valid for eighteen days for ponies six years old or more.

Every pony must be measured yearly until it reaches the age of six, at which time it is issued a measurement card valid for life.

MIDDLEWEIGHT HUNTER *See* HUNTER CLASSIFICATIONS.

MODEL CLASS A class in which the horse is judged solely on his conformation—that is, physical build, quality, substance, and overall appearance. The class is literally an equine beauty contest with no performance requirements.

MORGAN HORSE DIVISION Under AHSA auspices, horses shown in this division must be registered with the Morgan Horse Club, Inc., and must be entered under their full registered name. Morgans are shown with a full natural mane and tail. Braids or the addition of supplemental hair in the mane or tail, as well as any evidence of ginger or tailsetting result in disqualification. All entries must be serviceably sound and in good condition.

Morgans are most versatile performance horses and may be shown in harness and/or under saddle, in English or Western tack, as well as in various combination classes in which they are both ridden and driven.

NON-THOROUGHBRED HUNTER *See* HUNTER CLASSIFICATIONS.

NOVICE CLASS A class open only to horses or riders who have not won three first ribbons at Regular Member Shows of AHSA—Novice Hunters or Novice Hunt Seat Equitation.

OFF COURSE Failure to keep the prescribed course in competition constitutes elimination. Going off course includes negotiating obstacles in any sequence other than the designated order or in the wrong direction. It also includes failure to cross the starting or finishing markers.

OLYMPIC GAMES The Equestrian Olympic Games consist of three events. The *Prix des Nations,* which is the jumping competition that consists of several events, each of which is open to

59

three riders and three horses from each country. It is scored either as a team of three or as an individual.

The *Three-Day Event* is the tri-phase competition testing the versatility of horse and rider. It is open to a team of four from each country and judged both individually and as a team in each of three sections: 1) *dressage;* 2) endurance test, which includes cross-country and steeplechase performances; and 3) stadium jumping.

The *Individual Dressage Competition* is open to two representatives from each country and judged solely on the individual performances of the *dressage* test.

OPEN CLASS   A class open to all horses or riders regardless of their previous experience or winnings—Open Jumpers or Open Saddle Seat Equitation.

OUTSIDE COURSE   A hunter course not laid out within the confines of a ring; it is thus more apt to simulate the conditions found in the hunt field.

OWNERS' CLASSES   According to AHSA, an Owners' Class is one in which every contestant is an amateur, and the rider or driver is the owner or an amateur member of the owner's immediate family.

Owners' classes may be restricted to riders or drivers who are no longer eligible to compete as Junior Exhibitors and may be offered in any division using the specifications as set forth in the respective division rules.

PALOMINO HORSE DIVISION   To compete in this division, AHSA requires that all horses be registered with either the Palomino Horse Breeders of America, The Palomino Horse Association, or the Canadian Palomino Horse Association, or, if under age, must be eligible for registration.

The color qualifications for Palominos are specifically outlined in the *AHSA Rule Book,* and judges may eliminate animals of extreme variations of body color or those carrying more than fifteen percent dark or off colored hair in either mane or tail, or both.

Palominos may be shown as Pleasure Horses under English or Western tack with qualifying gaits described for each one separately, as Three-Gaited Saddle Horses under English tack and as Stock Horses under plain Western tack, including stock and trail horse sections.

PARADE HORSE DIVISION   AHSA states: "The Parade Horse must be a beautiful, stylish animal, displaying refinement and personality and presenting eye-appeal of horse and rider. Entries may be of any color or combination or colors, of any breed or combination of breeds, stallions, mares or geldings. Good manners are essential, both in executing gaits and while lined up in the ring."

Parade horses are shown with a full mane and undocked tail, which may be arched but not held in a vertical position. All entries must be over 14.2 hands, and the tack and rider should be suitable to the horse.

The Parade Horse is required to perform at two gaits—an animated walk and a "parade gait," both of which are carefully defined in the *AHSA Rule Book*.

PARK PACE and SHOW YOUR PONY   These are commands that may be given in Hackney and Harness pony classes to indicate that the entries are to move out at a "smart trot" without excessive speed.

PERFORMANCE   When performance is the sole requisite of a class, then obviously whatever an entry might do during the course of the judging is considered a part of performance—open jumping classes where all that counts is jumping obstacles without incurring faults. However, some classes are judged only in part on performance with the balance being divided among manners, way of going, conformation, suitability, and so forth. When this is the case, performance usually refers to the way or form in which the horse executes his specialty. For example, a brilliant jumper or saddle horse could receive top call in the judge's opinion for jumping style or fine action under saddle and still be marked down in a class limited to ladies or juniors for being overly strong or hard to manage simply because, despite outstanding performances, they were sufficiently unsuitable or unmannerly to be considered a poor mount for a lady or child.

PINNED   A horse or rider who receives a ribbon in a class is said to have been *pinned*. Also, the expression *to pin a class* refers to the selection of entrants to receive awards: "Has the judge pinned the class yet?"

PINTO HORSE DIVISION   To be shown in this division, AHSA requires that the horses be registered with the Pinto Horse Association of America, Inc. Since many breed types may be exhibited in this division, the specifications for the various classes that can be offered and how they might be divided are well defined in the *AHSA Rule Book*. However, in all cases, suitability of the horse and its action for the type of job at hand is essential.

Pintos are shown under both Western and English tack as well as in harness. Classes may be offered for Western or English pleasure horses, trail horses, stock horses, reining horses, cutting horses, matched pairs, hunter or saddle exhibitors, driving horses, roadsters, and parade horses. Additional classes for Pinto dressage horses, hunters, jumpers, and saddle horses may also be offered and judged in accordance with the rules of the respective divisions.

POLING   A schooling tactic for jumping horses in which the horse's legs are struck "smartly" with a bamboo pole as he jumps an obstacle. This rapping of the animal's legs is accomplished by a person standing beside the obstacle, usually hidden from the horse as much as is possible. (*Note:* AHSA has very stringent rules with regard to the practice of poling and the type of pole used. Violations of these rules can result in the horse's elimination from one or more events in which it had been entered, and such violations must be recorded in the Steward's report to AHSA. If there is any evidence of cruelty or abusive behavior indicated in the report, the violator may be brought before the Hearing Committee for such action as may be deemed appropriate to the particular circumstances.)

PONY   For purposes of competing in horse shows, the word *pony* is used to designate animals which stand 14.2 hands or less. To compete in classes restricted to ponies, the owner of the animal is required to possess a measurement card. *See* MEASUREMENT CARD.

PONY HUNTER DIVISION   The specifications for the Pony Hunter Division are basically the same as those for the Hunter Division with the following exceptions:

1. All exhibitors must be children as defined by AHSA. (*See* CHILD);
2. Entries must be handled by Junior Exhibitors in all phases of a class;
3. All entries in a performance class must possess a measurement card (*see* MEASUREMENT CARD);
4. Stallions are barred from all classes.

Classes for pony hunters may be divided by size of pony, and the height of the fences must be changed accordingly:

1. Not exceeding 11.2 hands—fences two feet;
2. Over 11.2 hands and not exceeding 13 hands—fences two feet, six inches; and
3. More than 13 hands and not exceeding 14.2 hands—fences three feet.

If a show only offers two pony hunter sections, then the division is made at 13 hands, with ponies over 13 hands jumping three feet, and ponies under 13 hands jumping two feet, six inches.

When showing pony hunters, manners and suitability of pony for rider are emphasized in all classes. Extreme speed is penalized.

PONY JUMPER DIVISION   The Pony Jumper Division is governed by the same rules for scoring and class specifications as the Jumper Division, with the exceptions that it is open only to ponies and Junior Exhibitors and subject to the same height limitations as the Pony Hunter Division. The only exception to these heights occurs in the case of a tie score, when the jumps may be raised a maximum of nine inches for each height division. *See also* JUMPER DIVISION and PONY HUNTER DIVISION.

PONY OF THE AMERICAS DIVISION   AHSA requires that all entries in this division must be registered either tentatively or permanently in the Studbook of the Pony of the Americas Club, Inc., and they must be entered under their full registered names.

There are both Western and English classes offered within the POA division, and the qualifying gaits for each of these are clearly described in the *AHSA Rule Book*. These ponies are also shown in harness and as jumpers.

POST ENTRIES   Entries that are made after the date specified by the horse show as the closing for receipt of entries. A show may choose not to accept post entries, but under AHSA rules is required to state its policy on the prize list. If post entries are accepted, it is not uncommon for there to be an additional charge to compensate for the extra work involved on show day and to discourage exhibitors from making late entries.

PRIZE LIST   A booklet or flyer sent out several weeks in advance of a horse show to prospective exhibitors. It contains information that includes the exact date, time, and place of the show; the judges and responsible parties; a complete listing of all events, trophies, and prize monies offered; the amount of entry fee per class; and any other information which that particular show feels is pertinent and will draw entries.

PROFESSIONAL   For purposes of showing under AHSA rules, a professional is anyone over the age of eighteen years:

1. whose principal means of livelihood is derived from horse activities, such as breeding, riding, driving, schooling, training, or boarding horses; dealing in horses—buying and selling; instructing in horsemanship; owning or managing a racing, show, schooling, livery, or boarding stable for horses or a riding academy, circus or rodeo;
2. who accepts employment in connection with horses in a racing, show, livery, or boarding stable; riding academy; circus; or rodeo;
3. who is paid directly or indirectly for exercising, schooling, riding, driving, or giving instruction;
4. who is paid for the use of his name, photograph, or other form of personal association as a horseman in connection with advertisements or articles to be sold.

A professional is also any member of the family of a professional who assists in the activities that qualify another member of the family as a professional.

PROTESTS   Any exhibitor or his agent, trainer, or the parent of a junior exhibitor may file a protest with AHSA for any violation of the rules that take place at an AHSA member horse show. Such protests may be made in writing and signed by the protester; protests, accompanied by a twenty-five-dollar deposit, should be addressed to the secretary of the show at which the alleged violation occurred and received by a member of the show committee within forty-eight hours of the incident. Unless it is in direct violation of AHSA rules, a judge's decision may not be protested because it represents his *individual preference,* and the soundness of a horse cannot be protested if it has been determined by an official show veterinarian or by a judge. Either party to a protest or charge may appeal the decision of the show committee to the hearing committee.

QUALIFIED HUNTER   *See* HUNTER CLASSIFICATIONS.

QUARTER HORSE DIVISION   Horses shown in performance classes in this division must be registered with the American

Quarter Horse Association and must be entered under their full, registered names. There are definite specifications set forth by AHSA as to the rider's personal appointments, the types of tack permitted and prohibited, and special "instructions" to riders.

There are five basic types of performance classes which may be offered in this division: Reining Classes, Western Riding Horse Classes, Trail Horse Classes, Pleasure Horse Classes, and Working Cow Horse Classes. Additional classes for Calf and Steer Roping, Barrel Racing, and Pole Bending may be held under regulations available from either AHSA or the American Quarter Horse Association. Cutting Horse classes run under the regulations set forth by the National Cutting Horse Association may also be offered.

RACK ON   The popular command of the Five-Gaited Saddle Horse Classes, which is the signal to turn on the speed at the rack and show the horse at his brilliant best.

RATING—*AHSA Horse Show*   At a horse show which is a Regular Member of AHSA, each division is rated A, B, or C for the purpose of reckoning points for the association's annual High Score Awards. These ratings are based on definite specifications which must be met by the show with respect to the number of classes and amount of premiums offered. To meet the requirements for an A division, the minimums are higher than for the B or C divisions—a show with an A rating in the Green Working Hunter section of the Hunter Division would have to offer at least five classes and a minimum of $750 total prize money, whereas a B rating in the same division would only require four classes and $300 total prize money. The point values towards the Division High Score Awards are quadruple for ribbons won at an A show, double for ribbons won at a B show, and single for ribbons won at a C show.

RECOGNIZED HORSE SHOW   A horse show which, as a result of filing an application for membership, payment of dues, and compliance with the requirements for its classification, has become a member of AHSA.

Recognized shows are classified as to their type of membership (*see* LOCAL HORSE SHOW and REGULAR MEMBER HORSE SHOW) and rated A, B, and C for the purpose of reckoning points towards the association's annual awards in the various divisions. *See* RATING—AHSA.

Not all horse shows are AHSA members, but the benefits derived by the shows and exhibitors alike make AHSA membership an attractive proposition. For example, exhibitors generally would much rather compete at a show where certain standards of safety are a must, and there is a minimum on the premiums (as would be the case with a AHSA member show) than at one without such stipulations. AHSA member shows, which can offer licensed judges, points towards the annual High Score Awards, and a uniformity of organization required by the association, are attractive to exhibitors and draw more entries. (The more entries a show has, the more money it makes, which is, after all, the main reason for holding a show.)

REGISTERED HORSE   A horse with its name, description, and number recorded in the recognized studbook of its particular breed in any country. Horses need not be registered to be shown (except in breeding classes); however, any horse may be registered with AHSA upon payment of a fee, either in addition to his existing registration or as his sole means of identification. (To be eligible for the AHSA High Score Awards, a horse must be registered with AHSA, and its owner must be a member of AHSA in good standing.)

REGULAR HUNTER   A Regular Hunter is a horse of any age not restricted by previous showing in any division. "Regular" hunters, which may be either "Working" or "Conformation," are shown over fences not lower than four feet (at A and B rated shows) and three feet, nine inches (at C rated shows) and not exceeding four feet, six inches.

REGULAR MEMBER HORSE SHOW   This type of show is one in which the divisions and sections offered are individually rated A, B or C for purposes of reckoning points towards the AHSA annual High Score Awards for ribbons won. *See also* RECOGNIZED HORSE SHOW.

RESERVE CHAMPION   The placing of a *Reserve Champion* grew out of the old-time practice of having the horse judged the champion certified sound by a veterinarian. To avoid the embarrassment of finding the selected champion unsound, a second horse was chosen in reserve. Today the term simply refers to the champion's runner-up.

RIBBONS   At recognized horse shows in the United States, ribbons are awarded in the following colors:

66

Grand Champion—*blue, red, yellow, white;* Reserve to Grand Champion—*red, yellow, white, pink;* Champion—*blue, red, yellow;* Reserve Champion—*red, yellow, white;* First Place—*blue;* Second Place—*red;* Third Place—*yellow;* Fourth Place—*white;* Fifth Place—*pink;* Sixth Place—*green;* Seventh Place—*purple;* Eighth Place—*brown;* Ninth Place—*gray;* Tenth Place—*light blue.*

RING MASTER   An employee of the horse show, the ring master is responsible for keeping order in the ring while the classes are in progress. He acts as a sort of go-between for the judge and exhibitors, calling out the commands for changes of gait and so forth as the judge indicates his wishes, sounding a horn or whistle to indicate that an entry has been excused, pinning the ribbons on the horses at the end of a class, and in general seeing that the events in the ring move along smoothly.

ROADSTER DIVISION   According to the description set forth by AHSA, a Roadster should be a standard or nonstandard bred horse of attractive appearance, balanced in conformation, and with manners making him a safe risk in the ring. Roadsters must be serviceably sound and are shown without artificial appliances, except quarter boots and an inconspicuously applied tail switch or brace.

There are two types of Roadsters for show—those suitable for bike and those suitable for road wagon. Occasionally some horses are suitable for both purposes; however, in most instances, the Road Wagon Roadster will have more substance and height than the Bike Roadster.

The main gait for Roadsters is the trot. They may be asked to trot at three different speeds—the slow jog trot, the fast road gait, and then at full speed. Regardless of the speed, they should work in good form—that is, with their chins set and their legs working underneath them in collection.

ROUND or TRIP   A single performance over a hunter, equitation or jumper course is called a round or trip.

RUB CLASS   A slang term for open jumper classes in which touches are counted as faults, as opposed to ones in which only knockdowns are scored.

SADDLE AND FINE HARNESS PONY SECTION   Classes for Saddle and Fine Harness Ponies are restricted to entries 14.2 hands

67

and under. The owner of all entries in performance classes must possess a current measurement card. *See* MEASUREMENT CARD.

The specifications for these classes should follow as closely as possible the standards of similar classes for horses. The graceful trot and easy canter, typical of the saddle horse breed, are required.

SADDLE HORSE DIVISION   In order to be entered in this division horses must be of the American Saddle Horse type. Beginning January 1, 1974, horses shown in the Three-Gaited Saddle Horse Section, Five-Gaited Saddle Horse Section, Fine Harness Horse Section, and American Saddlebred Pleasure Horse Sections must be registered with the American Saddle Horse Breeders Association and be entered under their full registered name. They must be serviceably sound and shown without artificial appliances, except inconspicuously applied hair in the mane and tail, a tail brace, and mouth controls. They are permitted to use quarter boots in Five-Gaited performance classes and Fine Harness classes. Three-Gaited Saddle Horses show with a roached mane and tail, while Five-Gaited Saddle Horses show with a full mane and tail.

SCHOOLING FENCE   A fence or fences provided by a horse show and set apart from the ring or other areas of competition for the jumping horse exhibitors to use as a practice or warm-up jump prior to entering a class.

SHAKEY TAILS   A slang term for a Saddle Horse.

SHETLAND PONY DIVISION   All entries in this division must be registered in the American Shetland Pony Club Studbook and shown under their full registered name and number. Ponies may not be shown in performance classes unless their owners possess a current measurement card. *See* MEASUREMENT CARD. In addition to breeding classes, Shetlands are shown in harness, hitched to a roadster cart, under saddle in English or Western tack, and in a special "Pony Fancy Turnout" class.

SINGLEFOOT   Another name for the "rack," one of the two artificial gaits of the Five-Gaited Saddle Horse, stemming from its four-beat gait in which each foot strikes the ground separately; hence the term *singlefoot*.

SMALL HUNTER   *See* HUNTER CLASSIFICATIONS.

STAKE CLASS   A performance class in any section emphasizing brilliance, in which the prize money offered—as well as the number of placings—is greater than that offered in any other class within the section.

STOCK HORSE SECTION   A section of the Western Division which may be divided into two distinct types of classes—those in which the horses are not worked on cattle, and those in which they are. In classes worked without cattle, the horses are judged on a basis of a hundred points for a perfect score, which is broken down as follows: rein work, fifty points; conformation, twenty points; manners, twenty points; and appointments, ten points. In classes worked with cattle, the horses are judged on a basis of 150 points for a perfect score, which is broken down as follows: cow work, fifty points; rein work, fifty points; conformation, twenty points; manners, twenty points; and appointments, ten points.

STOPPER   A jumping horse that frequently refuses to jump is known as a stopper.

SUITABILITY   In recent years, classes listing *suitability* as part of the judging criteria have been placing more emphasis on this requirement. Suitability means just what it implies: Is the horse a suitable mount for its rider and for performing the job being asked of him? For example, a 17-hand, strong going hunter ridden by a small, ten-year-old child in a junior class would be marked down on suitability, as would a small pony being shown by a tall, leggy child obviously too large for it. In both instances, the horse is not suitable for its rider.

TABLE I   In the open jumper division, classes which are judged under Table I are those in which touches of the obstacle count, whereas the time taken to negotiate the course does not. In a case of equality of faults, the fences are raised and spread as often as necessary to break the existing ties, and the winner is the horse that jumps the most obstacles with the least number of touches or knockdowns.

TABLE II   In the open jumper division, classes which are judged under Table II are those in which touches of the fences are not scored. Time is taken in all classes designated Table II and will decide the winner either on the first go-round or in a subsequent jump-off, depending upon the individual class specifications. The fences are raised and spread, and the course is shortened for the jump-off, thus the winner is the horse jumping the course with the least number of faults in the fastest time.

TANDEM   Horses which are ridden or driven in tandem are positioned one behind the other—Tandem Hunters or Tandem Hackney (Harness) Ponies.

TENNESSEE WALKING HORSE DIVISION   To be shown in this division, a horse must be registered with the Tennessee Walking Horse Breeder's Association. The Tennessee Walking Horse is shown under saddle at three gaits: the walk, running walk (the specialty of the breed), and an easy "rocking chair" canter. They are judged twenty-five percent each for the running walk, the flat walk, and the canter, and an additional twenty-five percent for conformation and quality. In classes restricted to amateur riders, there is added emphasis on manners.

The flat walk should be true and square with a rhythmic head motion and a speed of about four mph. The running walk is a smooth, gliding, overstepping four-beat gait and, again, the cadenced head motion. The canter should be straight and smooth on both leads with a slight rolling motion. The horse should be "comfortably in hand" and, once again, the decided head motion. The horse should be flexed at the poll at all gaits, with the muzzle slightly tucked. Any deviation from the true gaits—such as a tendency to rack, pace or slow-gait—is considered out of form, and the entry is penalized accordingly.

THOROUGHBRED   HUNTER   *See*   HUNTER   CLASSIFICA-TIONS.

THREE-GAITED SADDLE HORSE—*Qualifying Gaits*   AHSA specifies that Three-Gaited Saddle Horses are to be judged on their performance of the following gaits:

1.   Walk—animated and graceful;
2.   Trot—square, collected, and balanced with hocks well under;
3.   Canter—smooth, slow, and straight on both leads.

TIME OUT   Time out may be granted during a class for the replacement of a lost shoe or repairing broken equipment, provided the animal does not leave the ring and that the repairs are performed within the allotted time.

TRAIL HORSE SECTION   A section of the Western Division. In all classes in this section, horses are shown at the walk, jog trot, and lope, with special emphasis on the walk. Trail horses must work over and through obstacles. Without losing control, a rider should open a gate, pass through it, and close it. Other tests that may be required are carrying objects from one part of the arena to another; riding through water, over logs, or simulated brush; riding down into and up out of a ditch without lunging or jumping; crossing a bridge; backing through obstacles; mounting and dismounting from either side; and performing over any natural conditions encountered along the trail.

UNDER SADDLE CLASS   A hunter class in which the entries are exhibited as a group at the walk, trot, and canter (Regular Hunters, may be asked to gallop) and judged on their overall performance, with emphasis on manners and way of going.

WALK THE COURSE   After the course has been set for a particular jumper class and just prior to the competition, the riders may be permitted to walk the course on foot for the purpose of deciding how best to approach the obstacles, as well as ascertaining the distances from fence to fence. Since time applies in many jumper classes, the chance to walk the course is a valuable aid to the rider in planning the strategy of his ride and lets him see just where he can cut corners, save ground, and make time.

WALK-TROT HORSE or CLASS   A slang term referring to the Three-Gaited Saddle Horse or a class in which these horses are judged.

WAY OF GOING   When the phrase *way of going* is one of the standards on which a class is to be judged, it refers to the way in which the horse moves and carries himself—that is, does he move high or low to the ground, with or without a lot of "action," or are his gaits fluid or choppy, and so forth.

WELSH PONY DIVISION   Entries in this division must be registered in the Studbook of the Welsh Pony Society of America, Inc. and must be shown under their full registered name. Welsh ponies must be under 14.2 hands in height; to be shown in performance classes, the owner must possess a current measurement card. *See* MEASUREMENT CARD.

Welsh ponies are shown under saddle in both Western and English tack, as pleasure and trail ponies, as well as in harness as roadster ponies and in Welsh Formal Driving Pony classes. There are also classes offered for Welsh Fine Harness ponies and Welsh Hunter and Jumper ponies.

WESTERN DIVISION A division open to horses of any breed or combination of breeds standing 14.1 hands and over that are serviceably sound, in good condition, and of stock horse type. This division is divided into three sections: Stock Horse, Trail Horse, and Western Pleasure Horse. *See* STOCK HORSE SECTION, TRAIL HORSE SECTION and WESTERN PLEASURE HORSE SECTION.

WESTERN PLEASURE HORSE SECTION A part of the Western Division. Horses competing in this section are shown at a walk, jog trot, and lope on a reasonably loose rein without undue restraint. Extended gaits may be requested by the judge, and special emphasis is placed on the walk. All horses considered for an award are required to back in a straight line.

WORKING HUNTER A Working Hunter is judged on performance alone. With the exception that he must be "serviceably sound" physically, he is not rated on his conformation. *See also* HUNTER. It helps if the horse is a good mover and jumps naturally in good form. But depending upon the conditions at a given show, a high-moving, short striding "safe" horse that chips in front of most of his fences can be pinned over a beautifully moving average jumping horse that is overly strong or jumping in sufficiently bad form as to be almost dangerous.

PETER WINANTS

FOX
HUNTING

ACCOUNTED FOR   When the hounds have killed or run a fox to ground, they are said to have *accounted for* their fox.

ALL ON   When the Whipper-In takes a head count of the entire pack of hounds and finds that every one is there, they are said to be *all on.*

AMAZON PACK or BITCH PACK   A pack of hounds comprised only of bitches.

APPOINTMENTS   The prescribed dress of horse and rider that is suitable for hunting.

ARTIFICIAL EARTH   A man-made place for a fox to hide or live. Usually made of drain pipe.

BABBLING   The cry of a hound when he is not on the line.

BAY   *See* SPEAK.

BILLET   Fox droppings.

BITCH   A female hound. Unlike males which are referred to as doghounds, females of the species are referred to as bitches, not bitchhounds.

BITCH PACK   *See* AMAZON PACK.

BLANK   When the hounds have drawn a covert and no fox has been found, they are said to have *drawn blank.* A day on which the hounds never find a fox is called a blank day. *See also* DRAWING THE COVERT.

BLOOD, to be IN BLOOD   Hounds that are *in blood* are those having made a recent kill. A pack of hounds which has gone for quite a while without making a kill is said to be *out of blood.*

BLOODED   Persons who are present for the first time at the kill are *blooded*—that is, dabbed on the forehead with blood from the fox. A hound is said to be *blooded,* when he has made his first kill.

BOLT A FOX   Forcing a fox to leave the refuge of an earth or drain is known as *bolting*. This may be accomplished by sending a small dog, usually a terrier, down the hole after him.

BOWLER HAT   A flat-brimmed derby reinforced with cork.

BREAST HIGH SCENT   When fox scent is very strong and hanging up off the ground, allowing the hounds to follow it without keeping their noses to the ground.

BREEDING   A hound's pedigree or lineage is referred to as his breeding.

BREEDING EARTH   A small hole in the ground which the vixen makes for the birthing of her cubs.

BROOD BITCH   A bitch selected for breeding because of her outstanding qualities in conformation and substance, brilliant work in the field, and, usually, superior lineage.

BRUSH   The fox tail is referred to as the brush. On a kill it is a part of the fox awarded by the Master to a deserving member of the day's hunt.

BURNING SCENT   A *burning scent* is one which is extremely strong; although it is lying on the ground, it allows the hounds to proceed rapidly and without hesitation.

BUTCHER BOOTS   Plain black boots.

CAPPING FEE or CAP   A small fee charged to guests, not regular members of the hunt, for the privilege of the ride. The term originated in the days when the fees were collected in a hat. There is usually a limit on the number of days a person may go out with a pack without becoming a regular subscriber to the hunt. The fee is generally paid to the Secretary of the Hunt before the hunt begins.

CASTING   The action of the Huntsman in leading the hounds over ground which he thinks has been recently traversed by a fox in hopes that the pack will pick up the scent.

CHARLES, CHARLES JAMES   Old English terms for the fox.

CHECK   When the scent is temporarily lost and the hounds stop, they are said to *check*. During such a time, the field remains quiet, allowing the hounds to recover the line or the Huntsman to cast them again. *See* CASTING.

CHOP A FOX   When a fox is killed either while sleeping or before it has gathered its wits and begun to run, it is said to have been *chopped*.

COFFEE HOUSING   Persons who engage in chitchat instead of keeping their minds on the hunt are said to be *coffee housing*.

COLD SCENT or LINE   When it is very difficult for hounds to track the fox because of a very faint scent either because the trail is old or because scenting conditions are poor.

COUNTER   *See* RUNNING HEEL.

COUPLE   Hounds are always counted by twos or in *couples*. This terminology stems from the early custom of keeping hounds coupled or held together in pairs with a short chain on a swivel. Fifteen hounds are thus referred to as seven and a half couple.

COUPLINGS   A piece of equipment carried by the Whippers-In; it consists of two leather collars hooked together and is used to join two hounds together for various reasons—a young hound to an experienced hound, for example.

COVERT   Any area in which a fox might be expected to hide, usually a wood or thicket.

CROPPER, TO COME A CROPPER or COMING A CROPPER   Coming a cropper refers to the fall of a horse and/or rider.

CRY, also VOICE, GIVE TONGUE, SPEAK   The sound the hounds make to indicate whether they are on a hot or cold scent.

CUB   After being weaned, a young fox is called a cub until the opening meet in November after which he becomes a fox.

CUB HUNTING or CUBBING   The time prior to the opening meet in which the young foxhounds are initiated to the ways of the hunt, and the fox cubs are taught to leave the covert as quickly as possible rather than stay home and be routed out.

DEN   The fox's home.

DOG FOX   Like hounds, a male fox is referred to as a *dog fox*.

DOGHOUND   A male hound.

DOG PACK   A pack of hounds comprised only of male dogs (dog-hounds).

DOUBLE   When a hunted fox retraces his original line in reverse, he is said to *double*.

DOWN WIND   Hunting with the wind at your back is known as hunting *down wind*. This is not a desirable position to be in, since the wind blowing over you carries both sound and scent to the fox and is certain to frighten him.

DRAFT   Removing one or more hounds from their regular pack.

DRAG   The artificial fox scent laid by a forerunner of the hunt.

DRAG HUNT   A hunt that follows an artificial line laid by a runner a short time prior to the hunt.

DRAIN   Any large ditch or waterway which may afford the fox a hiding place is called a drain.

DRAWING THE COVERT   The act of searching for a fox. When the Huntsman seeks to flush the fox out of a thicket or covert where he may have taken refuge, this is said to be *drawing the covert*.

DRAW BLANK   *See* BLANK.

EARTH   Any hole in which a fox might hide or take refuge is called an earth. These frequently are the vacated homes of other animals such as woodchucks or badgers. Also, the fox's home.

EARTH STOPPER   A person whose duty it is to stop (or block) the earths in a given territory the night before the hounds are to hunt in that area to force the fox into flight. He then returns and opens the earths the following day. Earth stopping is an English custom which is not too common in America.

ENTERED HOUND   Once a hound has hunted regularly for one or more seasons, he is called an *entered hound*. (In England, to earn the title, the hound must have been there at the kill and eaten his share of fox.) Until such time, he is referred to as an "unentered" hound.

FEATHERING   When a hound is sniffing at a scent, waving his stern, but giving little tongue (sometimes whimpering) to indicate some uncertainty, he is said to be *feathering*. *See also* STERN and TONGUE.

FIELD   All followers of the hounds either on horseback or afoot who are not members of the Hunt Staff—that is, the Master, Huntsman, Field Master, and Whippers-In.

FIELD BOOTS   Brown boots with lacing at the instep, which are only worn with ratcatcher dress. *See* RATCATCHER. Occasionally black field boots are seen.

FIELD MASTER   The person responsible for the followers riding in the field. A member of the Hunt Staff.

FIND   When hounds first pick up the trail of a fox, they are said to *find*.

FIXTURE CARDS   Cards that are sent to the hunt members announcing the time and location of the meet.

FLASK   A flask (plastic or glass) encased in a leather holder, which is carried on the saddle of male riders or within the sandwich case of female riders. Tradition requires that it be filled with either tea or brandy.

FOIL   A diversionary tactic of the fox, which entails either crossing his own line (a circle) or that of another animal, so that its scent will confuse the hounds and cause a check. Also, another animal or object crossing the line of the fox and confusing or covering the scent.

FOX   Charles, Charles James, Reynard, all are names for the fox.

FRESH LINE   A more recently laid scent as opposed to cold scent. *See* COLD SCENT.

FULL CRY   When the entire pack of hounds is running a line and speaking in a chorus.

GIVE TONGUE   *See* SPEAK, CRY.

GONE AWAY   The call indicating that the fox has left covert and the hounds are running.

GONE TO GROUND, also GONE TO EARTH   When a hunted fox enters an earth or drain to hide, he is said to have *gone to ground*.

GRAY FOX   The gray fox is almost twice as large as his relative the red fox and weighs about thirty pounds to the red fox's fifteen. He has neither the speed nor the endurance of the red fox and depends upon his ability to baffle and confuse the hounds rather than his stamina to save his life. For this reason, the gray fox is constantly doubling back, crossing his line, and literally running in circles in his efforts to outwit the hounds. *See* RINGING FOX.

HARK   The order given by the Master or Huntsman to the field to be silent and listen to hounds. Also, when one hound goes to the rest of the pack, he is said to be *harking*.

HEADING THE FOX   Crossing the path of a fleeing fox in such a way as to turn him back. The fox is not to be "herded" or his course intruded upon or diverted in any way by a rider. This most serious offense is guaranteed to bring down the wrath of the entire hunt upon the offender.

HEADS UP   When the hounds lose a line because of outside interference, they are said to have their *heads up*.

HILL TOPPER   A person who follows the hunt by observing as much as possible from hilltop to hilltop. Also persons who follow the hunt from an automobile, stopping on the hilltops to view the chase.

HITTING IT OFF or HIT OFF THE LINE   When the hounds regain the scent after losing it and stopping for a check.

HOLD HARD   A call used by the Field Master to halt an individual or the entire field.

HOLD THEM FORWARD   *See* LIFTING.

HONOR   When a hound not running or giving tongue goes to the rest of the pack when they are running.

HONORING A LINE   *See* SPEAKING TO A LINE.

HOUNDS   A group of foxhounds, referred to collectively as a pack of hounds. In mentioning the pack or any one of its number, hunting people always use the term *hound* or *hounds,* never dog.

HUNT   The term *hunt* refers only to the actual chasing of the fox and does not include the meeting beforehand or the hunt breakfast which may follow. *See* MEET, HUNT BREAKFAST, RUN.

HUNT BREAKFAST   The hunt breakfast was originally the meal served to members who arrived at the host's house a couple of hours before the advertised time of the meet. Now the term refers to the meal served after the day's hunting is over.

HUNT BUTTONS   A matched set of buttons for a rider's coat or jacket on which the insignia of the particular hunt is engraved; they may be worn only by invitation.

HUNTING ATTIRE   The clothing worn by hunt participants, as opposed to appointments, which include tack and equipment by inference.

HUNT COLLAR, also HUNT COLORS   A hunt collar is the colored collar of a member's riding coat, the color being officially registered to denote a particular pack of hounds and worn by those members of the hunt entitled to do so by invitation. Hunt colors may be worn only on one's appropriate hunt attire.

HUNTING CAP, also HUNT CAP   A reinforced velvet skullcap with a peak, which may be worn by the Hunt Staff, hunting farmers, ex-Masters, juniors under eighteen years of age, and by gentlemen members in certain attire but only at the discretion of the Master.

HUNTING CROP   A whip including the thong and lash, with a crook bone handle designed to help in opening gates.

HUNTSMAN—*Amateur*   A man who is chosen to hunt hounds and does so at his own expense.

HUNTSMAN—*Professional*   The member of the hunt staff whose singular concern is with the hounds, which look to him for instruction and attention. He calls them each by name. In the field, the Huntsman rides first and plots the strategy of the hunt, guiding the hounds with his voice and horn with the assistance of the Whippers-In.

KENNELMAN   The man who is responsible for cleaning the kennels and feeding the hounds.

KENNELS   The place where the hounds are housed.

KILL, THE   The ever hoped for climax to a day's hunting is the catching or killing of the fox.

LAIR   The fox's daytime hiding place. It may be an abandoned hole or ex-home of some other animal, but it is definitely not the fox's present home. A clever fox will know the location of numerous *lairs* in his territory for they could mean the difference between life and death when being pursued.

LARKING   The ill-considered jumping of fences at times when it is unnecessary, such as when returning home after a hunt or when the hounds are not running.

LASH   The long braided-leather end of a hunting crop or whip.

LEATHER GLOVES   Traditionally worn for protection against brambles and the like, as well as for warmth and to save wear and tear on a rider's hands during a long hunt.

LIFTING, also HOLDING THEM FORWARD   When the hounds have lost the trail of the fox, the Huntsman *lifts* them, or leads them to a spot further ahead to cast them again, hoping to regain the line. *See* CASTING.

LINE, A FOX'S   The direction taken by the fleeing fox, as revealed by his scent.

LINE HUNTER   A hound that hunts close to the fox's scent.

LOO-IN   Call used by the Huntsman to encourage hounds into a covert. From the French *lieu en.*

MAIN EARTH   A large den with multiple entrances and exits used by adult foxes.

MARKING TO GROUND   Running a fox into an earth and then baying around the mouth of the hole. At such times the hounds make a special sound known as a "den bark" or "den cry," announcing that their quarry has run to ground.

MASK   The fox's head is called the mask which, on a kill, is awarded by the Master to the most deserving member of the day's hunt.

MASTER OF FOXHOUNDS (MFH)   The man who assumes the final responsibility for the success or failure of the hunting season. His duties are extensive and range from overseeing the stable and kennel management to deciding the terrain to be hunted. He also obtains permission from the farmers over whose land the hunt will pass and acts as social organizer for members of his hunt. In some instances, the Master works the hounds himself instead of having them handled by a professional huntsman. *See* HUNTSMAN.

MEET   The gathering of the Hunt Staff, followers, and hounds prior to the day's hunting.

MIXED PACK   A pack of hounds comprised of both sexes.

MUTE   Hounds are said to be running *mute,* when they track a fox in silence. Such a practice is undesirable as it renders impossible any interpretation of the hunt's progress.

MUZZLE   The fox's nose is called his muzzle.

OPENING MEET   When the period of cub hunting is over, the first meeting prior to the first hunt of the actual hunting season is called the opening meet. *See also* CUB HUNTING, MEET.

PACK   The number of hounds regularly hunted together are known as a pack.

PAD   The fox's foot is called a pad, which on a kill is awarded by the Master to a deserving member of the day's hunt.

PINK COAT, also RED or SCARLET COAT   The Pink Coat or "Hunting Pinks" refer to the scarlet livery worn by the Hunt

Staff and honored members authorized to wear it by the Master. Named for the British tailor of that name who designed and made the original coat, "Pinks" are available in three types— long, short, and swallowtail.

POINT   The farthest point as measured in a straight line from the actual place where the fox was found during the hunt.

POLO BOOTS   Brown boots.

PUPPY   A young foxhound that has been weaned from its mother but not yet entered is referred to as a puppy. *See* ENTERED HOUND.

PUPPY WALKER   Persons living in the hunting country who care for foxhound puppies after they are weaned until they return to the kennels.

QUARRY   Any hunted animal—in this instance, the fox.

RATCATCHER   The less formal attire worn by all but members of the Hunt Staff during the cub-hunting season. This type of dress usually consists of breeches; a checked or tweed coat; butcher, polo, or field boots; spurs; and a colored stock or collar and tie. Gloves are optional. A hunting crop should be carried at all times, but it is permissible to substitute a cutting whip if mounted on a horse which may require schooling.

RATCATCHER DAY   Most hunts have one *ratcatcher day* per week on which it is not necessary to appear in formal hunting attire.

RECOVER THE LINE   *See* CHECK.

RED FOX   The smaller and fleeter of the two main foxhunting quarries—the red fox and the gray fox. The red fox, which weighs about fifteen pounds to the gray fox's thirty, has remarkable stamina and is renowned for running straight away. *See also* GRAY FOX, STRAIGHT-NECKED FOX.

RED RIBBON   A horse that is a kicker must wear a red ribbon in his tail as a warning.

RINGING FOX, also RINGER   A fox that runs in circles when being hunted instead of heading straight across country. In most instances, the fox leading a circular chase will be a gray, a tactic for which they are famous.

RIOT   When hounds leave the fox's line and begin to run any other sort of animal or to bolt away from the Huntsman, they are said to *riot.*

RUN   Another term for hunt or chasing a fox.

RUNNING HEEL, also COUNTER   When hounds pick up the scent of a fox and run the line in reverse, namely back to the point from which the fox began.

SANDWICH CASE   A leather case carried on the saddle containing a metal or plastic box to hold a sandwich. Traditionally, the sandwich should be made of the white meat of chicken or turkey without mayonnaise. A lady's sandwich case also contains a flask. *See* FLASK.

SCENT   The odor given off by the fox.

SECOND HORSEMAN   The men who ride out at an appointed time to meet their employers for the purpose of exchanging their fresh mounts for those wearied by the hunt.

SINKING FOX   A wearied fox that is very nearly beaten is said to be *sinking.*

SKIRTER   A hound that runs on the outskirts of the pack and does not do his share of the hunting.

SPEAK, also GIVE TONGUE, BAY, CRY   When hounds are on the scent of a fox, they bay or give tongue to indicate that they have found the line. Since their sound will vary according to whether the scent is hot or cold or if the fox runs to earth, they are said to speak.

SPEAKING TO A LINE or HONORING A LINE   When hounds bark on a scent, they are said to be speaking to a line and as such *honor* it.

STAINED   A line interrupted by the scent of another animal is said to be *stained.*

STALLION HOUND   A dog hound used for breeding, usually because of superior conformation, performance in the field, quality, and lineage.

STERN, HOUND'S   The hound's tail is referred to as his stern.

STIRRUP CUP   A drink offered to the members of the hunt at the meet prior to the day's hunting. It is called a stirrup cup because the waiters bearing the drinks serve at the level of the stirrup iron.

STOCK   A hunting cravat or necktie. Originally a long piece of white, heavy cotton or linen that could be used as a tourniquet or bandage in case of injury to horse or rider.

STOCK PIN   Traditionally of the large safety pin variety, which could be used to secure a bandage in case of injury.

STRING GLOVES   An extra pair of gloves to be carried under the billet straps by all participants on a hunt; in case of rain, they can be substituted for the regular leather gloves, which may become slippery when wet.

TAG   The white tip of the fox's tail is called the tag.

TAIL HOUND   A hound left behind when the others found and followed a fox from the covert.

TALLY-HO   Another English distortion of French hunting terminology—*Ty a hilaut* or *Il est haut,* meaning He is up, or possibly *taïaut*. Tally-ho is the presentday cheer announcing that the fox has been sighted.

THONG   The small piece of braided nylon cord attached to the end of a hunt crop or whip; traditionally it is the same color as the main color on the hunt collar. This piece of cord creates the sharp crack or snapping sound when the crop is used.

THRUSTER   A person who goes to any lengths to keep up with the hounds. Often this means following a straight line as the fox leaves its cover, overriding the hounds, and jumping any fences which might be in his path. Such thoughtless behavior, usually reflecting a lack of experience in the hunt field, is a sure way

85

to become a general nuisance to the other members of the hunt. *See also* LARKING.

TOP BOOTS   Black hunt boots with either tan or patent leather tops. Originally these tops were not sewn down to the boot and could be pulled up over the rider's knees for protection against bushes and brambles.

TOP HAT   A silk hat that must be worn with a Pink Coat except by the Hunt Staff and farmers who are permitted to wear Hunt Caps.

TROPHIES OF THE HUNT   The brush, mask, and pads are the *trophies of the hunt;* they are awarded by the Master to the most deserving members of that day's hunt. *See* BRUSH, MASK, PAD.

UP WIND   When you are hunting with the wind in your face—that is, blowing towards you, you are up wind. It is most desirable to hunt up wind, so that the scent of the people and the noise of the hunt will not be carried toward the quarry.

VIEW (A)   When the fox is actually sighted.

VIXEN   A female fox.

VOICE   *See* CRY.

'WARE   A shortened form of *beware,* 'ware is used as a warning in the hunt field along with a term describing the type of danger, such as *'ware hole* or *'ware wire,* indicating a hole or wire in the way. The term is also used in the phrase *'ware hounds,* warning the followers that one or more hounds are approaching from the back or side and to be careful not to step on them. 'Ware Staff means to get out of the way to allow a Staff member to pass through.

WAVING HIS STERN   When a hound wags his tail he is said to be waving his stern.

WHELP   Before it is weaned from its mother, a foxhound puppy or a fox cub may be referred to as a whelp. Also, to give birth to puppies or foxes (whelping).

WHIPPER-IN   The Whippers-In assist the Huntsman in controlling the hounds and are usually responsible for their discipline. The first Whipper-In is the person who is second in authority to the Huntsman and rides with him. Before sighting a fox, he rides ahead in order to see the fox leaving the covert. The second Whipper-In rides behind the hounds scolding and urging any strays or laggards up with the rest of the pack.

WORK A LINE   When hounds are searching for a fresh scent or on one which might be foiled, they are said to be *working a line.*

WORRY, THE   When a fox has been killed and the mask, brush, and pads have been awarded, the carcass is given to the hounds to be devoured. *The Worry* may also refer to the reward given to the hounds after a drag hunt in which there is no carcass.

YOICKS   A term of encouragement to the hounds; it is an English corruption of the French *illoeques,* which was derived from the Latin *illo loco,* meaning Here's the spot, boys.

WESTERN
WORDS

À LA COMANCHE   Riding a horse hanging off one side in imitation of the battle style of the Comanche Indians.

ALL-AROUND COW HORSE   A horse that is adept at multiple duties such as cutting, dogging, roping, and so forth.

ANVIL   The Western equivalent of *forging* (*see* CONFORMATION and WAY OF GOING), meaning a horse that strikes his forefeet with his hindfeet when in motion.

APRON-FACED HORSE   A Westerner's phrase to describe a horse with a large white streak or blaze on its forehead.

ARCHING HIS BACK or GETTING HIS BACK UP   A phrase describing a person on the verge of anger or a horse about to buck.

BAKE   A term referring to a strenuous or inconsiderate ride resulting in an overheated or exhausted horse.

BAND   Used to describe a group, bunch, or herd of horses. This term refers only to horses, since cattle and other livestock are said to be in herds or bunches, never in bands.

BANGTAIL   Originally the word referred to a wild horse or mustang. Easterners later borrowed the word, using it with reference to race horses—that is, one might be said to *play the bangtails.*

BAREFOOT   A horse without shoes is said to be barefoot.

BAYOU COYOTE   An idiom of the Southwest describing a dun horse with a black dorsal stripe down its back. *See* DUN; CONFORMATION and WAY OF GOING.

BEDDED   A cowboy term referring to an animal that has been roped and thrown down with such impact as to make it remain motionless.

BEEFSTEAK   Refers to riding a horse in such a way as to cause his back to become sore and raw.

BELLYFULL OF BEDSPRINGS   A particularly good bucking horse may be described as a *beast with a bellyfull of bedsprings.* An extension of this phrase occurs when a good rider takes the edge off a horse for someone else to ride, in which case he is said to have made sure there *ain't no bedsprings loose*.

BITE THE DUST   A cowboy expression meaning to be thrown from a horse.

BLIND BUCKER   A horse that goes crazy under saddle and will buck into or through anything without regard for his own safety.

BLINDING   To get a saddle onto a nervous or fractious horse, it is sometimes the practice to cover his eyes with a sack or cloth to keep him quiet. Such procedure is called *blinding*.

BLOW THE PLUG   A bucking horse that displays all the tricks of the rodeo trade is said to *blow the plug*.

BLOW UP, also BOIL OVER, BREAK IN TWO   Said of a horse when he starts bucking.

BOGGED HIS HEAD   A horse that drops his head between his fore-legs prior to bucking is said to have *bogged his head*.

BOIL OVER   *See* BLOW UP.

BORING   A horse that leans all the weight of his forehand, neck, and head into the bit is said to be *boring*.

BREAKING PATTER   The constant yet soothing chatter employed by horse tamers to divert the animal's attention while they are being saddled and broken.

BREAKING PEN   A small fenced area (or corral) in which horses are broken to saddle and ridden for the first time.

BREAK IN TWO   *See* BLOW UP.

BREAK RANGE   Horses that stray off the home property are said to *break range*.

BRIDLEWISE   A horse that is so well schooled as to require only the slightest touch of the reins on the side of his neck to guide him in any direction is said to be *bridlewise*. He might also be said to neck-rein.

BRONC BUSTER, also BRONC TWISTER, BRONC SQUEEZER, BRONC PEELER   A man who earns his livelihood breaking horses. He must be especially good at it since most good cowhands are able to ride the rough ones but don't, because this is the job of the buster. His salary is usually a little higher because of the nature of his work. It is a thing of pride to be known as the rider of the semiwild horses of a big outfit, but the buster also takes care not to ruin the horses he rides and to make them into useful cow horses.

BRONCO   A word borrowed from the Spanish used to describe a wild or unbroken horse. Frequently shortened to simply *bronc,* the term usually stays with a horse until he has been ridden enough times to be considered fairly reliable and useful.

BROOMTAIL or BROOMIE   One of the many terms Westerners use when speaking of horses on the range. This one in particular refers to a mare with a long and full tail.

BUCK   Westerners have many varied and colorful words and phrases to describe the bucking action engaged in by the horses they ride: blow the plug, blow up, boil over, break in two, buck on a dime, buck straight away, chinning the moon, come undone, crawfish, crow hop, fallback, fence cornering, fold up, frog walk, hop for mama, kettling, kick the lid off, laying a rail fence, moan, pinwheel, pump handle, rainbowing, sheep-jump, slattin' his sails, stuck his bill in the ground, sunfish, swallows his head, take you to church, throwing the pack, turn a wildcat, unwind, warp his backbone, whing-ding, and windmilling, not to mention a few unmentionables!

BUCKEROO   Distortions of the Spanish *vaquero* or *boyero* both of which refer to a *cowherd.* Buckeroo (sometimes spelled buck-*a*roo) is another name for a cowboy. It carries the particular connotation of a hard riding cowhand principally concerned with breaking broncs. On occasion this term is also applied to rodeo riders. (Some further corruptions of the original Spanish are *baquero, buckhara,* and *buckayro.*)

BUCKING ON A DIME   A horse that confines his bucking to one place is said to be *bucking on a dime.*

BUCKING STRAP   A common misnomer for *flank strap* (*see* RODEO SECTION), a real bucking strap is a type of handhold attached to a saddle near the base of the horn. Such a device is barred from any competition and really good riders view one with contempt.

BUTTERMILK HORSE　The cowboys of some regions refer to a palomino horse as a *buttermilk horse.*

CABALLADA, also CAVVY, REMUDA　Another adaptation from the Spanish used to depict a band of extra saddle horses kept by the ranch, which are not at that time being ridden. Wild and/or unbroken horses are never included in the *caballada,* which may be used interchangeably with *cavvy* and *remuda,* depending upon the region.

CALICO　A cowboy's term for a pinto horse.

CAPONERA　A word from the Spanish meaning a herd of horses consisting only of geldings.

CAVVY　The northern region's word for caballada. *See* CABA-LLADA.

CAYUSE　A name taken from the Cayuse Indians originally to designate the wild horses of Oregon. It has now come to mean any horse, when used by the cowboys of the north. It may also be used to refer to a true Western horse to distinguish it from one brought from the East. It is also a term of contempt denoting any ratty, small, or inferior horse. Still another meaning is that of an Indian pony.

CHAIN HOBBLE　A method of hobbling whereby one end of a short length of chain is fastened around the horse's foreleg and the other end dangles loose. The principle is that if the horse attempts to run, the loose end of chain will whip around his legs and the resulting pain will discourage him. Unfortunately, the animal may also trip upon the lengths of chain and could cause himself harm. For this reason, chain hobbles are not in common usage.

CHAPS　An American abbreviation of the Spanish *chaparejos* (or *chaparreras*), which means breeches or overalls made of leather. They are essentially a seatless overall or trouser which is worn over the cowboy's working pants to protect his legs from brush and chaparral, rain, cold, and serious injury if thrown.

CHEW GRAVEL   When a cowboy is thrown from a horse, he might say he had been *chewin' gravel*.

CHINNING THE MOON   One of the more colorful Western expressions for a horse that bucks unusually high or rears up on his hind legs while pawing the air.

CHOPPING HORSE, also CARVIN' HORSE   A slang name for cutting horses.

CINCH BINDER   A horse that falls over backwards as a result of rearing and losing his balance is called a cinch binder.

CINCH UP   A cowboy never *cinches* his horse when explaining the final act of tightening the cinch to secure the saddle on his horse's back. His is always said to *cinch up*.

CIRCLE BUCK   A horse's bucking pattern, which follows a circular path by means of rapid, rhythmic leaps during which time the animal's body is inclined towards the circle's center.

CIRCLE HORSE   A horse used to round up cattle scattered over the range. The cowboys, who are assigned a different area each day by the foreman, gather the cattle within that section and then drive them to an appointed place called the roundup ground. Since this tends to be a job requiring brawn rather than brains on the part of the horse, no specialized training is necessary, and the wilder horses in the remuda are frequently used.

CLAYBANK   A term denoting a horse of nondescript, yellowish color, which is usually the offspring of a sorrel and a dun.

CLEAR-FOOTED   An extremely nimble, agile horse that is successfully able to miss gopher holes, brush piles, and other obstructions on the range is said to be *clear footed*.

CLOUD HUNTER   Another of the many names for a rearing horse that stands for seconds pawing wildly at the air.

CLOUD WATCHER, also STARGAZER   A horse with a head carriage too high to permit him to watch his cattle work.

COASTING ON HIS SPURS   Said of a cowboy who is riding with his spurs secured in the cinch or just beneath the horse's shoulders.

COMB   When a cowboy spurs a horse to make him buck, he may also be said to *comb.*

COYOTE DUN   A word representing a dun horse with a dark or black stripe extending down his back, often into his tail. This type of coloring may also include leg marking.

CREMELLO   A member of the albino horse family with a cream-colored coat, very pink skin, and "china" blue eyes. Frequently a cremello is the offspring of a chestnut and an albino, which were bred for the purpose of producing a palomino—thus a washed-out palomino.

CROPPY   Another name for an outlaw horse that has been virtually earmarked as a rogue by means of cropped ears. In some of the colder regions of the west, a horse's ears may also become cropped from frostbite.

CROSS-HOBBLE   A rather dangerous method of hobbling horses by tying one front foot to the diagonal hind foot. When employed, there is always the chance that should the horse become frightened and panic, he could easily entangle himself sufficiently to be thrown to the ground and thereby do injury to himself.

CROW BAIT   A slang term for a horse or indeed any article of poor or inferior quality.

CROW HOP   Used to express the rather mild bucking attempts of a horse that is simply leaping and jumping around with stiffened knees and a *hump in his back.*

DALLY   *See* RODEO SECTION.

DIGGERS   A slang name for spurs. Also used rarely to refer to old, beat-up horses around the ranch.

DUDE   Anyone who is not a native of the West and thus unacquainted with the customs and ways of the range. Such "tenderfeet" were often readily identifiable by their clothes, which frequently were unsuitable to the life-style in cattle country.

DUST A HORSE, also DUST HIS EARS   When a cowboy fans a horse with his hat while he is riding him, he may be said to be *dusting his ears.*

95

DUSTED   A cowboy who has been thrown from a horse is said to have been *dusted*.

EATIN' GRAVEL   One of the most picturesque descriptions meaning to have been thrown from a horse; the complete phrase actually is: *to be eatin' gravel without stoopin'*.

FANTAIL   Another word for a horse with an unusually long and often bushy tail. Or simply a wild horse.

FIDDLE or FIDDLEHEADED   In this instance, *fiddle* simply refers to the horse's head as when a bucking horse rider attempts to keep the horse's head up so that he can't get *his fiddle between his feet*. The term *fiddleheaded* refers to a horse with a poor or ugly shape to his head.

FILLY COLT   Unlike the East where all baby horses are foals, males called colts, and females called fillies, the Western baby horse is called a colt, the male and female distinction of which is stud and filly. A *filly colt* is thus a young female horse.

FROG WALK   A horse that is fresh, particularly on a crisp morning, may indulge himself in a few antics when first mounted. When the game is mild and confined to a series of short easy hops, he is said to be doing a *frog walk*.

FUZZ-TAIL and FUZZ-TAIL RUNNING   Still another example of the cowboys' colorful vocabulary in which there are always many ways to describe almost anything. *Fuzzy-tail* is a different way of saying broom tail, mustang, wild horse, or range horse, particularly one with an abundant tail. *Fuzzy-tail running* is the act of hunting these wild horses or mustangs.

GALVES   A term for spurs.

GEED UP   A cowman's horse is said to be geed up when it is sufficiently lame as to be laid up or injured in such a way that it is unusable.

GIMLET   Causing a horse's back to become sore by improper riding, poorly fitting saddle, or overuse.

GOOD ENOUGHS   In areas where there are no blacksmiths available to shoe the horses by means of using a fire and shaping the shoe to fit each horse, horseshoes are bought by the keg in a number of different sizes and simply nailed on the horses' feet cold, when necessary. Such shoes are called *good enoughs.*

GRABBIN' THE APPLE or THE NUBBIN or THE POST   Clutching the saddle horn during a ride on a bucking horse. Also to *pull leather.*

GRASSED HIM   A horse that has thrown his rider may be said to have *grassed him.*

GRASS HUNTING   A cowboy who has been thrown from his horse may be said to be *grass hunting.*

GROUNDING or GROUND TIE   A method of "tying" a horse or keeping him in one place by allowing the reins of the bridle to hang down on the ground. A horse which has been trained to stand *tied to the ground* will not move from the spot.

GRULLA   An adaptation from the Spanish word meaning *crane,* grulla is used to designate a grayish-blue or mouse-colored horse. Horses of this coloration are usually the offspring of mixtures of dark bay, liver chestnut, and some blacks. Despite their color, they are nonetheless members of the major group called dun, and indeed, *grulla* is synonymous with mouse-dun and smokey-dun.

HAME-HEADED   A slang term for anything stupid, although usually applied to a horse.

HAY BALER   Another word for a horse.

HAY BURNER   Still another cowboy phrase for a horse, although this one usually denotes a horse kept in and fed hay and grain, as opposed to one that lives out to pasture. It may also be used with a connotation of contempt for an almost worthless animal.

HOBBLING STIRRUPS   A method of anchoring the stirrups of a saddle by means of passing a rope or strap beneath the horse's belly to connect them. While this method may enable some riders to stay on a bucking horse, such a device is banned in rodeo contests and frowned upon by skilled riders. Hobbling the stirrups is also considered quite dangerous, since the rider has little chance to kick loose of the horse should he rear over backwards or fall.

97

HONDA   A ring of rope, rawhide, or metal on a lasso through which the loop slides.

HONEST PITCHER   A respectful name for a horse that generally endeavors to unseat its rider from the moment it is mounted, as opposed to one that waits for the moment when he feels he has the advantage because the rider has dropped his guard.

HORSE MAN   A person who breeds and raises horses, as opposed to a *horseman,* which refers to a person on horseback or a particularly skilled rider.

HURRICANE DECK   Another example of the vivid vocabulary coloring Western conversation. This type of *hurricane deck* is found on the back of a bucking horse; it is another term for a saddle.

JERKED DOWN   A horse that is pulled to the ground by the weight or thrashing of a roped steer is said to have been *jerked down.*

JIGGLE   A Western equivalent of nautical knots, namely the average gait of a moving cow horse, which averages about five mph.

JINETE   Borrowed from the Spanish, *jinete* refers to a rider of superior skill or a bronc buster.

JINGLER   A cowboy who herds horses.

KACK   A saddle.

KACK BISCUIT   In cattle country, a kack biscuit is a saddle sore.

KICKBACK RIDER   A phrase meaning a rider who uses his spurs extremely high behind the saddle while riding a bucking horse. This style of riding frequently brings the rider to a fall because spurring in this manner causes him to lose his grip.

KISSED THE GROUND   Having been thrown from a horse.

LACED HIS TREE UP   Saddled a horse.

LANDED, also LANDED FORKED END UP or ON HIS SOMBRERO   A rider who has been thrown from a horse has simply *landed*. However, a rider who has been thrown headfirst from a horse has landed either *forked end up* or *on his sombrero*.

LARIAT   An adaptation of the Spanish *la reata,* meaning rope. A lariat is a rope of horsehair, rawhide, or hemp, with a running noose used for roping cattle and horses or for picketing.

LETTING THE HAMMER DOWN   Riding a wild or unbroken horse enough to take off the roughest edges.

LIVIN' LIGHTNING   When a bucking horse really puts on a good show and is obviously talented in the pitching department, he may be referred to as *livin' lightning*.

LOCKED SPURS   A literal description of spurs that have been tied with a string or horsehair to prevent them from moving. When spurs fastened in this manner are pushed tightly against the cinch, the rider is practically guaranteed a seat on the horse no matter how hard he bucks. For this reason, riding with locked spurs is forbidden at all rodeos.

LOGGIN'   A manner in which a horse may be staked but still have a certain amount of freedom. In this way, the horse is tied to a log, and because the log is not rooted or fixed in the ground, the animal may move around without running the risks involved in staking to a secured object.

LONG HORSE   Said of a horse that can cover a great deal of ground without losing his speed.

LOPE   The Western name for an uncollected, free-striding gait, which lies somewhere between a canter and slow gallop.

MANSADOR   An adaptation from the Spanish *manso*, which means tame; a mansador is a bronc buster—literally, a horse tamer.

MAVERICK   Named for Samuel A. Maverick, a Texan who did not brand his cattle; a maverick is an unbranded calf, frequently motherless, of unknown ownership.

MASTEÑERO   Derived from the Spanish *mesteño,* meaning without a home. This word is used to describe a wild horse hunter or simply a mustanger. It is also used directly in the English language to mean a mustang.

MET HIS SHADOW ON THE GROUND   Another colloquialism meaning a horse has successfully bucked off his rider.

MONTURA   Adapted from the Spanish, it means a horse used for riding and rarely for a saddle.

MOUNT   When a cowboy signs on at a ranch, he is assigned certain horses to use during his employment. The size of the ranch and the type of work to be done usually determines the number delegated to each hand, although seven to ten comprise the average mount. Also called a string.

MULE-HIPPED   Westerners refer to a horse with extremely sloping hips as being *mule-hipped.*

MUSTANG   A corruption of the Spanish word *mesteño,* which means "strays from the *mesta.*" In early days, cattle and horse breeders were collectively called *mestas,* thus evolved the term *mustang,* literally, a horse that had strayed from the mestas and was running free. Now *mustang* has come to be used only to identify the unmixed type of wild horse. Used as a verb, to *mustang* is the act of trapping wild horses, and a *mustanger* is a man who earns his livelihood in this manner.

NAG   A contemptuous word for the most inferior horse imaginable.

NECK-REIN   *See* BRIDLEWISE.

NIGHT HORSE   A horse selected by his rider for outstanding qualities that make him a safe, reliable mount for work in the dark. Good eyesight, surefootedness, and an unerring sense of direction are prerequisites for a night horse, since in cases of stampede or other crisis, the cowboy's life might depend upon his horse. Such an animal was only used at night and was always picketed in a handy spot so that he might be caught and saddled without delay.

OUTLAW   An untamable horse, which despite the fact that it might be possible to ride it, would remain essentially "wild" and constantly devote its thought and energies to unseating its rider.

100

PALOMILLA   A direct incorporation of the Spanish word into English, palomilla means a horse of milk white or cream coloring with a white mane and tail, on the order of a faded palomino.

PALOUSE HORSE   A distortion of the Appaloosa Horse.

PECKER NECK   A horse, which although broken to ride, has not been schooled to work cattle.

PEG HORSE, also PEGGER or PEG PONY   A horse that is extremely useful in cattle work and particularly cutting, because of his ability to gallop full tilt in one direction, halt abruptly, and spring away in another direction with a minimal loss of time.

PELTER   A saddle.

PILED   Thrown by a horse.

PILE DRIVER   A rather apt description of a bucking horse the favorite trick of which is leaping into the air with a hump in his back and landing stiff-legged with all four legs locked.

PINTO   *See* Section "Conformation and Way of Going."

PIONEER BUCKER   An apt portrayal of a bucking pattern in which the horse follows an irregular path of circles and figures of eight. The name *pioneer* is derived from the fact that he always seems to be looking for new territory.

PITCHING FENCE-CORNERED   Said of a bucking horse the path of which progresses at right angles to itself—that is, he is heading one direction as he leaps into the air, and lands turned roughly forty-five degrees from the point of departure.

PORTRANKA   A sometime name for a filly or young female horse.

POTRO   Any young horse, colt, or filly until the time when he loses his milk teeth. This occurs when the horse is about four-and-a-half years old.

101

PUDDIN' FOOT   More than one clumsy, awkward horse with a larger than average foot has been dubbed *puddin' foot.*

PULL LEATHER   *See* GRABBIN' THE APPLE.

PUMP HANDLE   A bucking pattern that follows an easy one-two motion as the horse lands first on his front feet and then on his hind. Such a horse is considered an easy ride. Should a rodeo contestant draw a horse known for this type of action, he generally feels cheated.

RANAHAN   A top-notch cowhand, good rider, and so forth, sometimes shortened to *ranny.*

REATA   Spanish word for lasso, rope, or lariat.

REEFING   Allowing a rider's legs to slip back and forth against the horse's sides as he spurs.

REMUDA   A term favored in the Southwest to describe the extra horses assigned to each cowhand. When not actually being ridden, these horses are herded together into a band which is collectively called the *remuda.* The word itself is from the Spanish meaning replacement and is thus a literal description of their use. *See* CABALLADA.

RIB WRENCHES   Spurs.

RIDGE RUNNER   A watchful, wild stallion that seeks out vantage points high on the hills and ridges to protect his mares from danger.

RIDING ON HIS SPURS, RIDING SAFE   A rider who secures his spurs into the cinch throughout his ride, as well as sitting close to his saddle with his legs clamped against the horse's sides. Barred in competition.

RIDING SLICK   A vernacular phrase for riding without any aids to staying on such as hobbled stirrups, locked spurs, or a saddle-roll wedged behind the rider to help him stay pressed in the saddle.

RODEO   *See* RODEO SECTION.

ROUGH STRING   That group of wild, unbroken horses which will put up a very convincing argument every time they are saddled. The rough string rider is an accomplished bronc buster. *See* BRONC BUSTER. His main duty is to get the green ones broken in a minimum of time with maximum efficiency to save his boss money.

ROUNDUP   The periodic gathering of all of a rancher's horses or cattle for the purpose of branding, inventory, and choosing the stock to be sold.

SABINO   From the Spanish, the word depicts a horse whose with a light red coat generously interspersed with white hairs so as to make it appear almost pink. Its belly is definitely white.

SACKING OUT   The practice of accustoming a horse to being handled and making him less apt to shy by means of tying up one hindleg and then waving a saddle blanket or other cloth around him before saddling him for the first time.

SAFETY FIRST   A phrase to describe the ride on a bucking horse during which the rider holds the saddle horn.

SALTY BRONC   An unusually nasty or vicious horse.

SAVIN' SADDLE LEATHER   Frequently the act of a saddle sore dude, the practice of standing in the stirrups to raise the rider's seat out of the saddle in an effort to ease the pain.

SAVVY   Essentially it means to understand; many horse are said to have *cow savvy,* if they are particularly adept at cattle work.

SCALAWAG BUNCH   A tough group of horses that are rough to ride and handle.

SERAGLIO   The harem or band of mares belonging to a stallion of the range.

SHAVETAIL   It is the custom in the northern part of the country to identify the broken horses from the unbroken ones by means of their tails. When a horse has been broken by a bronc buster, his tail would be "pulled" or thinned and shortened. When he was returned to the range to mix with those still unridden, the shavetail was readily identifiable when it came time to separate them for the next season of work.

SHOE   While a horseshoe remains a horseshoe under any circumstances, the cowboy has his own names for the different types. A *shoe* refers to a horseshoe made with a calked heel, as opposed to a *slipper,* which is completely flat with no calks, while a *boot* is calked at both heel and toe.

SIDELINE   A type of hobbling wherein the front and hind foot on the same side of the horse are tied to prevent it from wandering off at any great rate of speed.

SLICK   The term *slick* frequently means the *absence of* in cowboy expressions such as walking around *slick-heeled,* meaning not wearing spurs. A slick fork is a saddle with very little protrusion at the fork.

SNORTY   An excitable, high-spirited horse may be called *snorty.*

SOBRE PASO   A Spanish phrase describing the slow trotting gait of a horse.

SOUNDING THE HORN   Same as GRABBIN' THE APPLE.

SPINNER   A type of bucking pattern consisting mainly of small tight circles in any direction. While bucking in this manner can be rather violent and rough to sit upon, the rider is usually dislodged by dizziness rather than being thrown.

SQUEEZE THE BISCUIT or SQUEEZIN' LIZZIE   Same as GRABBIN' THE APPLE.

SUICIDE HORSE   A bucking horse that becomes so blinded either by rage or fear that he has no regard for himself or his rider and will often injure his rider and himself by crashing into a fence or other obstacle attempting to fight.

SUNFISHING   One of the better known terms for a bucking pattern. The horse twists his body into an arc with his hind legs high over his head, while simultaneously dropping first one shoulder, then the other towards the ground in a motion cowboys swear is designed to *turn his old belly right up to the sun.*

SUNNED HIS MOCCASINS   Another term meaning thrown from a horse but particularly landing headfirst.

SWALLOWS HIS HEAD   A horse whose bucking specialty is a high leap into the air with his head buried somewhere between his knees, his tail clamped between his hindlegs, and a definite arc to his body accentuated by a huge hump in his back. Such a bucking horse is said to swallow his head.

TAKE SQUATTER'S RIGHTS or TAKE UP A HOMESTEAD   To be thrown from a horse.

THREE SADDLES   A bronc buster considers a horse broken after he has been ridden three times; the expression *three saddles* thus actually means three rides. A horse may also be referred to as *second saddle,* meaning he has been ridden twice.

THROWBACK   Besides referring to a more primitive type or species, a *throwback* may also mean a most dangerous type of bucking horse to a cowboy—namely, one that will deliberately lurch over backwards, attempting to unseat his rider.

THROWN FROM A HORSE   There are many words and phrases to describe a fall from a horse for whatever reason. A few of the more popular ones are bite the dust, chase a cloud, dusted, eatin' gravel, grassed him, grass hunting, "Ketch my saddle!," kissed the ground, landed, lost his hat and got off to look for it, lost his horse, met his shadow, pickin' daisies, sunned his moccasins, taking up squatter's rights (or taking up a homestead), and went up to fork a cloud.

TRIGUENO   An adaptation from the Spanish word meaning *swarthy* or *brunette;* it is used by Americans in the Southwest to denote a brown horse.

TURNED THE PACK   A horse that has thrown its rider may be said to have *turned the pack.*

TURNED THROUGH HIMSELF   A horse that digs in quickly and is instantly off in another direction may be said to have *turned through himself.*

W   A type of breaking apparatus used in training wild horses to go in harness, consisting of a length of rope extending from the wagon through a ring attached to a surcingle and then tied to one of the horse's front feet. Should the animal attempt to fight or bolt, he can be halted in an instant by tripping him by pulling on this rope.

WALKING DOWN   A method of virtually exhausting wild horses to capture them. It is accomplished by following them in shifts and keeping them moving ahead of the hunters hard and fast enough so that they do not have time to eat or rest. Although the mustang is a tough animal with a great amount of stamina, after several days of constant motion, these horses become sufficiently tired to be approached and driven in a given direction. Despite the obvious grueling nature of this device, men afoot have been known to trap horses in this manner.

WAR BRIDLE   A rather crude device used as a bridle; it is simply a length of rope passed through the horse's mouth and secured around his lower jaw.

WASSUP   A vicious or outlaw horse.

WEAVER   A horse with a bucking path that never follows a straight line but rather lands first to one side, then the other in a sort of weaving motion.

WILLOW TAIL   A slang expression usually applied to a mare, denoting an inferior horse of nondescript breeding. Animals earning such a title often have a tail of course, thick hair, which is said to be indicative of its poor quality.

WINDMILLING   A bucking style in which the horse switches from forefeet and front end to hind feet and rear end as he pitches.

WIPED HIM OUT   A cowboy who uses his whip on his horse may be said to have *wiped him out.*

WITCH'S BRIDLE   A horse with multiple matts and tangles in its mane may be said to be wearing a *witch's bridle.*

WRANGLE   The work of herding horses, usually for the other hands who are working on the range. The hand assigned this task is called a *wrangler.* The term is derived from the Spanish *caballerango,* which means *one who cares for horses.*

RODEO

ADDED MONEY   The total purse or prize money for any event at a rodeo is comprised of the entrance fees paid by the contestants and an amount put up by the rodeo committee, which is called *added money*. If an event fails to draw enough entries, it is cancelled and the monies put up by the committee are added to the other contests.

ARENA DIRECTOR   The arena director of a rodeo has rather far-reaching responsibilities. He oversees every detail and all jobs directly connected with the arena itself—that is, keeping the arena clear, loading stock in the chutes, and so forth. He also coordinates the program so that the entire rodeo runs smoothly and according to the rules. He may be an individual hired by the rodeo committee, the producer, or the stock contractor, although both producer and contractor frequently double as arena director.

ASSOCIATION SADDLE   The only saddle that meets the Rodeo Cowboys Association specifications for saddle bronc riding competitions. Adopted in 1920, this saddle is now mandatory at all large contests. There is nothing about this saddle to aid the rider in maintaining his seat, which might seem somewhat unfair except when viewed from the standpoint of safety. Part of the reason for standardizing the saddle used for competition was the outcropping of unusual designs for helping a rider stay on, which unfortunately too often became traps and one-way tickets to the hospital. The present saddle is usually custom-made for the cowboy on a modified Ellenburg tree of medium height with a fourteen-inch swell and a five-inch cantle.

AVERAGE   When a rodeo event consists of more than one go-round, the prize money is awarded in accordance with the best ride or fastest time in each go-round and also for the best average for all the go-rounds. The contestant winnning the average wins the event.

BAREBACK RIDING   One of the five standard rodeo events. The rider has no saddle, bridle, or rein; he is outfitted with minimal equipment, consisting of a standard ten-inch-wide piece of leather with a handhold. It is cinched around the horse. The contestant may use only one hand during the ride and may not switch hands at any time. The other hand and arm must be free and waving about, so as not to touch any part of the horse, rigging, or any part of the rider's body for the ride's duration. The rider is further required to spur the horse over the shoulders on the first jump out of the chute and continue to do so for the entire ride. The spurs used in bareback riding must be dull roweled according to the rules. The event is scored by two judges, who mainly watch for violations of the few rules governing a ride and evaluate the bucking of the horse and control of the rider.

Each judge marks his book independently, scoring the bucking quality of the horse between sixty-five and eighty-five points and the spurring and general control of the rider from one to twenty. The ride lasts for eight seconds, except when a horse knocks his rider off while coming out of the chute or intentionally throws himself down after entering the arena, in which case the cowboy is entitled to a reride.

BARRIER At most rodeos the barrier is a rope pulled taut across the front of the box where the roper's or steer wrestler's horse waits for the signal to proceed. The stock that the contestant is to work with is released from a chute and then given a predetermined head start or score, which is marked by a score line. When the animal crosses the score line or gains enough ground from the chute, the barrier flagman lowers a flag, which indicates the start of time and at the same time releases the barrier.

BREAKING THE BARRIER A fault that penalizes a contestant with an extra ten seconds added to his time; it occurs when the competitor bolts through the barrier prior to its being released.

BUCKING REIN A single rope attached to the hackamore of a bucking horse. The rider holds this rope and can lean against it if necessary to help maintain his balance. When riding out of competition, he may use either hand at will, but he is not allowed to change hands during rodeo contests.

BUFORD A rodeo term referring to a particularly small or weak calf or steer that is comparatively easy to throw or tie.

BULLDOGGING, also STEER WRESTLING One of the five standard rodeo events which may be offered at Rodeo Cowboys Association (RCA)-approved rodeos. In this timed event, the steer is given a head start out of the chute, and the contestant may not begin until it crosses a predetermined "score line." At that moment the cowboy races after the running steer, leaps from his horse's back onto the head of the steer, brakes to a halt, and twists him to the ground. For the fall to be legal, the steer must land so that its head and all four feet are pointing in the same direction, with its side lying flat on the ground. If the cowboy lands too hard on the steer's neck, the sheer impact of his weight may cause the steer to fall without being twisted down, in which case he must get the animal to its feet and then twist him down. Another possible problem is the "dog fall," in which the steer's legs are either underneath him or facing in the opposite direction from his head. Still another illegal maneuver which can cause a "no time" ruling is that of "pegging," in which the wrestler twists the steer's horn into the ground resulting in a fall.

The origin of the term *bulldogging* is as colorful as the rodeos where it is featured. Legend has it that one day in the early 1900s, a Negro cowboy named Bill Pickett was tried beyond his patience attempting to haze a wily steer into a corral. Ultimately his temper got the best of him, and he leaped from his horse onto the creature's back, seized it by the horns, and virtually twisted it onto the ground. The tale goes on to say that Pickett was so enraged that he sank his teeth into the tender lower lip of the steer in the classic fashion of a bulldog worrying an attacking bull. There are many pros and cons as to this particular part of the story, but apparently it was repeated affirmatively enough times to lend the name "bulldogging" to the trick.

Pickett exhibited his new stunt of bulldogging at Wild West shows for a number of years thereafter. Other cowboys began to see a future in such a daring stunt, and more and more of them tried it. It developed into a regular contest event, although biting the lip of the steer was not one of the requirements. It came in later years to be called more appropriately *Steer Wrestling*, but nonetheless the name bulldogging stuck, and it is called that today.

BULL RIDING   It is probably the most spectacular of all rodeo events: The contestant rides a bull with only a "bull rope" between himself and disaster. The rigging used by these daring cowboys is unique and was developed solely for this event.

It consists of a rope, which is usually owned by the contestant, that reaches around the bull and is fastened with a honda knot so that it can be pulled tight by the rider during the ride.

But the knot will loosen and slip off as soon as the tension is released. A bell which hangs down under the bull's belly must be attached to the rig for the twofold purpose of annoying the bull and then providing a weight to pull the rigging off after the rider has been thrown or jumped off the bull.

Like bronc riding, the contestant may not touch the bull or any part of himself with his free hand, although judging is somewhat more lenient than in bronc riding. Unlike broncs, bulls are quite apt to pursue and seriously harm a rider once the two have parted company.

CALF ROPING This is one of the more traditional but nonstandard events of a rodeo, which finds its origin in actual practice. The contest calls for a mounted cowboy to drop a loop over the head of a calf, which has been released seconds before from a chute. Once the rope is settled, the cowboy's horse brakes to a stop as the rider leaps from the saddle and runs down the now taut rope to make the tie.

To accomplish this, he must first throw the calf to the ground and then tie two hind legs and one foreleg together in such a manner that the animal remains tied until examined by the judge and passed as a fair one. Should the tie become loose and the calf escape before the judge makes a ruling, the rider is not credited with "time."

CHUTE CRAZY or CHUTE FIGHTER A horse that rears, thrashes, throws himself against the sides of the chute, and shows other indications of extreme nervousness or panic when put in a rodeo chute is said to be *chute crazy* or a *chute fighter*.

CLOSED EVENT An event at an approved rodeo limiting the entrants to "local" and thus not open to all members of the Rodeo Cowboy's Association in good standing. If an approved rodeo wishes to hold a local, closed event, it must also offer a duplicate event for RCA members.

CRYING ROOM The main office or headquarters of a rodeo—dubbed the *crying room*, because it is here that excuses are offered and disappointments and complaints aired.

DALLY From the Spanish phrase *dar la vuelta*, which literally means *to take a twist or turn with a rope*; it has given rise to the terms dally, daled, vuelted, dale vuelted, and dolly welter. All of these terms refer to the act of taking a half hitch

111

around the saddle horn with the held end of a rope after a catch has been made, although dally, being the short form, is the most commonly used.

DALLY ROPING   A recognized rodeo event, though not one of the five standard contests, in which a world's champion team is named. The team consists of two ropers—the header and the heeler. The header must make a qualified catch around the head of the steer and then maneuver the animal into a position, so that his partner, the heeler, may send a loop around its heels. After each catch is made, the roper must dally his rope to stop the steer. Time is taken when the steer is roped and both horses are facing the steer in line with the ropes that have been dallied and are tight. Another rule is that the steer must be standing up when its head or heels are being roped.

DAY MONEY   The prize money awarded to the winner of each go-round at a rodeo.

DAY MONEY HORSE   A horse that can be relied upon to put up a good bucking round sufficiently rough to rate a high score for the rider but not tough enough to cause him to fall off.

DINK   A rodeo term for a steer wrestling or roping horse which performs inconsistently or badly or has been poorly trained.

DRAWS DEAD   Drawing an animal of consistently poor performance, such as a saddle bronc that will not buck or a steer that quits or ducks back making it almost impossible for a cowboy to win.

ENTRY FEE   The amount of money paid by the contestant to enter a rodeo event. Each event has an entry fee, usually determined by the amount offered in the purse.

EVENT   To qualify as approved by the Rodeo Cowboys Association, a rodeo must offer five standard events—bareback riding, saddle bronc riding, calf roping, steer wrestling, and bull riding. This does not mean that the committee is limited to these classifications, and in many parts of the country other events are equally popular and usually worked into the scheduled contests—steer roping, team tying, and team roping.

FINAL HEAD   While it is not required, a rodeo will frequently put up additional prize money for a short, final go-round in any event. This last or *final head* is open to only those cowboys who have topped the event.

FINAL HORSE A horse that is extremely difficult to ride and consequently used only for the final ride determining the championships.

FLAGMEN or FLAG JUDGES Those rodeo officials who monitor all timed events. One judge is stationed at the barrier and signals the start of time. The second flagman, stationed in the field, is responsible for indicating the end of time and ruling on the legality of a tie, and so forth. He must also allow six seconds after signaling for time in a roping event to see if the tie holds. The same men who serve as judges for timed events may also serve for riding events.

FLANK STRAP or RIGGING A strap passed and fastened around the flanks of a horse or bull to improve the ferocity of bucking. Although most *bucking horses* will buck without the aid of the rig, pulling it tight as they leave the chute seems to bring out the best in the buckers.

GOOSE EGG A zero or "no score" in a riding event in which the contestant has been thrown or otherwise disqualified.

GO-ROUND The length of time required for every contestant to compete on one head of stock is called a go-round. The size of the rodeo determines the numbers of go-rounds per event, beginning with one in the smaller one-day competitions to seven or more in the larger contests.

GRAVY RUN Drawing an animal that usually performs well, such as a good bucking horse or a steer easily caught and thrown, thus making it easy to win.

GROUND MONEY When none of the contestants in an event are able to qualify, there is no winner. Entry fees and the purse in such cases are divided equally among all participants.

HEADER The first rider of a two-man roping team, who is required to rope the steer by the head. He is allowed to throw two loops; if he misses with both, the team retires with no score. *See also* HEELER. When the throw is successful and the catch made, he must then position the steer so his partner can rope its hind legs.

HEELER   The second man of two-man roping team. It is his duty to rope one or both of the steer's hind legs after his partner has already roped the head. The heeler is permitted to cast two loops. If he misses with both, the team retires with no time. *See also* HEADER.

JACKPOT   An event in which the prize money consists solely of the entry fees paid by the contestants. The rodeo does not offer any purse, and the winners split all or part of the entries.

NO TIME   The fateful ruling spelling failure to a bull-dogging or calf-roping contestant, because he has not managed to accomplish his work within the allotted time and thus will not gain a chance at the final money.

PICK-UP MAN   It is the job of the pick-up man to release the bucking strap and lift the contestant off the bucking horses or bulls when the time limit has expired.

PIGGIN' STRING   The short piece of rope carried by the contestants in events requiring an animal to be tied; it is used to tie two hind legs and one foreleg together.

POINT-AWARD SYSTEM   The way in which the annual champion cowboy is determined for each rodeo event. Every dollar a cowboy earns at a Rodeo Cowboys Association-approved rodeo is worth one point in the final tabulation. The cowboy who has amassed the greatest number of points at the end of the year is awarded the championship.

PRODUCER   The title of the person actually running the rodeo. It is a job that varies from rodeo to rodeo, and it may be undertaken in a number of ways. Sometimes the stock contractor doubles as producer. Other producers have a rodeo committee, which is responsible for hiring the stock contractor and acts and supervising all other necessary work. Still other producers have a sponsoring organization to handle such details. Producing is quite a job for an individual; in cases where there is no sponsoring organization or committee, the producer wears many hats and becomes promoter—renting the arena and paying the expenses and, in turn, becoming the recipient of the gate.

RERIDE   A second ride on a different horse or bull in the same go-round of an event; it is permitted by the judges because of an unsatisfactory performance on the part of the stock on the first ride.

RIDING JUDGES   All stock to be ridden is identified by a number. When a cowboy's name is called, one of the riding judges draws a number from a hat to select the contestant's mount. Before the ride, a judge is posted at each side of the chute gate, thus allowing the horse and rider to come out between them. Each judge independently marks the horse's bucking quality and the rider's ability. The four resulting figures are totaled for the final score. Riding judges may also serve as flag judges.

RIDING THE SHOWS   A professional bronc rider who follows the rodeos to compete for prize money is said to be *riding the shows.*

RODEO   From the Spanish word *rodea,* which means *to encircle or surround.* The Americanized word *rodeo* has come to mean a contest or proving grounds for cowboys in events in a number of categories. Mexicans use the word colloquially to mean a cattle roundup.

RODEO COWBOYS ASSOCIATION, INC. (RCA)   The Rodeo Cowboys Association, Inc., located at 320 Boston Building, Denver, Colorado 80202, establishes the rules and approves the prize lists of all rodeos in which its members may compete. Nearly all regular rodeo contestants are members of the association, which—among other things—keeps a running compilation of each member's winnings for the year. At the end of the season, the RCA National Finals are held through which the World's Champions are determined for each event. Qualification for the finals is based upon annual earnings, and the top fifteen cowboys in each event are invited to participate.

ROMAN RIDING   A contract stunt for entertainment in which one or more horses are ridden by a rider in a standing position with only the reins to guide the horses and help him maintain his balance. The truly spectacular exhibitions of Roman riding usually feature a team of four or five horses running abreast being handled by a single rider.

RUSSIAN DRAG   A rodeo stunt ride in which the rider's head hangs off the side of the horse while he maintains his position by placing one foot in a strap on his back.

115

SADDLE BRONC RIDING   One of the five standard rodeo events. In this riding competition, the cowboy is equipped with a halter —a single rein that is simply a braided rope—and his saddle. The saddle, the most important and prized possession of a bronc rider, is carefully made to meet the specifications for the "association saddle." *See* ASSOCIATION SADDLE.

Like bareback riding, the rider must be spurring the horse as he leaves the chute and throughout the whole ride. He may not touch any part of his horse, rigging, or himself with his free hand and may not change hands or wrap the rein around his hand. Loss of a stirrup may also disqualify a rider. Scoring is the same for bareback riding. Duration of the ride is either eight or ten seconds.

SPLITTING   A practice involving two contestants in the same event whereby they agree prior to the competition to combine their winnings and divide the total equally between them.

STANDARD EVENT   *See* EVENT.

STEER DECORATING   The Canadian version of steer wrestling, which evolved as a result of the Humane Society's complaints against steer wrestling. In this event the contestant leaps from his running horse onto the head of the steer and places a small ribbon or elastic band around his nose or over his horn instead of twisting him to the ground.

STEER ROPING   A rodeo event in which the contestant throws a steer to the ground with his rope. To accomplish this single-handedly, the roper first rides as close as possible to the animal before throwing his loop around its horns or neck. When the loop has been secured with a jerk, the rope's slack is then thrown around the far side of the steer under its right hipbone and around its buttocks.

The rider then reins his horse off at an angle to the left, bracing himself for the fall. As soon as the slack is taken up in the rope, the steer is abruptly reversed in midair and falls to the ground. The animal usually lands in such a way as to make it practically impossible for it to regain its feet before the roper can jump off his horse, run down the rope, and make the tie.

TEAM ROPING   Same procedure as Dally Team Tying, with the exception that once the catch's head and heels have been made, the head roper dismounts and ties the steer's hind legs above the ankle joint with a short length of twisted rope, raising his hands to signify the taking of time after he has completed a double knot. *See also* DALLY TEAM ROPING.

TIMERS   Experienced members of the Rodeo Cowboys Association or committee members of the rodeo who time each contestant. There must be at least two timers who agree on the time of each individual. For the events such as calf roping or steer wrestling, time commences when the contestant leaves the chute or upon signal of the score-line judge. In riding events, time begins at the first jump out of the chute; then the timer sounds a buzzer, gun, or whistle to signify when the cowboy has stuck on long enough to make a qualified ride.

TWISTER   Rodeo terminology for a cowboy. A shortened form of *bronc twister,* when first used it probably referred exclusively to bronc riders.

WILD-COW MILKING   Another timed rodeo event but not one of the five standard ones. In this contest the object is to obtain a few drops of milk in a pop bottle from a wild cow turned loose in the arena. Upon her release, two cowboys race after her. While one of them ropes her, the other dismounts and subdues her sufficiently to allow the team to obtain a few drops of milk in a small necked bottle.

WILD HORSE RACE   A Rodeo Cowboys Association recognized event that carries no championship award. This contest is attempted by teams of three cowboys who begin on foot. The object is to catch, saddle, and then ride a wild mustang turned loose in the arena. When the horse is ridden across the score-line by a member of the team, the test is complete. The teams compete against each other and are ultimately placed first, second, and third.

DRESSAGE
AND
HAUTE ÉCOLE

AIDS　The hand, leg, weight, spur or whip actions of the rider in eliciting responses from the horse are called *aids*.

BALANCE　When referring to an educated horse, the term *balance* generally is used to describe a rather intangible blend of collection and impulsion along with the accompanying flexibility and elasticity of the horse's musculature that results in a cadenced yet free forward motion.

BALOTADE　One of the aerial moves similar to the *capriole*, except that the hind legs are folded beneath the horse's quarters instead of being horizontally extended behind him. *See* CAPRIOLE.

CADRE NOIR　The section of the French Samur Cavalry School which specializes in *haute école. See* HAUTE ÉCOLE.

CAPRIOLE　A movement above the ground in which the horse leaps into the air with folded forelegs, while the hind legs kick out behind him in a horizontal line.

COLLECTED CANTER　Actually a slow gallop with increased lifting of the neck and head, increased engagement of the hocks, decreased forward motion, and intensified impulsion and strength of each stride.

COLLECTED TROT　A "highly charged" gait of great energy executed with a slightly raised head (the result of collection) and accentuated by well-elevated steps. Despite the reduced speed and shortened strides, this gait maintains all the "drive" and impulsion of an extended trot.

COLLECTED WALK　A walk in which the horse moves with neck raised slightly and arched from poll to withers, face approaching a vertical line, and hindquarters working well beneath him. The steps should be absolutely even, clearly defined, and not overly long.

COLLECTION　The attitude of the in-motion horse whereby the length of his stride is shortened and the height of his action is increased. Collection occurs as the result of a sort of "compression" of the horse from rear to fore, causing the horse to enter a state of self-carriage and to lighten his forehand. *See* SELF-CARRIAGE.

COUNTER or FALSE CANTER   When a horse works a circle or curved line while leading with his outside foot, he is said to be on the false or *counter* lead.

COURBETTE   One of the more advanced airs above the ground wherein the horse leaps forward in rapid cadence on his haunches while maintaining the levade position. *See* LEVADE.

DEMI-VOLTE—*Half Circle*   A change of direction during which a half circle is executed with a return to the track in a straight line at a forty-five-degree angle to the track.

DEMI-VOLTE RENVERSE—*Half Circle in Reverse*   A change of direction during which the horse leaves the track in a straight line at a forty-five-degree angle and returns to the track by executing a half circle.

DRESSAGE   A term from the French *dresser* (to train), *dressage* may be translated as *training*. This does not mean, however, that every person who schools, trains, rides, or otherwise seeks to educate a horse is practicing *dressage*. Training is an integral part of the definition of *dressage,* but the word actually implies that such "training" shall be accomplished according to established principles and schools of thought (as opposed to anyone's haphazard theories on horse training) with predictable results (taking into account each individual horse's conformation and temperament), which are practically guaranteed to improve an animal's flexibility and balance provided that the trainer is a qualified horseman. In fact, the *Federation Equestre Internationale* (FEI) states that the purpose of dressage "is to make an animal keen and obedient."

Dressage may be divided into three levels: Elementary, Secondary, and Superior, which indicate an increasing difficulty. However, regardless of the level, *dressage* involves suppling and collecting horse exercises that range from the very simple to the very difficult. Although some of the more complicated movements are almost identical with certain of the easier high school airs, dressage is not to be confused with *haute école* (high school). Perhaps dressage and Haute École are best differentiated by the fact that *dressage* is actually intended as training for horses destined for other work, whereas high school is an end unto itself. *See* HAUTE ÉCOLE.

EXTENDED TROT   The extended trot is executed with less restriction or "compression" than the collected trot, but the horse should maintain good self-carriage and elasticity of stride. His steps should be long and even, although it should be noted that an exaggerated long reach with the forelegs denotes tension and means an incorrect extended trot.

EXTENDED WALK　A gait marked by its steady cadence, the extended walk is performed with less collection than the collected walk. Each step should be pronounced with the hind feet overstepping the forefeet tracks.

EXTENSION　A gait is said to be "extended" when the length of the stride is increased and the elevation diminished; at the same time the hind legs are engaged as intensified driving aids, so that the horse may be encouraged to use his forelegs freely from the shoulder.

FLEXION　The relaxation or softening of the muscles controlling the jaw and poll of the horse in yielding to the aids of the rider. Proper flexion of a well-schooled horse would put the animal's nose very nearly on a horizontal line with his hips which he accomplishes by raising his neck, while his nose and forehead are positioned just barely out of the vertical.

FLYING CHANGE OF LEAD　A maneuver wherein the horse changes from one lead to the other at the gallop without interrupting the gait.

FULL HALT　The action of bringing the horse to a standstill with his legs *squarely* placed and his hindquarters well underneath him.

FREE WALK ON THE BIT　The natural walk of the horse while under the influence of the rider and accepting a light hold of the bit.

FREE WALK ON A LOOSE REIN　The natural walk of the horse with no existing contact between the rider's hands and the bit.

GRAND PRIX DE DRESSAGE　A *dressage* competition at the highest level as defined by the *Federation Équestre Internationale*.

HALF-HALT　The brief pause or hesitation effected by a horse that is making a transition from one movement or one pace to another (usually when he is moving from a more extended movement to a shorter one). Perhaps the most important aspect of the half-halt is that the horse's hindquarters must momentarily receive his forward impulsion in a transient increased collection, so that the horse may then strike out smoothly in the gait or speed requested by his rider.

HAUTE ÉCOLE—*High School* The art of riding in its highest form and the training of horses to execute a series of extremely complicated and controlled movements is known as *haute école.* Although some of the movements in *haute école* actually belong to *dressage,* for the most part *haute école* begins where the other leaves off. The movements, or "airs" of *haute école* may be divided into two types: Those performed "on the ground," and those executed "in the air" (also referred to as the "airs above the ground").

True and classical *haute école* attempts to develop the horse's natural motions by means of specialized exercises in a slow, painstaking but relentless progression towards perfection. There is only one institution in the world dedicated to the preservation of this art of developing horse and rider—The Spanish Riding School of Vienna. *See* SPANISH RIDING SCHOOL.

IMPULSION The driving or propelling force that affects the horse's forward motion is called "impulsion." Since the horse is essentially a "rear-engined" animal, his "drive shaft" is located in his hind legs. It follows that the greater the development of the hindquarters, the more powerful and versatile the animal. This is not to imply that some horses are incapable of creating their own impulsion in their own ways, for they most definitely do. However, a horse that has been educated and taught to engage his hocks and work off his hindquarters (as opposed to tipping onto his forehand) will be far better equipped to live up to and/or surpass his potential in whatever type of work he does than an animal without such training.

Because impulsion originates in the hindquarters and is literally the driving force with which the animal motors, it is directly responsible for the liveliness, cadence, and energy of any particular movement or gait. Without impulsion the performance is dull and flat and, in some instances, impossible. With impulsion the horse appears to be vital and elastic, as if his body is a coiled spring ready to "pop" with great energy. Furthermore, if a horse is expected to be schooled to execute any type of advanced *dressage* or *Haute École* movements, it is essential that he first be taught to use his own body to create

123

a constant source of forward motivation rather than be dependent on the leg, weight, hand, whip, or spur aids of his rider.

LEVADE   One of the airs above the ground in which the horse raises his forelegs from the ground in a low rearing motion; he then crouches with forelegs folded under and all his weight on his hindquarters with his body at a forty-five degree angle to the ground.

ORDINARY CANTER   A free-moving gait executed at a pace that in the rider's opinion is most conducive to maintaining his horse's balance.

ORDINARY WORKING TROT   A cadenced, even trot in keeping with the horse's stage of education; a pace designed to encourage him to stay in balance.

PASSAGE, also called the SPANISH TROT or STEP   One of the most beautiful and graceful movements of *haute école,* the *passage* is actually a compressed, shortened, and extremely elevated condensed trot characterized by a marked increase in the flexion of the knees and engagement of the hocks as well as an intangible quality simultaneously suggesting great strength and elasticity.

PIAFFE   Literally trotting in place, the *piaffe* is essentially a slightly elevated version of the *passage* executed in one place. Since the horse is not moving forward, his impulsion is directed upward, and each of his legs when raised in suspension is higher than the passage. One of the more difficult movements of *haute école,* the *piaffe* requires that both rider and horse have a solid foundation of training before it is possible to accomplish the movement with the necessary cadence, elasticity, lightness, and lack of effort on the horse's part.

PILLARS—*Pilliers*   Two posts between which the horse is cross-tied during instruction in the *piaffe.*

PIROUETTE   Executed at the collected canter, the *pirouette* is a *volte* (or circle) on two tracks, which is approximately equal to the length of the horse. In this movement, the horse, with his hocks well under him, pivots on his haunches in the smallest circle he can manage, while his forelegs describe a wider circle around his hindquarters.

124

PRIX ST. GEORGE   A *dressage* competition that is the next level below the *Grand Prix*.

REIN BACK or BACKING   The retrograde movement of the horse executed at the walk. The most important aspect of backing is that the horse must step backward in a straight line without swinging his quarters to either side.

RENVERS—*Haunches Out*   A movement on two tracks in which the horses moves forward towards a point, but in a sideways position approximately forty-five degrees from the wall. In this exercise he is positioned with his tail pointing toward the wall, and his loins and quarters are distinctly flexed around the rider's outside leg. His head, neck, and shoulders follow a straight track approximately three feet from the wall, and the inside legs cross over the outside legs.

SELF-CARRIAGE   It is most desirable to teach a horse to carry himself by his own impulsion—that is, without depending on the rider's hands for support or to "hold up" his "front end." In order to accomplish this condition of self-carriage, the animal must engage his hindquarters and hocks, relax his back muscles, and accept the responsibility of supporting his own body.

SHOULDER-IN   A movement on two tracks in which the horse is bent symmetrically through his spinal column, from poll to croup, around the rider's leg with his body set obliquely to the line of motion.

SPANISH RIDING SCHOOL   A unique institution that preserves the teaching of Italian and French riding masters of the 16th and 17th centuries as its exclusive basis of schooling. Located in Vienna, the school was founded (1680) by the Emperor Leopold and was later established (1735) in a permanent building. It is renowned throughout the world for its excellence and performance of the most difficult movements and airs of the *Haute École*. The name Spanish is not indicative of the style of riding practiced; it stems from the fact that the famous Lippizaner horses used at the school are descended from an Andalusian strain, the foundation stock of which was exported to Austria from the Spanish Court by Queen Isabella.

TRAVERS—*Haunches-In*   Another of the movements on two tracks, this exercise is directly opposite to the *renvers*. The horse is

125

positioned so that his head, neck, and shoulders are pointing toward the wall, and his quarters are approximately forty-five degrees, or three feet, from the wall. His body is bent around the rider's inside leg; as he moves, the outside legs cross over the inside legs.

TURN ON THE FOREHAND　An exercise worked from the halt, the turn on the forehand is just what the term implies. A turn of the horse in which his inside foreleg acts as a pivoting center around which the outside foreleg and hindquarters are slowly and rhythmically moved.

TURN ON THE HAUNCHES　An exercise in which the horse executes an about turn by pivoting on his inside hind leg (which is not rooted to the ground, but moves around naturally while always returning to the same spot), while the outside hind leg and forelegs move around it. Turns on the haunches are performed at the halt, the walk, the trot, and the canter; however, it should be noted that such turns at the canter are actually *pirouettes* and belong to the *haute école.*

TWO TRACK　Any movement in which the horse travels on two tracks with his body simultaneously moving forward and sideward. Two tracking may be accomplished at the walk, trot, or collected canter, but it is most important that both tracks remain absolutely parallel to each other. The horse's body should be positioned so that his forehand is always leading his hind quarters, but the angle of the sideward inclination should not exceed forty-five degrees.

VOLTE　Actually a complete circle, the term *volte* usually implies a circle of prescribed diameter in which the animal returns to the track at the exact point of departure.

POLO

Polo

BACK One of the three playing positions on an indoor polo team, and of the four playing positions on an outdoor team.

CHUKKER or CHUKKA Both indoor and outdoor polo games are divided into seven-and-a-half-minute periods of play called *chukkers*. There are six such periods in an outdoor polo game and four in an indoor game. The word *chukker* is an East Indian term.

CROSSING One of the most common fouls committed during a polo game, *crossing* may be called when a player moves across the line of his opponent who has the right of way in such a way as to be dangerous or cause a possible collision.

CROSS TAIL SHOTS Hitting the ball in a backward shot executed over the pony's hindquarters.

CUP MATCHES Championship matches are called cup matches.

FOUL Like many other sports, a foul may be called for any infraction of the rules of play. In polo, a foul is generally incurred by some form of reckless or dangerous riding. Some of the more frequently committed fouls are: crossing the line of the traveling ball in such a way as to endanger oneself or the player who has the right of way; failing to yield to the player who has the right of way when approaching from a different direction; failing to yield to two players riding from the opposite direction; galloping a zig zag pattern in front of another player; halting or pulling up on the ball; and unusually rough, uncalled for play and any sort of dangerous riding. Any dangerous and/or illegal use of the mallet such as hooking the mallet of an opponent so as to cross in front of his pony's forelegs or across the back of his mount is also considered a foul.

GROUND The polo field is also called the ground.

HANDICAP All polo players are handicapped—rated in accordance with their experience—on a scale from zero to ten goals. A zero handicap denotes a player with the least experience, while a ten-goal player, something of a rarity, is of course extremely proficient. To arrive at the handicap for a team, the ratings of the individual players are combined.

HIT IN When the ball is hit from the end zone of the field, it is said to have been *hit in*.

128

HOOK   A playing technique in which one player hooks his mallet into the mallet of his opponent.

INDOOR POLO   Indoor polo is played in riding arenas of varying size, but the ideal specifications approximate one hundred yards long by fifty yards wide. The goalposts of the outdoor game are replaced by a ten-foot-wide designated area frequently painted or otherwise marked on the walls at either end of the ring. The entire arena is often bounded on all sides by kneeboards averaging three feet, six inches in height. There are three players on a side (as opposed to four in outdoor polo)—Number 1, Number 2, and the Back. The ball used for indoor polo is approximately one and a half times as large as that used in the outdoor game. It consists of an inflated rubber bladder encased in a leather covering; it resembles a small white soccer ball or basketball. The same mallet is used in both indoor and outdoor games.

KNEE BOARDS   *See* INDOOR POLO.

MALLET   The stick that players hit the ball with is called a mallet. The head is usually made of maple, sycamore, ash, or elm, the shaft of tapered cane or Malacca. The length is approximately fifty inches and weighs a pound. To aid the players in keeping hold of their mallets, a tape thong, attached at the held end, is wound around the rider's thumb. Hits are made with the flat side of the mallet head.

NEAR SIDE SHOTS   Either backhand or forehand hits of the ball executed from the left side of the pony.

NUMBER OF PLAYERS   There are four players on a side in outdoor polo, three in the indoor game.

OFF SIDE SHOTS   Either backhand or forehand hits of the ball accomplished from the right side of the pony.

OUTDOOR POLO   Outdoor polo is played on a regulation field, which is 160 yards wide by 300 yards long. It is enclosed by ten-inch-high boards to keep the ball on the playing field. The goalposts, located at each end of the field are set twenty-four feet apart. Each side has four players—Number 1, Number 2, Number 3, and the Back (as opposed to three on an indoor team). The ball is made of solid wood, weighs approximately

129

four-and-a-half ounces and is three-and-a-quarter inches in diameter. The mallet is the same for both indoor and outdoor.

PENALTY   A variety of free shots at the goal, which may be with or without defenders, are awarded when a foul occurs.

PERIOD   *See* CHUKKER.

PICK UP STICK   A stick with a net at the end; it is used to pick up the polo ball from the ground without dismounting.

PLAYER POSITIONS   Players are designated Number 1, Number 2, Number 3, and Back.

POLO   The origins of the game of polo find their roots in Persia, where records exist of such a sport as early as A.D. 590, as well as in ancient Greece and China prior to the Christian era. Before the 16th century polo was well known in India, and it was introduced into Japan from Tibet and China more than 400 years ago. In fact, the Japanese form of the game, called *Dakiu,* is still played today. The game was first played in England in 1869, and in 1876 polo was brought to the United States by James Gordon Bennett (the renowned newspaper publisher), when he introduced the indoor game in New York City. The outdoor game quickly followed.

The word *polo* seems to be an adaptation or corruption of the Tibetan work *pulu,* which means ball.

POLO BALL   *See* INDOOR POLO and OUTDOOR POLO.

POLO BOOTS   A heavy felt protective covering strapped around the legs of a polo pony to prevent injury.

POLO PONY   The designation *pony* for the mounts used in polo games stems from the fact that in the years prior to 1915 the height of the animals eligible to be played was limited to 14.2 hands: a pony. Between 1915 and 1920, the limit was raised to 15.1; since 1920 all height restrictions have been dropped.

REFEREE   A mounted official who judges the play of the game, throws in the ball after an out-of-bounds play or begins play after a goal is scored, and calls fouls and assigns penalties for them.

RIDING OFF   A playing technique wherein the player and his pony bodily force their opponent out of the line of play.

SIDES   In the game of outdoor polo, the sides are changed after each goal has been made. In the indoor game, sides are changed at the end of each *chukker*.

UMPIRE   The dismounted official who acts as the final judge on the referee's decisions; an umpire generally officiates at important championship matches.

UNDER THE NECK SHOTS   Hits of the ball accomplished by means of the player's bending over and striking the ball with the swing of his mallet being underneath the pony's neck.

CONFORMATION
AND WAY
OF GOING

Conformation and Way of Going

ACTION   The way in which a horse moves his feet and legs while in motion is called his *action* or way of going.

ALBINO   The Albino is the only true white horse—that is, his coat is white from birth and the skin under it is uniformly pink. He is devoid of pigmentation and suffers from the same weaknesses as other albino creatures: namely, sensitivity to the sun and impaired vision. The Albino tends to breed true, and there have been attempts to establish it as a color breed. However, because of its characteristic weaknesses, interest in this project has been limited. *See also* ALBINO—Breeds Section.

APPALOOSA   A coat color that combines white with any other solid color. Usually the loins and hips are white with dark round oval spots. These spots may range in size from small dots to dots three or four inches in diameter. The spotting, which may occur all over the body, predominates in the area over the hips. However, there may be white without any spots over the hip area, or there may be a mottled effect over the entire body. There are also instances of white specks or spots on a dark background. Appaloosas are marked by three additional features, so that even if the polka-dot spattering is not present the animal may be identified as an Appaloosa. First, the eye is encircled by white similar to the human eye. Second, the skin beneath the coat has a muddy, mottled pink and gray speckling that may be most readily detected around the nostrils. Third, the hoofs are likewise particolored with vertical black and white striping. The presence of these characteristics and consistent transmission of them among animals of the type suggest that, of all the "color" horses, the Appaloosa has been most successfully resolved into a true breed. *See also* APPALOOSA—Breeds Section.

BALD FACE   *See* CALF FACE. —

BANDY LEGGED   A horse the hind feet of which turn in at the toes while his hocks turn outward is called bandy legged.

BAY   May range in color from a yellowish tan called light bay, through a bright reddish color referred to as blood bay, to a mahogany shade called dark bay. Mane, tail, and lower legs are black.

BENCH KNEED   *See* KNEE SPRUNG.

134

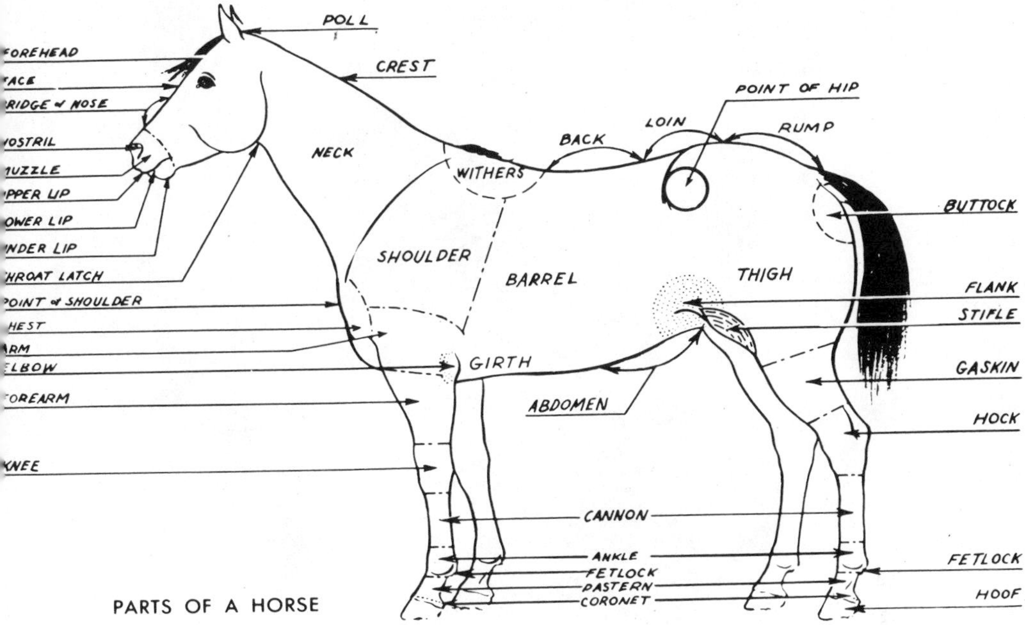

PARTS OF A HORSE

Labels: POLL, FOREHEAD, CREST, FACE, BRIDGE of NOSE, NOSTRIL, MUZZLE, UPPER LIP, LOWER LIP, UNDER LIP, THROAT LATCH, POINT of SHOULDER, CHEST, ARM, ELBOW, FOREARM, KNEE, NECK, WITHERS, SHOULDER, BARREL, GIRTH, ABDOMEN, BACK, LOIN, POINT OF HIP, RUMP, THIGH, BUTTOCK, FLANK, STIFLE, GASKIN, HOCK, CANNON, ANKLE, FETLOCK, PASTERN, CORONET, FETLOCK, HOOF

NATIONAL 4-H SERVICE COMMITTEE

PARTS OF THE PASTERN AND FOOT

NATIONAL 4-H SERVICE COMMITTEE

Labels: FETLOCK, PASTERN, CORONET, HOOF, BULB, CANNON BONE, LONG PASTERN, SHORT PASTERN, CORONARY BAND, COFFIN BONE, SENSITIVE LAMINAE, DEEP FLEXOR TENDON, PLANTAR CUSHION, SENSITIVE FROG, INSENSITIVE FROG, WHITE LINE, QUARTER, HEEL, TOE, FROG, BUTTRESS, WALL, SOLE, COFFIN BONE, LATERAL CARTILAGES

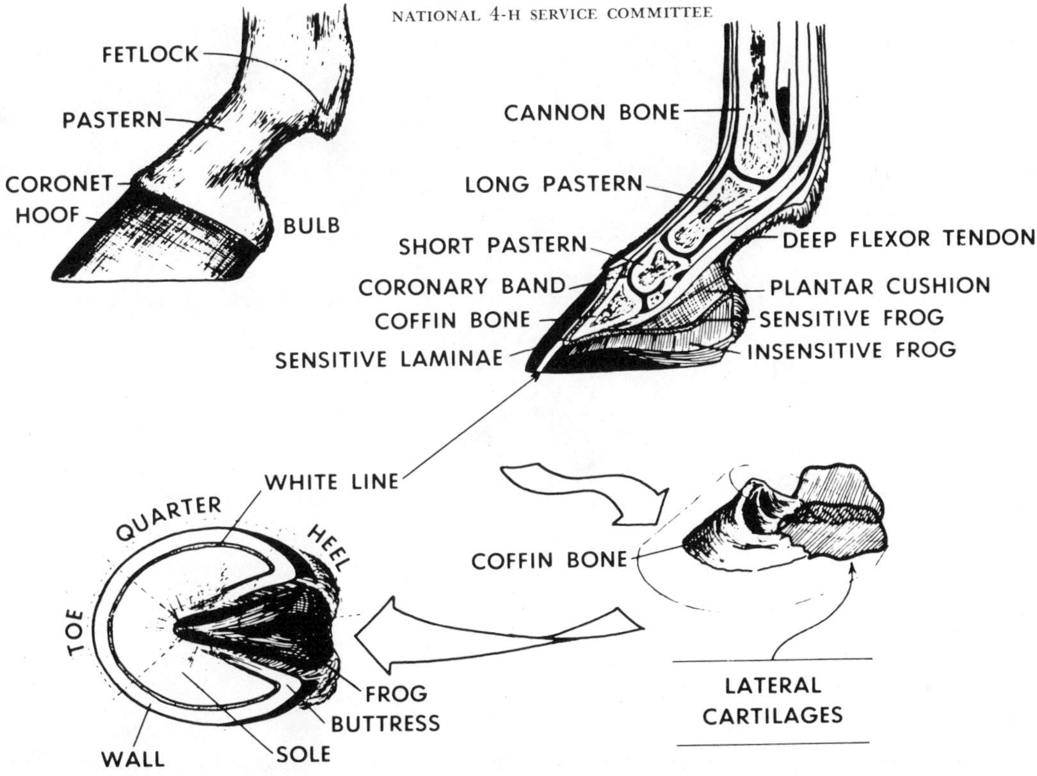

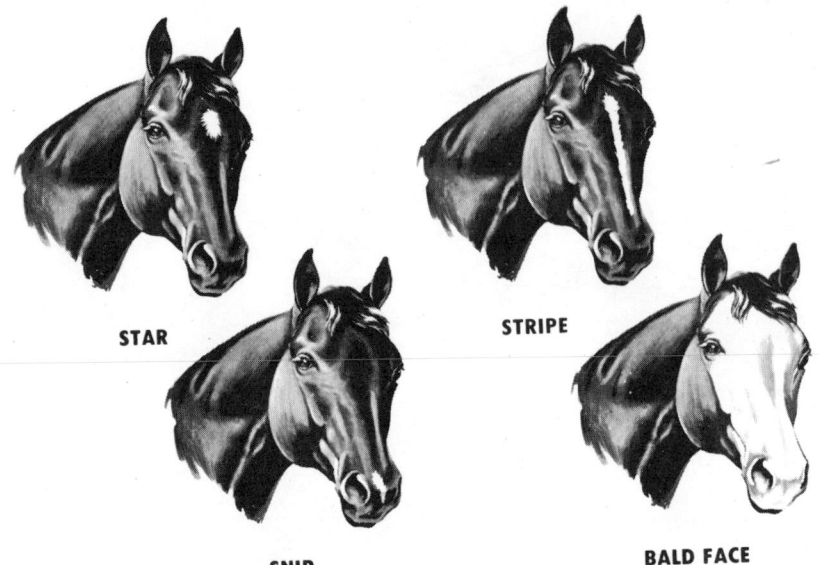

STAR

STRIPE

SNIP

BALD FACE

BLAZE

STAR, STRIPE AND SNIP

STAR AND STRIPE

NATIONAL 4-H SERVICE COMMITTEE

ALL THESE HORSES HAVE
UNDESIRABLE CHARACTERISTICS

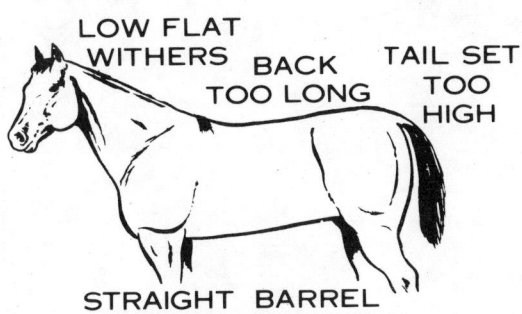

LOW FLAT WITHERS BACK TOO LONG TAIL SET TOO HIGH

STRAIGHT BARREL LOIN TIES-IN POORLY

GOOSE RUMP

TAIL SET TOO LOW

ROMAN NOSE

PARROT MOUTH

PIG-EYED

NATIONAL 4-H SERVICE COMMITTEE

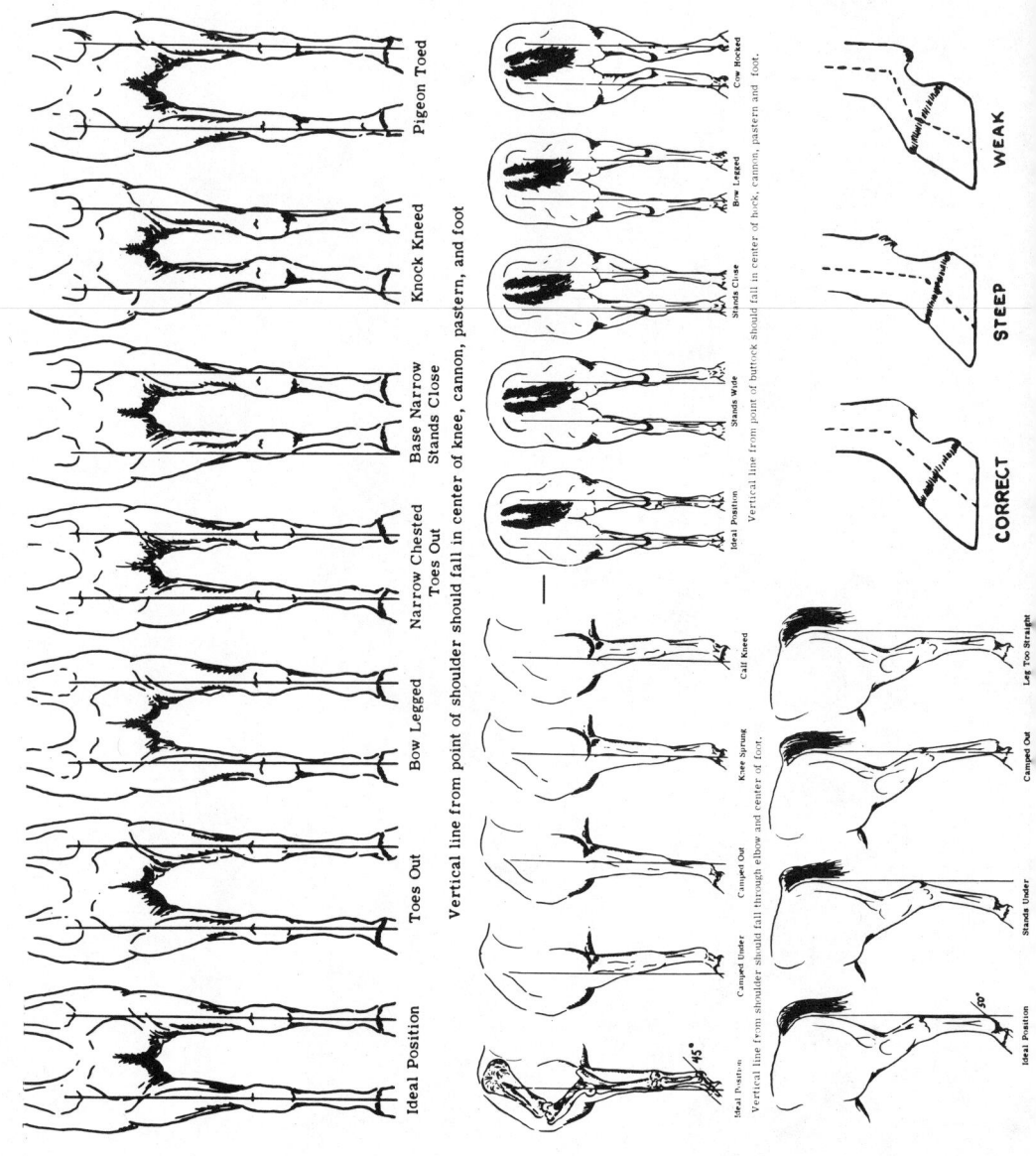

Ideal Position   Toes Out   Bow Legged   Narrow Chested Toes Out   Base Narrow Stands Close   Knock Kneed   Pigeon Toed

Vertical line from point of shoulder should fall in center of knee, cannon, pastern, and foot

Ideal Position   Stands Wide   Stands Close   Bow Legged   Cow Hocked

Vertical line from point of buttock should fall in center of hock, cannon, pastern and foot.

Ideal Position   Camped Under   Camped Out   Knee Sprung   Calf Kneed

Vertical line from shoulder should fall through elbow and center of foot.

Ideal Position   Stands Under   Camped Out   Leg Too Straight

CORRECT   STEEP   WEAK

NATIONAL 4-H SERVICE COMMITTEE

BLACK   A true, absolute pitch black, which is rare.

BLACK POINTS   A horse with a black mane and tail and legs which are either black or darker than the rest of his body is said to have *black points.*

BLAZE   A wide white streak running from the horse's forehead down to his nose.

BROKEN CREST   *See* LOP NECK.

BROWN   Ranges from a lustrous, rich shade of brown to almost black. *Brown* horses which appear to be black over most of the body surface usually have light tan hairs around the muzzle and underbelly.

BRUSHING   *See* INTERFERING.

BUCK KNEED   *See* KNEE SPRUNG.

BUCKSKIN   *See* DUN.

BUG EYED   *See* POP EYED.

CALF FACE, also BALD FACE   A large irregular splash of white covering generous portions of the face and frequently accompanied by one or two watch eyes. Calf-faced horses are also called bald faced.

CALF KNEED   The direct antithesis of *buck'kneed* or knee sprung. It thus means standing with the knees too far toward the back.

CANTER   A three-beat gait in which the horse's feet strike the ground in the order—left hind, right hind, and left fore almost simultaneously, followed by right fore. Then just before the sequence begins again, there is a time when all four feet are off the ground. The progression described here is for a horse *cantering* on the right lead—that is, leading with his right fore foot. The *canter* is actually nothing more than a "controlled" or "educated" version of the horse's natural gallop.

CHESTNUT   Ranges widely from a light, yellowish red—sometimes known as sorrel—to a deep liver-colored hue with many red, gold, and coppery tints in between. Chestnuts have a mane and

139

a tail that may be either a little darker or distinctly blonder than the body color, but they can be distinguished from reddish bays in that mane, tail, and legs are never black.

CHESTNUTS, also NIGHT EYES   A protruding horny growth located on the inner surfaces of the horse's four legs. On the fore legs they appear above the knee, while on the hind legs they are situated along the lower inside portion of the hock. These formations are the *residua* of the final digit to recede from the foot of the prehistoric horse. These growths are thus normal, and they are more pronounced on cold-blooded horses than on the hot-blooded strains, such as the Arab on which they are nearly undetectable. The swirls of the horn are completely individual and are thus used for purposes of identification, like a human being's fingerprints.

CLAYBANK   *See* DUN.

CLEAN-LEGGED   A horse that is not blemished by any permanent enlargements or calcifications such as splints, osselets, bows, sidebones or ringbones, big knees, and so forth is said to be *clean-legged*. The term also implies soundness of limb.

CLYDESDALE EYED   *See* WALLEYED.

COARSE   A horse lacking refinement and appearing rather rough or harsh is said to be *coarse*.

COLT   An entire male horse under five years of age.

COON FOOTED   An excessively long, low pastern in combination with a shallow heel. Such construction denotes a weakness of the part.

COW HOCKS   A conformation flaw wherein the points of the hock turn in and the toes turn out. This condition causes a loss of impulsion, as the animal expends energy in an outward motion instead of moving directly forward in a straight line.

CROSS CANTER   *See* DISUNITED CANTER.

CROSS FIRING   A defect in gait most frequently seen in pacers in which the diagonal fore feet and hind feet make contact on the inside while in the air, just as the stride of the hind leg is nearly completed and the stride of the foreleg is begun. *See also* FORGING.

CRYPTORCHID   *See* RIDGLING.

CURBY HOCKED   A term used to describe hocks that are rounded on the back side and thus constitute a flaw in conformation. This is not to be confused with the existence of a curb. *See* CURB—Health and Condition Section.

DAISY CUTTER   A horse that moves with an unusually long low stride which barely clears the ground at the trot. This is generally an indication of a good shoulder movement with the horse able to cover a fair amount of ground at each stride.

DAPPLED   When spots about the size of a silver dollar that may be lighter or darker overlay the basic coat color, the horse is said to be *dappled*.

DISH FACE   A concave line of the face, frequently denoting Arabian ancestry.

DISHING   *See* PADDLING.

DISUNITED CANTER or CROSS CANTERING   A horse that is cantering with his forelegs on one lead and his hind legs on the other is said to be *disunited* or *cross cantering*. This is generally considered a rather serious fault, and in many cases it is an indication of unsoundness.

DOCKED TAIL   A horse with tail bones that have been cut for the purpose of shortening the tail is said to have a *docked tail*.

DOGTROT   *See* JOG.

DUN   A dull yellow-brown or tawny-gray. Duns have a black mane, tail, and black legs—the latter sometimes being marked by zebra-like striping. Duns commonly have a black dorsal stripe down the spine and, less commonly, may have a transverse stripe across the withers. The body color may also be imposed on any of the basic colors—that is, bay, brown, black, or chestnut. When combined with black, brown, or dark bay, the result is a smoky-color mouse dun (or grulla). Imposed on light bay, the result is a sandy yellow called buckskin; imposed on light chestnut, the outcome is the reddish yellow of the claybank dun.

141

Conformation and Way of Going

ENTIRE   A stallion may simply be referred to as an *entire* horse.

ERGOT   A semihorny growth located at the posterior base of the fetlock joint and usually completely covered by a tuft of hairs called the fetlock, which also grows at the same point.

EWE NECK   A defect in conformation in which the top line of the neck from the poll drops sharply just in front of the withers. Such construction is the direct opposite of the desired form, and it is thus also referred to as a neck that has been set on "upside down."

FALLEN NECK   *See* LOP NECK.

FEATHER   The longish hair that grows down the back edge of the cannon bone and fetlock joints. Since the Clydesdale and Shire horses have this hair in the greatest abundance, they are known as the *feather-legged* breeds.

FILLY   A female horse under five years of age.

FLEA-BITTEN GRAY   A dark gray coat interspersed with small patches of whitish hairs.

FOAL   The term applied to a newborn horse regardless of sex, usually up until the time it is weaned, when it is identified as being a colt or a filly.

FORGING or OVERREACHING   Overreaching of the hind foot so as to strike the forefoot on the same side. This condition is in part a result of conformation; long-legged, rangy horses are the most prone to forging. The added weight of a shoe on a horse's foot can provide the impetus for carrying the foot beyond its normal point and therefore strike the forefoot, or the thickness of the shoe (a-half-inch average) may exceed nature's narrow margin for the placement of the animal's feet while in motion. In most instances, removing the shoes for a time and then re-shoeing with the advice of a competent farrier or veterinarian will eliminate this problem.

FOX TROT   A broken gait peculiar to the Missouri Fox Trotting Horse of the Ozark region of the United States, which consists of a brisk walk with the front feet and a trot with the hind feet. This gait is performed in cadence at speeds from five to ten mph.

142

GALLOP   An accelerated canter (*see* CANTER), which becomes a four-beat gait (as opposed to three at the canter) as the horse strikes the ground with his feet in the order—inside hind leg, outside foreleg, inside or leading foreleg. This is then followed by a long moment of suspension after which the horse lands on the outside hind leg. The change from the three-beat cadence at the canter to the four-beat rhythm at the gallop results from the fact that with the increase in speed there comes a moment when the simultaneous hoof beats of the inside hind leg and the outside foreleg suddenly separate from each other.

GELDING   A castrated male horse of any age.

GLASS EYED   *See* WALLEYED.

GOOSE RUMP   A horse with quarters that descend in an exaggerated slope from the point of the croup to the root of the tail is said to be goose rumped. This particular construction seems to denote jumping ability, and the high point just in front of the slope is frequently referred to as a *jumping bump.*

GRAY   A mixture of white and black hairs, which lightens with age and may range from a deep gunmetal hue to white. Dappling is common among grays.

GRULLA   *See* DUN.

HALF STOCKING   A white stocking that reaches over the ankles but stops well short of the knee or hock.

HAND GALLOP   The gallop performed with definite collection.

HANDS   A horse's height is measured in hands from the highest point of the withers to the ground. A hand is a four-inch unit, thus a horse standing 16.0 hands is sixty-four-inches tall, and one standing 15.3 hands is sixty-three-inches tall. A grown animal must stand over 14.2 hands to be classified as a horse (with the exception of some breeds—that is, Arabs, which frequently mature to heights under this minimum and are nonetheless considered horses). Animals that stand 14.2 hands and under are called ponies.

HEAVY FRONTED   A horse with an unusually wide and overly muscular chest may be said to be *heavy fronted.* This particular

143

conformation is frequently a sign of coarseness, and a horse with such configuration is often a bad mover.

HERRING GUTTED or WASP WAISTED   A horse with a belly that is drawn up toward his quarters with no depth of stomach is said to be *herring gutted* or *wasp waisted.* This construction is an inconvenience as well as a defect, for it is most difficult to keep a saddle in place without the use of a breastplate to keep it from slipping too far back and resting on the horse's kidneys.

INTERFERING or BRUSHING   Hitting the fetlock or cannon of the opposite (supporting) leg with the foot of the leg that is in motion. Animals which toe out or are splay footed have a predisposition to this way of going. *See* SPLAY FOOTED and TOE OUT.

JIG   A horse that will never walk when being ridden and is constantly jogging a few paces, throwing his head, and generally behaving in a natty or fretful manner is said to *jig.*

JOG or DOGTROT   A slow trot is called a *jog* or *dogtrot.*

JUMPING BUMP   *See* GOOSE RUMP.

KNEE SPRUNG   A state in which the knees project too far forward beyond the normal line from forearm to hoof. Also known as *over at the knees, buck kneed,* or *bench-kneed.*

LOADED SHOULDER   A horse with a *loaded shoulder* is one with little or no definition of withers coupled with a thick muscular shoulder. Such horses are frequently bad movers and tend to roll at the trot and gallop.

LOPE   Another variation of the horse's natural gallop, the lope is the Western version, which is performed freely and easily with little or no collection at approximately the same speed as the canter.

LOP EARRED   Dropping the ears sideways so as to carry them in a semihorizontal position, or being born with ears set on the head too low is known as being lop earred. Lop ears are frequently thicker at the base than normal ears; this, coupled with the inability to *perk* them up at attention, tends to make the head look plain or common and is considered a conformation flaw.

144

LOP NECK, also FALLEN NECK, BROKEN CREST   A term describing a condition in which the superior border (or crest) of the neck becomes invaded with fatty tissue to such an extent that it can no longer remain upright under the weight and falls to one side.

MARE   A female horse more than five years of age.

MUTTON WITHERS   A conformation flaw wherein the withers are more or less undefined, being of rather round flat construction over the top of the shoulder. Horses with such conformation are often poor movers, tending towards choppy and clumsy gaits. It is also difficult to keep a saddle in place on a horse with mutton withers, as it often slips to one side or the other.

NARROW IN FRONT   *See* ONE GUTTED.

NIGHT EYES   *See* CHESTNUTS.

ONE GUTTED   A horse with very little space between his forelegs is said to be *one gutted* or *narrow in front*. This configuration is suggestive of limited space for the heart and lungs, and horses of this build tend to interfere when in motion. *See also* INTERFERE.

OPEN BEHIND   A horse standing *open behind* is one with hocks that are far apart while his feet are close together. The opposite of *cow hocks*.

OVER AT THE KNEES   *See* KNEE SPRUNG.

OVERO   *See* PINTO.

OVERREACHING   *See* FORGING.

OVERSHOT JAW   *See* PARROT MOUTH.

PACE   A two-beat lateral gait in which the horse moves the front and hind legs on the same side in unison (that is, right front and right hind step forward simultaneously, then left front and left hind). As the horse shifts from one pair of lateral legs to the other, there is a moment when all four feet are in suspension above the ground.

PADDLING or DISHING   A way of going in which the front feet are thrown outward as they are raised from the ground. Horses that are pigeon toed have a tendency to this gait flaw.

PALOMINO A creamy, golden body color with mane and tail of extremely pale, flaxen color. Horses of a variety of breeds may appear with palomino coloring, and Quarter Horses seem to produce a greater percentage of animals of this shade. The Palomino Horse Breeders of America have attempted to set forth standards whereby palominos may hopefully be organized into a true breed. Their requirements specify that the official coat color should be no more than three shades darker or three shades lighter than the glister of newly minted gold. Permissible markings include white facial marks and white below the knees.

PARROT MOUTH or OVERSHOT JAW A congenital imperfection in which the incisor teeth of the upper jaw are longer than the lower, thus causing them to overlap. An animal with such a deformity is hard to keep in good condition, since he will have difficulty biting off any attached foods (such as grass). As this condition worsens with age, the best treatment is frequent inspection of the involved teeth and proper adjustment by means of rasping from time to time.

PIEBALD A coat color consisting of large irregular patches of black and white. *See* PINTO.

PIGEON TOED A conformation flaw affecting the forefeet: The toes turn in, thereby causing the animal to throw out the feet as they are raised from the ground.

PIG EYED A slang term used to describe an eye that is too small, extremely narrow, and has a tendency to squint. The eyelids are usually thick. Horses with this feature are often coarse and frequently display a sluggish and unpredictable temperament.

PINTO A Spanish term meaning *painted* or *colored,* used to describe a coat color that is white in combination with any one of the ten basic coat colors recognized by the Pinto Horse Association—that is, bay, black, blue roan, brown, chestnut, dun, palomino, red roan, sorrel, grulla. The distribution of the white and color comes in two patterns, *overo* and *tobiano.* The *overo* is a colored horse with an irregular pattern of white extending upward. The head is usually white or bald, the tail and mane are dark or mixed. The *tobiano* is a definitely marked pattern of color on a white base, usually divided about equally throughout the coat. The mane and tail are the same as the coat color in their region; the legs are usually white. The head is either dark or dark with white markings such as a stripe, blaze, or star.

PLAITING   *See* WINDING.

POINTING   A way of going in which there is little flexion and considerable extension. Horses with this type of gait show little break in the knees and tend to be low-gaited in front. Thoroughbreds and Standardbreds with their excessive speed and long strides tend to be pointy-strided. *See also* DAISY CUTTER.

POP EYED   Eyes that tend to bulge out and in form are extremely convex. Considered a conformation flaw, such eyes also show a predisposition towards nearsightedness, and horses with this configuration frequently shy.

POUNDING   A way of going in which the feet make heavy contact with the ground as opposed to a more desirable light, airy tread.

RACE   *See* STRIP.

RACK   One of the two specialty gaits of the Five Gaited Saddle Horse, the rack is the four-beat pattern of the slow gait done at speed. The horse's four feet still strike the ground separately at equal intervals and mark a definite four-beat rhythm. Speed is the "key" to the rack, and despite the form and elevation required to execute this difficult gait properly, the American Saddle Horse has been known to cover a mile in 2:19 when not within the confines of the show ring.

RAY   Another name for the black dorsal stripe commonly found along the spine of dun-colored horses. *See* DUN.

RIDGLING or CRYPTORCHID   A male horse in which one or both testicles have not descended and are retained within his body cavity.

RIG   A slang term for ridgling. *See* RIDGLING.

ROACH BACKED   A structural defect in which there is a definite convexity of the back disallowing sufficient freedom for the extension and flexion of the legs in taking long and rapid strides. There is a predisposition of horses with this conformation, in combination with long legs, to result in forging.

ROAN   Any of the varieties of chestnut, bay, brown, or black with a more-or-less even dispersal of white hairs running through the coat. Black roans are black horses with roaned coats and often hard to distinguish from grays. Blue roans are similar but also have reddish hairs in the mixture. Red roans are bay horses with the mixture of white hairs, and strawberry roans are roaned chestnuts.

ROLLING   A way of going marked by extreme lateral shoulder motion, such as is seen in wide-fronted horses or horses with projecting shoulders.

ROMAN NOSE   When the flat surface of a horse's face is convex between the eyes and the nostrils, the horse is said to have a roman nose. A roman nose is considered a sign of coarseness and, as such, a conformation flaw.

ROPE WALKING   *See* WINDING.

RUNNING WALK   The characteristic gait of the Tennessee Walking Horse. The running walk is a smooth, fluid, gliding four-beat rhythm, which is actually an extended accelerated walk. This means that each hoof rises and strikes the ground separately. The unusual aspect of the running walk is that the horse does not involve his upper shoulder or back surface in the execution of this gait, which means that the saddle is all but motionless, and the rider experiences a sort of "floating" sensation. The official speed of the running walk is between six and eight mph.

SCALPING   Striking the hind foot at the coronet against the toe of a forefoot as it breaks over.

SICKLE HOCKS   A conformation fault in which the cannon bone leans forward so as to bring the hind leg underneath the body. This is a serious flaw; it causes a great deal of strain to be put upon the hock joint above and the tendons below, and quite often it brings about lameness.

SINGLEFOOT   Another term for the rack. *See* RACK.

SKEWBALD   A coat color which is white in combination with any definite color, except black. *See* PINTO, PIEBALD.

SLAB SIDED   A horse whose girth and ribs are decidedly flat, instead of being long and well-sprung to provide ample room in which to house a well-developed heart and lungs.

SLOW GAIT or STEPPING PACE   A slightly syncopated four-beat gait in which each foot strikes the ground singly in easy succession. It is performed under collection at a speed only slightly faster than the walk, with considerable elevation and precision. It is one of the two "specialty" gaits of the Five-Gaited Saddle Horse.

SNIP   A small patch of white on the lower nose or a flesh-colored mark on the lip between the nostrils.

SOCK   A white anklet reaching about to the fetlock.

SORREL   *See* CHESTNUT.

SPEEDY CUTTING   A condition occurring at speed when, as the foreleg breaks over, it hits the hind leg above the scalping line. This is most frequently seen in trotters and pacers, involving the legs on the same side in trotters and diagonal legs in pacers. *See* SCALPING.

SPLAY FOOTED   A horse whose toes turn out and heels face each other while the hoof grows flat and towards the outside is said to be *splay footed*.

STALLION   An entire male horse more than five years of age.

STAR   Small patch of white on the forehead.

STEPPING PACE   *See* SLOW GAIT.

STRIP, STRIPE or RACE   A narrow white streak that runs down the nose.

STRIPE   *See* STRIP.

STOCKING   White reaching from hoof almost to the knee of the foreleg or the hock behind.

STRAIGHT PASTERN   A horse of extremely vertical conformation in the pastern area will have a choppy, uncomfortable gait and often a predisposition to navicular disease.

SUCKLING   A foal, usually under six months of age, that is at his mother's side prior to weaning.

SWAN NECKED   A swan necked horse is one whose neck is excessively arched and extremely pliable.

SWAY BACKED   A conformation defect wherein the back is hollow or concave, suggesting weakness.

THREADING   *See* WINDING.

TIED IN BELOW THE KNEE   The phrase *tied in below the knee* refers to a horse with poor tendon construction; it is evidenced by a sharp indentation just below the back of the knee. Such conformation generally denotes a weakness of the part.

TOBIANO   *See* PINTO.

TOE OUT   A horse with feet that are definitely turned out has a predisposition to brushing or interfering.

TRAPPY   A quick, choppy, short but often high stride; it is frequently seen in horses with straight shoulders and short straight pasterns.

TROT   A two-beat gait in which the horse's feet move forward and strike the ground in diagonal pairs—that is, right hind and left fore almost simultaneously, then left hind and right fore simultaneously. At the time when the horse shifts from one diagonal pair to the other, all four feet are momentarily off the ground.

UNDERSHOT JAW   A hereditary deformity that is the reverse of *parrot mouth,* wherein the lower jaw is longer than the upper jaw.

WALK   A four-beat gait in which the horse's feet strike the ground in the order: right hind, right fore, then left hind, left fore.

WALLEYED, WATCH EYED, or CLYDESDALE EYED   Eyes in which the iris is without pigment and appears to be a pearly

150

white color. Considered a conformation fault, such eyes are nonetheless functional and do not constitute an unsoundness.

WATCH EYED   *See* WALLEYED.

WEANLING   A foal that has been weaned from its dam but is not yet a yearling.

WAY OF GOING   *See* ACTION.

WINDING—ROPE WALKING, THREADING   A way of going in which the striding leg crosses over in front of the supporting leg in the fashion of a tightrope artist. It is also known as threading or plaiting and most often seen in horses with extremely wide fronts.

WINGING   Increased paddling, which is particularly noticeable in horses with high action.

YEARLING   A horse that is one year old but not yet two—that is, a horse chronologically 20 months old is still a *yearling*.

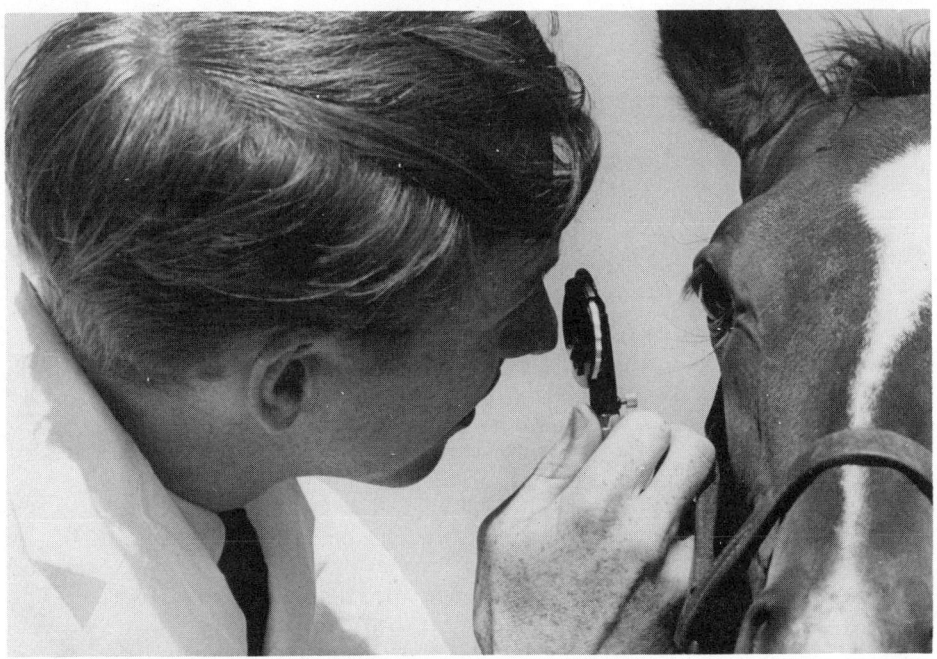

HEALTH
AND
CONDITION

ALTER   *See* GELDING.

ANTERIOR   The veterinarian's term for the forward aspect of a particular area.

AZOTURIA, MONDAY MORNING DISEASE or BLACKWATER
A disease of undefined origin that is nonetheless peculiarly constant in the conditions under which it occurs. It usually affects horses that have been idle for a few days but receiving the same amount of feed as when working. The animal will be fine while at rest, but when moved suddenly evidences a reluctance to use the hind legs (seldom a fore limb). The affected muscles stiffen into a rigid position. There is profuse sweating and blowing. The animal struggles to stand but soon falls; if able to regain its forefeet, he assumes a sitting position. Abdominal distress is obvious, and urine, if passed, is of reddish color.

A veterinarian should be called because of this condition's severity; however, while awaiting his arrival, treatment consists of absolute rest and quiet and application of warm cloths and/or blankets to the hardened muscles alternated with massage. During the illness and through convalescence, the diet must be easily digested and of a laxative nature: bran mashes and so forth. As this disease rarely attacks horses in constant work or those turned out to pasture, prevention rests in limiting the daily ration to an amount commensurate with the work of the animal, as well as providing some sort of exercise when the horse is idle.

BALL UP   A horse is said to have balled up when snow packs in lumps in his shoes in such a way as to prevent him from placing his foot squarely on the ground. Greasing the insides of a horse's feet with vaseline before he steps out into packing snow can often stop balling altogether; however, extremely wet snow will pack under any circumstances. Once the snow becomes a solid lump in the horse's foot, it is almost impossible to remove it with a hoof pick or similar instrument. In this case a sharp rap on the outer edge of the horse's shoe with a hammer or rock will usually dislodge the clump from the foot.

While balling up is mainly a nuisance factor, in that no one wants to be continually dismounting to dislodge snow from his horse's feet, it may also be considered somewhat dangerous, since a horse balled up in one or more feet could conceivably fall or otherwise sprain, wrench, or damage himself because of his inability to gain purchase on the ground.

BLACKWATER   *See* AZOTURIA.

BLISTERING   Inducing a strong inflammation in a given area by the application of a blister-producing agent for the purpose of bringing blood to the area to effect healing. No part should be blistered until all fever has been cooled out. Prior to the application, the part should be washed, the hair removed, and, in the case of a leg being blistered, the entire area around the affected area should be greased with vaseline to prevent the blister running down and causing a cracked heel or affecting a part which was not intended to be treated.

    After the blister has been applied, the horse's head should be set in such a way as to prevent his licking or biting the blistered part. A cradle—an apparatus embracing the horse's neck and restricting his bending motions but not his eating—is quite effective to this end.

    Within twenty-four to forty-eight hours after the initial application of the blister, there is marked swelling, inflammation, and evidence of blisters forming. These will eventually burst and discharge a clear fluid. For this reason, blistering is to be avoided in hot weather and during the fly season because of the danger of infection. Blistering is a severe measure; it should only be performed by or under the supervision of a veterinarian. *See* COUNTER-IRRITANT, FIRING.

BLOOM   The *bloom* on a horse usually refers to an overall appearance of good health, which is particularly evidenced by a clean and glossy coat. The term also, by implication, means a horse that is in good flesh.

BOG SPAVIN   A large mushy swelling of the hock joint resulting from an unusual amount of *synovia* (joint fluid) as a consequence of joint stress. In most instances a bog spavin first appears as an acute problem evidenced by varying degrees of heat and swelling involving the front, outside, and back of the hock—or in some cases, the entire joint. A veterinarian should be called immediately, since treatment within twenty-four to forty-eight hours can frequently result in a complete cure. But if a bog spavin is neglected and the filling becomes cold, the condition may become chronic resulting in the joint capsule being permanently distended.

BONE SPAVIN or "JACK" SPAVIN   A bony enlargement on the inside of the hind leg towards the forward region of the hock at precisely the point where the base of the hock tapers into

155

the cannon part of the leg. Stress must be considered the primary source of bone spavins; however, defects in conformation and congenital weaknesses are predisposing factors. This condition usually begins as a cunean bursitis, evidenced by an abnormal gait that worsens with continued work. Since normal flexion is painful, the toe of the affected foot may be worn by the peculiar "spearing" action of the horse's foot. This is a result of the shortened anterior phase of his stride. In recent years, treatment has expanded to include cutting the cunean tendon (which passes over the bursa) to relieve this source of irritation. This cunean *tenotomy,* which may be used alone or in conjunction with firing, blistering, or both, has proved to be the most effective remedy for bone spavins thus far developed.

BOWED TENDON   A swelling, and therefore stretching, of the flexor tendon and/or its sheath (the tissue covering the tendon), occurring along any section of the tendon ("a high bow" located just below the knee or "low bow" found near the ankle or even the coronet) or extending the entire length from knee to coronet. The severity varies in degree from inflammation of the tendon sheath to the complete tearing and rupture of the tendon and its fibers. It is most often caused by overexertion or concussion or external violence such as a fall or blow. Its immediate symptoms of extreme soreness, inflammation, and swelling are readily identifiable. Once bowed, a tendon rarely regains its original shape because it loses its elasticity and becomes rigid. In the area of racing soundness, surgery is the most successful treatment, but it still must be regarded as a weakened part and the potential seat of recurrent lameness.

BROKEN WIND   *See* HEAVES.

BUCKED SHINS   An extremely painful irritation of the bone covering (*periosteum*), affecting any or all of the area between the knee and the ankle on the front surface of the cannon bone. Believed to be the result of concussion and high speed, it is found most frequently in two-year-olds and lightly raced three-year-olds toward the end of their preparation to race. Despite the increased sensitivity of the afflicted area, which can render the horse totally disabled during the acute form, this condition is considered a temporary unsoundness responding to treatment without the likelihood of recurrence. (There is increasing evidence at postmortem indicating that many instances of bucked shins are actually fractures, a fact that may ultimately change the entire concept of this condition.)

BURSITIS Inflammation of a bursa: the fluid-filled sacs that protect such structures as tendons or ligaments from the trauma of normal bony projections.

CANKER A chronic disease attacking the horn-producing tissues of the foot. The origin of this ailment is undetermined, and there is one theory that classifies it as a skin disease. Another theory attributes it to being the result of an infective germ. In many instances, it begins in the frog and is likened to thrush, except that the tissues secreting horn are affected and swell. The subsequent horn produced is soft and of a cheeselike consistency.

There is a great amount of tissue degeneration, and the affected parts are easily polluted by any number of organisms. A typically foul odor is present. Once this condition has been established, it always progresses, though slowly. It may include the sole and/or the wall and seriously undermine these areas. In cases involving only the frog, there is a fair chance of cure, but if the disease has extended to the sole and/or wall, chances of recovery are slim. In any event, there does not seem to be a definite remedy, and treatment requires constant professional attention.

CAPPED ELBOW *See* SHOE BOIL.

CAPPED HOCK Due to the protrusion of the point of the hock, it is extremely prone to injury resulting from blows, kicks, bruising, and so forth. Once a swelling begins on the point of the hock, it is continually irritated whenever the horse lies down, because the entire outer surface of the leg is in contact with the ground. This constant aggravation not only increases the damage but also eliminates all chances of lasting shrinkage of the enlargement.

The condition, while unsightly, is seldom regarded as serious, and it rarely interferes with the usefulness of the animal. The filling is fluid at the onset; if it is recognized and immediately treated, there is a possibility of some resorption before the fluid has a chance to form fibrinous tissue in the sheath or bursa. If not, the "cap" may become fibrinous, whereupon the only treatment is reduction of inflammation followed by repeated blisters, which may diminish the size of the cap but will not remove it.

157

CAST When a horse is down and in such a position that he cannot regain his feet, he is said to be *cast*. This occurs most frequently in the stall, where a horse may roll and wind up with his feet caught underneath a water bucket, manger, or hay rack or simply with his body too close to the wall to allow him to get his legs under him to rise.

Horses can and do get cast in other confining quarters, such as a trailer, van, or starting gate—even in a field or paddock by getting caught up against a fence, gate, tree, or other object. In such cases, efforts should be made to keep the horse as quiet as possible to prevent him from hurting himself in his attempts to get up. Then the animal should be pulled or turned over by means of ropes (or in some cases simply by pulling his head by the halter) into a position from which he can get to his feet by himself.

CASTRATION *See* GELDING.

CATARACTS Opacities involving the lens, or the capsule of the lens, of the eye and causing partial or complete blindness.

CAUDAL The veterinarian's term for the area toward the tail from the part in question.

CHRONIC A longstanding condition is said to be chronic.

COGGINS TEST *See* SWAMP FEVER.

COLD-BACKED A condition wherein the horse tries to sink away from the touch of the saddle. This is often because of an abnormality or irregularity in the structure of the withers or saddle-bearing area, which may only be detected by unusually perceptive scrutiny or by viewing the top line from croup to withers from a point behind the horse. Any deviation in the shape of this region is readily ascertained from such a vantage point.

COLIC A term used to describe a group of symptoms that are the outward evidence of any abdominal pain, ranging from extremely mild to acute. These warning signs—restlessness, looking at the flank, frequent attempts to roll, spasmodic tail twitching, stretching as though to urinate, and pawing—must be heeded; treatment should be begun as quickly as possible. Since there is always danger of rupture of the stomach or twisting of an intestine as the result of the horse's thrashing around or attempting to vomit, as well as from the disorder itself (such as rupture resulting from impaction), colic must be regarded as one of the most potentially dangerous conditions affecting the horse. There a number of abdominal disorders that can cause colic; each requires special treatment. The pain does not remain constant; in the intermissions, the horse may appear to be normal.

For these reasons, as well as the necessity of a prompt and accurate diagnosis, a veterinarian should be called as soon as colic is suspected. While awaiting the doctor's arrival, the horse should be kept warm and carefully watched. At the first signs of any attempt to roll or become violent, he should be hand walked. The most common types of colic are: 1) Thromboembolic Colic, which results from parasitic damage of the intestines and the blood vessels servicing the intestines; 2) Spasmodic Colic, which is a spasmodic contraction of the bowel covering; 3) Flatulent Colic, which is a distension of the stomach with gas; 4) Impaction Colic, which is obstruction of the intestines from overfeeding and/or irregular feeding—particularly of bulky, hard-to-digest feeds; 5) Engorgement Colic, which is overloading the stomach with feed, either from overfeeding or failure of the stomach to digest the feed and the resulting accumulation in the stomach; 6) Obstructive Colic, which is the presence in the stomach of gastric calculi (stomach stones) or foreign bodies, such as sand, bits of metal, oat husks, and so forth.

CONGENITAL   It refers to an abnormality or deformity that the horse possesses at birth, such as a clubfoot.

CONJUNCTIVITIS   An inflammation of the conjunctiva (the thin moist membrane covering the inside of the eyelids, the third eyelid, and the cornea) as a result of either infection or aggravation by any number of irritants, such as dust, pollen, disinfectants, and the like. At the onset, there is a watery discharge from the eye; the discharge then becomes sticky, thicker, and in some instances consists of pus. The horse is reluctant to allow examination of the eye, and there is fitful closing of the eyelids and tearing. Conjunctivitis is a common symptom of many general diseases. A veterinarian is best able to treat this condition with regard to its immediate cause, but bathing the eye with a tepid solution of common salt or boric acid and water may aid in removing the irritants.

159

CONTRACTED FEET   A condition most often affecting the fore-feet wherein the heels become drawn in or contracted, cramping the bones of the foot. Although most frequently compounded by poor or careless shoeing, a tendency towards this weakness may be inherited. Unless further complicated by circulatory malfunctions, removal of the shoes for a time, trimming the toes, and/or the application of corrective shoes allowing as much frog pressure as possible usually restore the foot to a normal shape. If, however, the contraction is sufficient to produce a situation of "too many bones in too small a space" that hinder the blood's natural circulation through the foot, the problem is far more serious. The blood becomes trapped in the foot, resulting in severe inflammation and rendering the animal quite lame. Rest, cooling, and spreading the foot may alleviate the pain, but more energetic measures are often required at the discretion of a veterinarian.

CONTRACTED HEELS   *See* CONTRACTED FEET.

CORNEAL ULCERS   Ulcers on the cornea of the eye usually result from a foreign object entering the eye or some type of trauma such as a blow. Treatment is generally successful, but a veterinarian should be consulted immediately; a neglected corneal ulcer can cause the horse to lose his eye. This occurs in cases where the ulcer is large enough or severe enough to cause the eye to rupture, resulting in contamination of the internal eye from which point the infection can travel along the optic nerve to the brain.

CORNS   A bruise beneath the horny sole of the foot, characterized by a reddish discoloration of the sole just below the point of injury. Often caused by poor shoeing, flat soles, weakened bars, or excessive work on rough roads, this condition may cause intense pain and severe lameness that worsens with work. Treatment consists of shaving the affected area as thin as possible and applying poultices until the pain has been relieved. This is followed by corrective shoeing, with particular care to insure that all pressure from the shoe is removed. Such shoeing adjustments as are required usually meet with satisfactory results and render the horse serviceable.

COUNTER-IRRITANT   Any artificial irritant designed to cause inflammation for the purpose of making a *chronic* condition *acute* under positive control. Such treatment is indicated because, once a condition becomes chronic, the body ceases to fight with any vigor. But should the condition become acute, the body responds strongly to effect healing.

CRANIAL   The veterinarian's term for the area toward the head from the area in question.

CRIBBING   Grasping by the teeth some object or projection, such as the edge of the feed box or the rail or a fence so as to brace the jaws and expand the throat while sucking air. This produces the characteristic "gulping" sound peculiar to cribbers. The quantities of air taken in may render the horse a bloated appearance; he is more difficult to keep in condition; in severe cases, he may even become emaciated. Quite often this vice is an immediate cause of other ailments such as colic. Since the horse must flex his neck to crib, a leather strap buckling around the neck and compressing the larynx upon flexion is a common corrective measure. There is a surgical operation for this condition that has met with limited success.

CURB   A *true curb* is a soft swelling and subsequent thickening of the ligament on the posterior side of the rear leg, approximately four inches beneath the point of the hock. A horse may "spring a curb" as a result of a sprain, and the initial treatment is exactly that accorded to sprains. If detected early, shoeing adjustments can alleviate the strain, but in cases where lameness is obvious and persistent, blistering or firing may be required. Also categorized as a curb is the *false curb,* which is a hard unsightly enlargement of the small external metatarsal bone located on the outer side of the rear leg. *True* or *false,* in either instance, a curb is a distinct protrusion that deviates from the straight line extending between the point of the hock and the fetlock.

DESMOTOMY   The last-resort operation performed on a horse with a locked or slipped stifle in which the medial ligament is severed. *See* STIFLED.

DEW POISONING   An allergic reaction that occurs on unpigmented areas (white muzzle, socks, or stockings) and is associated with wet grass, particularly clover. It is evidenced by an ulcerative moist lesion; if the case is severe enough, the affected legs may swell. It is treated with the topical application of steroids.

161

DISTEMPER *See* STRANGLES.

DORSAL The veterinarian's term for the area toward the back (*i.e.* spine) or top of the area in question.

ENDOSCOPING An endoscopic examination (frequently shortened to simply "scoping") is used to detect any abnormality in the pharynx, cranial part of the larynx, gutteral pouch, and nasal passageways (such as those that would cause roarers, hemorrhaging, polyps, and the like).

FAVOR A horse who *favors* a foot or leg is one who is showing some sign of soreness in that limb but is not decidedly lame or refusing to use it at all.

FEATHER A white scar visible on the cornea of the eye is called a *feather*.

FILLED LEGS or STOCKING UP *Filled legs* or *stocking up* may be used as generic terms to describe swelling of the legs caused by any injury or internal disorder (frequently urinary problems). More specifically, however, horsemen use these terms to refer to swellings of the limbs, resulting from no particular injury or disease but simply from irregular work and/or feeding habits. Horses allowed to stand in over long periods of time may stock up merely from lack of exercise, and the swelling diminishes with proper work. Abrupt changes in diet and excessive or overly rich feed may produce circulatory congestion that produces the same effect. A properly adjusted diet, routine work pattern, and massaging the limbs may relieve the swelling.

FIRING Inducing the most drastic form of counter-irritation by means of applying a heated metal instrument to the skin and, in some instances, to the deeper tissues as well. Used frequently in the treatment of bony deposits such as splints and bone spavins, this method is not usually indicated until all other methods have failed or have not produced any lasting results. The principle of such action is to change a pathology from chronic to acute and thereby promote healing.

The two main types of firing are line firing and pin (or point) firing. The former is accomplished by the use of a barlike instrument and is most frequently seen in the treatment of bowed tendons, in which case the lines are placed horizontally along the tendon. The latter is produced by means of a needlelike instrument that makes little holes in the skin. These are far less unsightly than line firing, and are used most often in the treatment of splints, osselets, spavins, and so forth because the small punctures can penetrate to the bone.

Preparation for firing entails reducing any existing inflammation of the part; immediately before the operation the hair should be clipped from the area. This treatment is performed by a veterinarian, usually under local anesthetic. Once the firing has been completed, the horse must either wear a cradle (*see* BLISTERING) or be tied in some way so that he cannot bite and tear at his legs.

FISTULA   An inflammatory and usually suppurating condition frequently resulting from a foreign body, such as dead tissue or grit, that cannot be expelled. Treatment consists of determining the nature of the irritant, removing it, and effecting adequate drainage. In most cases, this should be performed by a veterinarian.

FISTULOUS WITHERS   An inflammatory condition much like poll evil, which is found in the region of the withers. It is often the result of pressure from an ill-fitting saddle or harness. Treatment is the same as for poll evil and should be handled by a veterinarian.

FOUNDER   *See* LAMINITIS.

GELDING   Castrating, or removing the testicles from a male horse is called *gelding*.

GIRTH GALLS   A soreness or laceration of the skin resulting from chafing or undue pressure from the girth. The tender skin just behind the point of the elbow on the ribs is most frequently affected. The main causes of girth galls are: sensitive and thin skin on the horse; a girth drawn up too tightly on a horse not been ridden for some time; a girth left too loose, which slides back and forth creating friction; and a dirty girth on which dirt and sweat have hardened into rough edges and lumps. Treatment of girth galls generally consists of cleansing the area and applying some type of astringent lotion or antiseptic powder or ointment. An old-time remedy consisting of a solution of water, salt, and vinegar splashed on daily can aid in healing and does seem to "toughen" the skin. Girth galls must be allowed to heal completely before the saddle is used again.

GOING SHORT   The expression *going short* denotes a horse that is taking noticeably shorter steps with one leg than with the other, or that is moving with an overall shortened stride. In either case the shortness of stride is indicative of some sort of lameness, and *going short* is used in the sense of going lame: "The bay horse is 'going short' in the near fore."

GRAVEL   An invasion of the sensitive tissue of the hoof by tiny pieces of gravel or dirt. Such foreign matter usually gains entrance to the hoof at the "white line"—the junction of the wall and the sole because the horn at this point is somewhat softer—and readily produces an infection. The accompanying inflammation, gas, and pus create a great deal of pressure and pain in the foot. If allowed to continue without treatment, the pressure will become so intense as to break out at the coronary band, thus expelling the gas and pus. If gravel is suspected as the cause of lameness, then the point of entry must be determined. Once ascertained, the pathway used by the gravel going into the foot must be opened, allowing drainage at the bottom and relief of the pressure. Then the opening should be dressed and protected from further infection.

GREASE HEEL   *See* SCRATCHES.

GREEN OSSELETS   *See* OSSELETS.

HEAVES, BROKEN WIND   A chronic respiratory condition in which the horse has difficulty in exhaling air from the lungs. This occurs because the lungs have lost much of their elasticity and are unable to contract sufficiently. It results from degeneration of the walls of the air cells and paralysis of the muscular tissue. The direct cause of this ailment has not been definitely determined, but any condition weakening the lungs will predispose an animal to heaves. The condition is readily identified by two marked symptoms: the peculiar action of the flanks and abdomen as the animal makes a double expiratory effort, and a cough, characteristic of this disease. The cough is intermittent, hollow in sound, and often spasmodic. On breathing, the intake of air is normal, but much of the lung power required to expel it is lost; after a short normal contraction, the muscles of the abdomen nearest the flank are brought into play, producing the distinctive double bellows-like motion. There is no cure for heaves, and treatment is designed to subdue the symptoms as much as possible by strict attention to the diet, environment, and exercise. (One recent thought on the cause of heaves is that it is an allergy to hay pollen.)

HIDEBOUND   The skin of a horse is said to be *hidebound* when it is hard to the touch and adheres closely over the ribs. Disturbances of nutrition (as in starvation) or chronic wasting diseases can cause a hidebound condition, which is, in effect, a removal or absence of fat from the tissues beneath the skin.

HIGH BLOWING   The rhythmic snorting sound produced by some horses upon exhaling during exercise. It may disappear after the horse has worked for a time but recurs when he is fresh. This condition is not indicative of any unsoundness; it is caused by a minor deviation in the shape of the nostrils.

HIP DOWN   A condition in which the prominent tip of the hip-bone breaks away from the main portion of bone as a result of severe injury, causing the point of the hip to drop down. The animal will usually be lame until the inflammation accompanying the injury is reduced, after which he may work sound. However, the *hip down* blemish remains and is considered a conformation defect.

INFLUENZA or SHIPPING FEVER   A highly contagious viral respiratory disease of horses that is often referred to as *shipping fever* and appears in many strains. There is an available vaccine.

INTERNAL PARASITES   Horses are subject to a large number of internal parasites, which may be found in almost every tissue of the body. Affected animals usually eat well but tend to lack condition, tire easily, lose weight, and, in the case of young animals, may have stunted growth and poor development. The most common types found in horses are: strongyles (bloodworms) and roundworms, pinworms, and Bots. In any case, there is a definite cycle in which: 1) the eggs or larva are produced, often within the body of the animal; 2) they grow or mature; 3) they are passed with manure, and 4) then either lay more eggs or hatch and cause reinfestation on ingestion of infective feed or grass. The best treatment is worming four times annually and periodic laboratory examination of feces for worms (called a "fecal" exam). In cases of heavy infestation, a veterinarian should be consulted to determine the number of times the horse should be wormed and the strength of the medicine to be administered.

-ITIS   The suffix *-itis* means inflammation of the preceding part —that is, sesamoiditis, tendonitis, laminitis, and so forth.

LAMENESS   Lameness can be divided into three major categories: Supporting Leg: Disease or injury involving the tendons, ligaments, or bones; Swinging Leg: Disease or injury affecting the muscular system; Combination: Disease or injury involving any combination of muscles, ligaments, tendons, bones, and joints.

A horse may help in diagnosing the source of his problem by "nodding." For example, a horse that is showing a foreleg lameness will noticeably nod his head when in motion (best seen at the trot). This is because he lifts his head as the injured foot strikes the ground and then nods each time the sound leg touches the ground. Horses may also nod with a hind leg lameness, but rarely as markedly and in reverse of the above—that is, the head drops down when the injured leg strikes the ground.

"JACK" SPAVIN   *See* BONE SPAVIN.

JOINT CAPSULE   The membrane that encloses a joint through which nutrients for the joint must pass.

LAMINITIS or FOUNDER   An extremely painful ailment affecting the vascular system within the foot. The hoof is composed of fleshy and horny interlocking leaves (*laminae*). When, as a result of excessive work, overeating, lack of exercise, poor shoeing, inflammation of the uterus after foaling, or any condition that upsets the vascular balance within the feet, the fleshy leaves become engorged with blood and fluid, pressure is exerted upon the horny leaves, and a state of congestion exists. The degree of pain is dependent on the amount of pressure placed on the sensitive structures of the foot and thus varies greatly with the extent of congestion.

There are three forms of laminitis, each being categorized by the amount of pain manifested: acute, subacute, and chronic. In the acute form the animal is in obvious distress. He may sweat, blow, his temperature is usually higher than normal, and he is unwilling to place any weight on the affected feet. The end result of an acute attack is generally chronic laminitis in which the pain has been greatly reduced by decreasing the congestion and pressure within the foot, and there have been certain modifications in the shape of the foot compensating for the changes within.

While the horse is rendered useless during an attack of laminitis, the most dangerous aspect is the effect upon the foot and hoof. As a result of the distention of the fleshy and horny leaves, a certain amount of elasticity is lost; depending upon the degree, the *os pedis* is no longer supported properly and the sole is said to *drop*. This produces the characteristic dished shape of the wall of the hoof. Because the formation of horn from the coronet is not at a constant level rate, the hoof becomes *ringed* (ridges on the walls of the hoof), which represent the periods of most active growth. Any case of laminitis should be treated by a veterinarian, but until his arrival, applications of cold water, ice, or standing in a cold soaking tub can give the horse some relief. Laminitis in any degree or form is considered an unsoundness.

LINIMENT   A mild counter-irritant.

LYMPHANGITIS   Intense inflammation of the lymphatic structures of the leg, producing a definite swelling that is accompanied by a high temperature and general agitation. It frequently occurs in animals that have been well fed or overfed; in these instances, it may be the result of an excessive amount of nutritive elements in the blood. Sudden changes in the work pattern or a severe external violence may also induce an attack. In the early stages the animal may show evidence of a chill, then a rise in temperature, and some degree of restlessness.

These symptoms are swiftly followed by lameness is one leg and filling, which usually begins on the inside of the thigh. This swelling gradually progresses to include the whole leg to the foot and is extremely tender to the touch. The horse sweats profusely and has a quickened pulse rate and accelerated breathing. Treatment consists of bathing the leg with alternately hot and cold water as frequently as possible for the first few days, hand walking for short intervals, and feeding a light, easily digestible diet. If this treatment is initiated in the early stages of the attack, a marked change may frequently appear within twenty-four hours. The leg seldom returns to its original size, leaving some permanent enlargement. The horse is then subject to intermittent attacks.

MANGE   A contagious disease caused by tiny insectlike parasites of which there are three principle types. They are easily identified by microscopic examination, and each type affects a different part of the body and manifests its own symptoms. In any case, these parasites produce a definite irritation that results

167

in itching and scratching. This, in turn, causes the skin to give off moisture that coagulates on the surface forming a crust. The hair in the affected areas usually falls out, and the constant rubbing of these patches leaves the way open for secondary skin infections. There are a number of effective insecticides to control this disease, but it must be remembered that the parasites can live outside the host's body for varying lengths of time. Successful elimination of this disease depends largely upon efficient disinfecting of the quarters and premises.

MONDAY MORNING DISEASE   *See* AZOTURIA.

MOON BLINDNESS   *See* PERIODIC OPTHALMIA.

NAVICULAR DISEASE   A disease of controversial origin that affects the small navicular bone and bursa of the forefoot. This bone and bursa are contained entirely within the foot. As a result of multiple occurrences or one trauma, the bursa becomes the seat of a *bursitis*. Because of the inflammatory reaction of the bursa, there is pitting of the navicular bone, resulting in a vicious cycle of increasing inflammation, pitting, and *spur* formation.

The early signs of navicular disease often go undetected, as the horse does not appear to be lame but may travel with a shuffling, stumbling gait. In later stages, the horse may "suddenly" go lame, then after some time, he will appear to have recovered completely or settled down to a minimal form.

Careful observation at this time usually reveals that the horse seems restless when standing and may adopt a slight rocking action of the feet. After this stage, the horse will point the affected foot; in the case of both feet being affected, he will alternate first one and then the other. When the horse is exercised, the lameness will probably be relieved; but upon standing and then being asked to move again, the old lameness appears. Nature attempts to relieve the pressure and pain, and the horse travels with a short, choppy stride, reduced flexion and extension of the lower pastern and foot. The toe of the foot may evidence unusual wear. As the disease progresses, the shape of the hoof will change to compensate for the limited action, and the hoof tends to become "blocky" (high at the heel and short at the toe).

Corrective shoeing along the lines of nature's own design—that is, raised heel and shortened toe can often bring about a satisfactory resolution; in cases of very early detection it has been able to reverse the progression. Few horses completely recover from this disease, but the condition can be dealt with in such a fashion as to render the animal serviceably sound. In cases of persistent and severe lameness, the only recourse is to neurectomy—severing the sensory nerves to the affected area.

NERVING   *See* NEURECTOMY.

NEURECTOMY or NERVING   A last-resort surgical remedy in the case of persistent and severe lamenesses in which the sensory nerve(s) leading to the affected part are severed. In most cases, it is possible to select the nerve to be cut, thus ensuring at least partial areal sensation. Many horses so treated are able to resume a vigorous and useful life without pain. (It must be noted that a *nerved* horse is considered to be unsound; if the animal is to be sold, it must be declared that the operation has been performed on him.)

OFF HIS FEED   A horse that has gone *off his feed,* is one not eating his usual ration or as much as he should. Some horses are just naturally "picky eaters," but when the average horse *goes off,* it generally is a sign that something is wrong and certainly indicates that the animal bears watching.

OSSELETS   A condition resulting from excessive strain on immature bone and/or tugging on the joint capsule attachments; it causes the ankle (or fetlock) joint to swell. The swelling is caused by an increased amount of joint fluid, which forces the joint capsule to expand. In the early stages (*green osselets*), the affected area feels mushy with the degree of heat dependent on the amount of irritation.

The animal objects to flexing the ankle and travels with a shortened stride. The enlargement is usually evidenced just above or below the center of the joint and slightly to the right or left of the front of the leg. If the inflammation is allowed to persist, it enters a secondary stage: Calcium deposits form at the point where the joint capsule is attached to the bone or in the joint capsule itself.

If treatment is begun at the first signs of fever in the area and the joint sufficiently "cooled out" and rested—with the possible addition of firing and/or blistering, in many cases the second stage can be obviated. If, however, the warning signs are not recognized or are disregarded and calcium deposits form, there can be serious interference in the flexibility of the joint, and permanent stiffness or lameness can result.

169

PALPATE   Examining by touch for the purpose of rendering a diagnosis—that is, a veterinarian will *palpate* a mare to see if she is in foal. When he *feels* down a horse's leg searching for the source of a lameness, he is *palpating* the leg.

PERIODIC OPTHALMIA or MOON BLINDNESS   An inflammatory eye affliction that is characterized by recurrence and ultimate blindness. Despite many theories as to its origin, the immediate cause remains undetermined. In most instances, the attack is sudden and affects only one eye at a time. An animal that appeared normal the previous night is found in the morning to be suffering from an extremely inflamed, painful, swollen, weeping eye that is nearly closed. He is unwilling for the eye to be touched and shows definite sensitivity to light. The body temperature may be elevated, and the horse is listless.

Shortly after the onset of this condition, sticky tears are discharged. The cornea becomes clouded and takes on a bluish tone, which may intensify until the entire cornea seems to be milky white. After several days the acute symptoms begin to subside; usually after two weeks, the fever has abated, but the vital structures of the eye are left with varying degrees of permanent damage. One attack may result in blindness; more often, however, the initial attack is the first of a series, each of which compounds the damage to the vital parts. The severity in different cases extends from great to slight, but the tendency toward recurrence and shrinkage of the eyeball remain constant and, in all instances, lead to permanent blindness.

There are no definite cures for this disease, but the addition of riboflavin to the diet has met with some success, leading support to the theory that this disease results from a nutritional deficiency—at least in some cases. During an attack, the eye should be shielded from light and bathed with an appropriate solution, such as boric acid. The horse should not be returned to work or exposed to full light until all symptoms have completely subsided.

PHARANGITIS   An inflammatory condition of the pharynx. Chronic pharangitis is very difficult to cure; despite the fact that multiple theories exist on the subject, few cures are successful. Horses with this condition have a definite predisposition to hemorrhaging after vigorous exertion, as in racing.

POINTING   Pointing exists when a horse stands on three legs while extending the fourth to rest it. Although a sound horse may adopt this pose simply to rest a leg, pointing is often indicative of lameness.

POLL EVIL   A painful inflamed swelling located on one or both sides of the center line in the region immediately behind the horse's ears on top of the neck. This condition is usually the result of a bone chip or bruise, such as might come from hitting the top of the head on the manger or from the constant pressure of an excessively tight halter or bridle. At the onset the symptoms are acute with intense heat and pain, accompanied by varying degrees of swelling, which in most cases contain pus. Often, the largest ligament of the body is involved; unfortunately, it is situated in such a way as to press upon the affected parts when the head is moved, causing extreme pain. For this reason, the animal assumes a position to ease, as much as possible, the tension on this ligament, keeping the head erect with the nose thrust well forward. The application of poultices may help this condition; however, in most cases surgery is required to remove the source of irritation and create proper drainage. This condition should be handled by a veterinarian.

POPPED KNEE   A slang term describing a variety of injuries to the knees, all of which produce some degree of inflammation and characterized by a sudden enlargement of the area. The irritation is most commonly a result of extensive strain on any or all of the ligaments that maintain the position of the knee-bones or of damage to the knee capsule, which causes the capsule to become distended because of an increase in the secretion of joint fluid.

This condition can also be produced by external violence—a blow or fall—or by arthritic changes in the knee structure itself. Chip-or slab-type fractures of any of the knee bones will naturally produce fever and swelling and, in most cases, require surgery either to remove the small floating fragments or stabilize the larger ones with a screw. It might also be noted that poor conformation of the knees contributes to susceptibility, and an animal can *break down* as a primary result of his own structural inadequacy. The treatment of knee ailments follows the customary pattern of first reducing the inflammation and then applying counter-irritants. Unfortunately, treatment often meets with limited success. On the whole, the prognosis is at best only fair, and a horse suffering from such an injury is seldom able to return to the top level of soundness.

171

POSTERIOR   The veterinarian's term for the rear aspect of the area in question.

PULSE   A pulse rate of eighteen to forty-two is considered within normal limits for an average horse at rest.

PUT DOWN   The expression to *put down,* when used with reference to a horse, means that the animal was destroyed.

QUARTER CRACK   *See* SAND CRACK.

QUITTOR   An open pus-filled sore at or near the coronet, which results in severe lameness. Often it arises from an injury caused, for example, by overreaching or being stepped on by another horse. It may, however, be the effect of a foot infection, puncture wound, corns, or sand-cracks.

Usually the problem is deep-seated, involving the harder tissues of the foot such as the lateral cartilage. As a result of injury, disease, or irritation, this tissue becomes damaged; because of an insufficient blood supply, necrosis (death of tissue) occurs. Nature treats this dead tissue as foreign matter and tries to dissolve it by setting up an inflammatory reaction. Occasionally this process is successful, but in most cases an abscess forms. If all the dead tissue is expelled when the abscess bursts, it will heal well, and healthy granulation tissue will fill the wound. Unfortunately, this is seldom the case; a portion of dead tissue remains, becoming the seat of a chronic running sore or fistula, which must be removed by surgery.

RESPIRATION   A normal horse at rest breathes quietly and evenly at the rate of between eight and sixteen respirations per minute.

RINGBONE   A calcium deposit or growth resulting from an irritation of the pastern bone—most frequently of the forefoot but, in some instances, affecting the hind foot. Although the condition may be brought about by concussion, excessive strain, blows, or poor shoeing, predisposition to this condition, in some instances, is believed to be inherited. A ringbone may be located *low,* with the enlargement beginning in front of the short pastern bone and extending down into the wall of the hoof or *high,* with the enlargement being close to the joint and causing it to appear larger than normal. In either position, this condition usually produces lameness, with varying degrees of stiffness in the ankle. Occasionally a ringbone is formed in such a way

172

so as not to interfere with the action of the joint and is thus simply a blemish. However, in most cases where there is lameness, the application of cold water bandages, followed by blistering, firing or neurectomy brings only temporary relief; any permanent result of such treatments is doubtful.

RINGWORM   A highly contagious disease affecting the outer layers of the skin and caused by certain fungi. Man, as well as horses are susceptible, and it is possible for attendants to contract and/or carry this disease through clothing, equipment, and so forth. The disease is also easily transmitted from horse to horse or from contaminated fence posts, grooming utensils, and the like, so it is necessary to disinfect every possible source of contamination. Then the infected animal should be isolated, if any effective control is to be gained.

The first indication of this disease is the appearance of scaly hairless patches on the forehead, face, side of the neck, and at the root of the tail. The center of the lesion is the oldest part, and it grows outward from the edges. It is thus possible for the center to be healing, while the borders are actively forming spores (seed), which may live more than eighteen months. The skin in these patches is of a grayish color and may become crusted. There is mild itching. If not controlled, these areas will become greatly enlarged. There are two main types of ringworm that require culture methods to distinguish one from the other; each variety needs individual treatment. The assistance of a veterinarian is thus essential to the cure of this disease.

ROARING   The term used to describe the respiratory noise on inspiration, when the animal is worked. It is caused by paralysis of the muscle that opens the vocal fold on the left side of the larynx, thus allowing the fold partially to occlude the air passageway. The fold has no *tone*, is lax, and thus flutters as air passes. Diagnosis of the condition is definitive by endoscopic exam. Roaring is considered an unsoundness.

SAND CRACK, also QUARTER CRACK, TOE CRACK   A vertical split of varying length and depth that occurs in the horny wall of the hoof. It begins at or near the coronet and extends downward to the bottom edge of the wall. This condition most frequently appears in the area of the quarter but may also be found in the front part of the toe, in which case it is known as a toe crack. Sand cracks may be caused by a direct injury, resulting from external violence, improper shoeing, or any dam-

173

age to the coronet that is severe enough to interrupt the production of new horn and, at least temporarily, alter the continuity of the wall.

If as a result of injury, a portion of the coronet is permanently damaged; there will never be any new horn produced in that area, and the fissure in the wall also becomes fixed. In almost all cases, the hoof has been allowed to become extremely dry and brittle. Small shallow cracks reaching upward from the lower border of the wall are of little significance and rarely cause trouble. The real problem arises when a sand crack extends deep enough to expose the sensitive tissues to irritation or infection from foreign materials, such as dirt and sand. There is also the danger of direct injury and pinching, since the edges of the crack have a tendency to open and close when the horse places weight on the foot. Such movement causes pain in varying degrees from simple aggravation to severe inflammation, in which case the horse becomes quite lame. If there is no pain, heat, or infection involved, the usual method of treatment is to limit the movement of the split by means of special shoeing or riveting the edges of the fissure together. This is followed by stimulation of the horn-producing tissue to reestablish the consistency of the wall and may be effected by the application of a mild blister to the affected part of the coronary band.

In cases in which pain, inflammation, and infection are present, these conditions must first be dealt with, and the fever and pain must be alleviated. Poulticing in conjunction with hot foot baths and thorough cleansing of the opening are the best means to this end. Once the pain and fever have been relieved, the crack should be clamped and an appropriate shoe applied. If a crack is found before it becomes very long, grooves in the shape of a crescent, straight line, or the letter *V*, which are cut or burned across the fissure may successfully halt any further damage. Rebuilding these defective areas with acrylic in recent years has been successful.

SCRATCHES or GREASE HEEL   A skin irritation on the back of the fetlocks and pasterns. The skin becomes inflamed and moist, and the hair is covered with a foul-smelling exudation from the skin. If unattended, the skin will swell and become wrinkled. The hair may fall off in patches. Small clusters of grapelike protrusions may form in the area, which, as the result of chafing against each other or the opposite leg, may ulcerate and/or bleed, causing lameness.

174

This condition can easily become chronic and is worsened by cold damp weather. The most common method of treatment requires placing the horse in a clean stall, clipping the hair on the area involved, washing with soap and water and applying an astringent antiseptic medicine at least twice daily until completely healed. Making sure that the fetlock and pastern area are kept dry and oiled (or greased in wet weather) can do much toward preventing this condition.

SEEDY TOE   A separation of the hoof wall from the foot, rendering that part most susceptible to contamination. Founder predisposes to this condition.

SESAMOIDITIS   Inflammation of the sesamoid bones, this condition is most prevalent among racehorses. It is not particularly serious in most instances and usually responds well to rest.

SHIPPING FEVER   *See* INFLUENZA.

SHOE BOIL or CAPPED ELBOW   A mushy enlargement at the point of the elbow caused by bruising. This injury is most often the result of either contact with the floor of the stall (because of insufficient bedding) or irritation from the inner heel of the shoe when the horse lies down. Lameness may accompany this condition, depending upon the degree of inflammation and the size of the swelling. If detected in the early stages, the swelling may respond to treatment in combination with the use of a shoe boil boot. If, however, the condition is allowed to progress and a large amount of fluid collects, it must be surgically opened by a veterinarian and drained.

SIDEBONES   The ossification of one or both of the lateral cartilages in the area just above the rear quarter of the hoof. This affliction most frequently affects the forefeet. The exact cause is not known, though it would seem to be at least, in part, hereditary. In many cases, sidebones have developed with no apparent cause or history of injury. On the other hand, they may also arise as an aftermath of sprains, cracks, quittor, or extensive work on hard ground or pavement. Lameness is not always present and, if manifested, usually during the period when the sidebones are forming. Once set, sidebones seldom cause lameness, unless in conjunction with another condition, such as contracted foot or ringbone. There are many treatments for this condition; not all of them are deemed successful.

175

However, reducing the inflammation by means of cold water applications seems to be universal approach, followed by blistering, firing, corrective shoeing, and, as a last resort, *nerving*. If there is no lameness, the condition is best left alone.

SLEEPING SICKNESS, EQUINE ENCEPHALOMYELITIS An acute infectious disease of horses and mules that attacks the central nervous system—the brain and spinal cord, in particular —and can be transmitted to humans. Since 1930 the annual number of cases has been on the increase, and in the United States it is estimated that nearly one million animals have been affected. This disease is the result of four distinct viruses of which three are found in the United States. These are identified, reflecting the areas of the first outbreaks, as Eastern (mortality rate of 90 percent), Western (usually not more than 50 percent mortality), and as of 1971, Venezuelan, which has proved to be more devastating than either of the other two. The disease is of a seasonal nature, occurring during the warm months and disappearing after the first sharp frost. Transmission seems to be effected by insects—that is, several types of mosquitoes, the assassin bug, and the spotted fever tick. In its early stages this disease may go undetected, as it usually consists of mild apathy in combination with a rise in temperature, which is generally more than 102 degrees and may be as high as 107 degrees. It is during this period that the virus circulates throughout the blood and may be found in nasal (and possibly other) secretions and excretions. The disease can end in this stage or continue on to involve the central nervous system.

During the second stage, there are definite nervous symptoms. The animal may evidence a total lack of interest in food and water, or he may be unable to grasp food, chew, and swallow. There may be grinding of the teeth, paralysis and/or twitching of the lips or tongue, and paralysis and/or twitching of other groups of body muscles. The animal may appear drowsy and stupid and stand with the head hanging in an attitude of depression; if movement is attempted, he may crash into objects or tend to pull back or walk backwards, if untied.

In the final stage, the horse cannot stand without support; often there is impairment of vision or blindness, paralysis of the bladder, and rapid weight loss as a result of dehydration. When an animal reaches this point, death usually ensues. This disease habitually runs a swift course with death occurring within two to four days after the onset of symptoms. In some instances, the contagion takes a more chronic course; provided the animal does not die from pneumonia or some related complication, the animal may survive the disease only to be impaired by permanent damage to the brain or spinal cord. Thus disabled, the horse cannot react to normal stimuli and is called a "dummy." There is little to be done in the way of treatment aside from careful nursing at the veterinarian's direction. Anti-encephalomyelitis serum has appeared to be valuable in some cases, but the decision to use it rests with the doctor. Prevention entails vaccination, which is effective for about six months and is generally administered in the spring.

SPLINT   A bony enlargement that may occur on any leg (but most commonly on the forelegs), between the lower knee or hock and ankle, or between the splint bone and the cannon bone. These protrusions, which may be found on the inside or the outside of the leg, range from the size of a pea to a bulbous diffused formation extending for several inches. Splints most usually develop in younger horses—yearlings and two-year-olds—because of overstrain, inflammation, a torn ligament, or external blows or injuries. While at the onset splints are extremely painful because of acute heat and irritation, once the heat is reduced and the growth becomes permanent, there is seldom any damage except as a blemish on the leg.

STALL WALKING   The fitful habit of an extremely nervous horse that cannot rest or remain quiet in his stall. Instead, the animal keeps walking in circles, round and round his stall. Horses who get into this habit are difficult to keep in good condition since they tend to literally "run" off any weight gained.

STIFLED, also LOCKED STIFLE, SLIPPED STIFLE   A condition in which one of the ligaments of the stifle joint becomes loose. The horse locks his hind leg in the "rest" position, whereupon the ligaments on either side of the patella raise it over the condyle of the femur and then hook it over this condyle. The slackness of the ligament(s) associated with this problem does not allow the horse to raise the patella back over the condyle (which is much like a knob) so the leg remains in the "locked" position). Flexion of the leg is impossible in this state; in fact, the only evidence of flexion at all may appear in the fetlock of the affected foot. The horse drags his toe, and the leg maintains an extended attitude. To permit the patella to return to a normal position, it is necessary to extend and pull the leg forward simultaneously to relieve the tension

177

on the ligament. Inducing the horse to move around (as in hand walking) will frequently cause it to snap loose and return to normal; or the veterinarian can, in most instances, manipulate the leg into the necessary position. Should the problem become chronic or particularly disabling, a last-resort surgery exists in which the medial ligament is severed (desmotomy).

STOCKED or STOCKING UP *See* FILLED LEGS.

STRANGLES or DISTEMPER A highly contagious disease that most frequently attacks young animals; it is characterized by the formation of one or more abscesses, usually of the lymph glands of the head. Sometimes it will affect other lymph glands in the body, in which case it is called "bastard strangles." It is thought to be caused by the bacterium *Streptoccocus equi* and is most often transmitted through food or drinking water contaminated by discharges from an infected animal. This organism can exist outside the horse's body for as long as six months, so it is imperative that the stall and premises as well as any equipment or feed possibly contaminated by contact with an infected animal be thoroughly cleaned and disinfected.

The symptoms will appear anywhere from two to fourteen days after exposure, being first evidenced by a sudden listlessness and loss of appetite. This is followed by a nasal discharge, which is at first clear and watery but then becomes pus. There is a high fever. After three or four days a hot, painful diffuse swelling, including the lymph glands, takes form under the jaw. This causes the horse to extend his head stiffly, and he will exhibit trouble in swallowing. After a few days the abscess will ripen and frequently rupture without help, discharging a thick pus. Care must be taken not to open the abscess before it is mature, but at such time it should be lanced to afford sufficient drainage. There are times when the abscess interferes with breathing in which case a tracheotomy may be indicated.

Once the abscess has drained, the fever will gradually lessen. The animal will become brighter and more alert; if no complications arise, there is usually complete recovery in a few weeks. Horses that have recovered from this disease are usually rendered immune for life. The mortality rate from this disease is low, but isolation, prompt attention, and large doses of antibiotics administered by a veterinarian are essential.

STRINGHALT A condition affecting one or both hocks and characterized solely by an exaggerated and involuntary flexion

178

(jerking upward) when the animal moves forward. This condition is not necessarily obvious with every step; in early stages it may go unnoticed unless the animal is asked to turn around suddenly. There is no known cure for this ailment; however, a surgical operation that involves removing of a portion of the extensor tendon on the outside of the leg just below the hock has met with a fair degree of success.

SOUNDNESS Soundness relates to the performance expected of the animal. (There is a growing trend of late to do away with the terms *sound* and unsound and to replace them with statements of "physically capable to do the job for which intended.")

SPUR Protrusion of bone, usually due to trauma. Spurs do not necessarily create problems until a high-performance level is expected. For example, a horse with a spur might be fine when ridden in a field for pleasure, but he might be unbearably lame when put through training at the racetrack or competing in jumping classes at horse shows.

SWAMP FEVER or EQUINE INFECTIOUS ANEMIA The symptoms of this disease extend the complete spectrum from carrier state to fatality. No vaccination exists, and only recently has positive diagnosis become available through the Coggins Test. A blood-borne disease, it is transmitted by biting insects, dirty hypodermic needles, and other means.

SWEAT Any sweat lotion is a hydroscopic (drawing water) agent used to pull fluid from an affected part.

SWEENEY A cavity in the shoulder resulting from nerve damage that causes the muscles to become atrophied. Irritants injected into the affected area may fill in the depression, but there is no known remedy to repair the injured nerve.

SYNOVIAL FLUID The fluid secreted within a joint to lubricate the articulating surfaces. It is the "oil" of the horse's body.

TEMPERATURE The normal temperature for a horse ranges from 99.5 to 101 degrees Fahrenheit. A horse's temperature is lowest in the morning and highest in the afternoon.

TETANUS, LOCKJAW A disease, usually resulting from a wound infection, that attacks the nervous system. Although it is most often associated with a wound or laceration, it need not appear as the immediate aftermath of an injury. The microorganism that causes this disease can grow only in the absence of oxygen; it then produces the seed forms, which may live for years under certain conditions. This germ thrives at the point of entry, but its powerful nerve poison is absorbed and carried throughout the body, thus involving the entire nervous system.

Deep wounds such as from a nail are far more dangerous when invaded by this germ, because they are farther from the oxygen of the air. The earliest sign of this disease is a stiffness about the head and face. The horse may have difficulty chewing and swallowing, and his head may be extended. The third eyelid protrudes over the inner part of the eyeball. There is limited ability to open the jaws; any attempt to open them to their full extent brings about extreme nervous excitement and increases the spasm of the jaw and neck muscles. The muscles of the neck and spine later on become rigid, and the horse becomes stiff-legged. The tail is usually partly raised and held immovable. From this point the horse shows the characteristic spasms that affect the muscles of the face, neck, body, legs, and of all muscles supplied by the cerebrospinal nerves. Any movement or noise—no matter how slight—can increase the contractions.

Treatment must be administered by a veterinarian, but the horse should be placed in a remote dark stall or outbuilding, where the noise and movement of other animals and/or people will not cause unnecessary excitement and increase the spasm. Tetanus is a grave disease with a mortality rate of more than 50 percent, because it exhausts or paralyzes vital organs. General cleanliness and prompt attention to all wounds will obviate many cases of tetanus, and the use of tetanus antitoxin should be a regular part of treating wounds.

THOROUGHPIN   A puffy filling located just above the point of the hock and slightly in front of the hamstring. When pressed by the fingers on one side of the leg, it bulges out on the other side. It may appear as the result of an injury, in which case it will be inflamed, taut, and painful; more often, however, it is an abnormal accumulation of fluid, without heat or pain. Unless brought about by a blow or some other injury requiring treatment, the condition seldom causes lameness and is of little consequence, except as a superficial blemish.

THRUSH   A disease of the cleft of the frog, which may affect all four feet but which is most frequently found in the hind feet.

It is essentially a decomposing of organic matter in the cleft of the frog as a result of unsanitary conditions existing in the horse's stall or poor attention to the care of the feet. This breakdown process gives rise to the characteristic offensive odor. Caught in the early stages, thrush seldom causes lameness and responds to paring away any excess material, sanitation, and the application of antiseptics.

TIED UP SYNDROME　　A slang expression used to describe a condition affecting any group of muscles but most frequently involving those of the loins and croup. It generally manifests itself after the horse begins exercise or after a particularly strenuous work. The horse begins to sweat, the pulse rate quickens, the muscles in the affected area stiffen and bulge out, and general signs of distress may be present. The horse is unwilling to move and will do so only if forced—and then with difficulty. The horse should be blanketed immediately and the affected muscles massaged. Movement should be avoided; if necessary, the horse should be tied in the stall. In many cases an attack will be of short duration, and the animal will quickly return to normal.

TOE CRACK　　*See* SAND CRACK.

VEE, VENEZUELAN EQUINE ENCEPHALOMYELITIS　　*See* SLEEPING SICKNESS.

VENTRAL　　The veterinarian's term for the area which is toward the belly from the part in question.

VISION　　Horses see everything around them except what their hindquarters block out. Their monocular vision is better than biocular, which means that they can see better using just one eye than when two are employed. The act of shying at an immovable object happens as a result of passing along its side (as opposed to head on) during which time the animal's vision changes from biocular (on the approach) to monocular (as he passes it), causing the object to seem to move or "jump."

WEAVING　　The swaying motion of the head and body so that the horse's weight rests alternately from one foreleg to the other. In bad cases the horse will pick up each foot before placing weight upon it, and the motion of the head is grotesquely exaggerated. This condition may be initiated from boredom and/or idleness, and it shortly becomes a habit. From this point it is a rapid progression to become a vice and later a nervous disease. Weaving may be sporadic or constant; the latter makes it impossible to keep the animal in good weight. The horse does not get sufficient rest, and the rear muscles of the body become overtired causing stumbling when at work. This vice is considered incurable, although there are varying remedies, some of which have met with limited success.

WINDPUFFS or WINDGALL   A dilation of the fluid sac (bursa) located at the back of the fetlock joint. Usually the result of an external strain such as heavy pulling, excessive speed, or jumping, they generally appear as symmetrical, well-defined distentions of varying size. The amount of secretion that they contain determines the degree of tenseness, though they become softer as the foot is raised and the fetlock flexed.

In most cases windpuffs are painless and seldom cause lameness, except in instances where they become large enough to interfere with the functions of the tendon or become calcified. Treatment consists of applying cold packs followed by the use of liniments, blistering, or—in severe cases—firing or draining by a veterinarian. However, windpuffs are often left untreated, for while they constitute a blemish, they rarely hinder the performance of the horse.

WORMS   *See* INTERNAL PARASITES.

BISHOPING   An attempt to artificially create the marks peculiar to young teeth to make a horse appear younger than his natural age. It was named for the person who initiated this practice and consisted of imitating the normal cups through drilling, staining, and burning. Although some dishonest horsemen become quite proficient at bishoping, the fact remains that the ring of enamel surrounding the natural cup cannot be duplicated or replaced, and experienced horsemen and veterinarians are seldom fooled.

CAPS   A young horse's deciduous molars are called caps. The first set of caps are lost at the age of three and frequently removed in racehorses because of a feeling that they interfere with the animal's eating habits during the time it takes for them to come out. The second set of caps is lost at age four, when they are replaced by permanent premolars.

CUPS   The hollow space on the wearing surface of the incisor is known as the cup.

DENTAL STAR   The star-shaped or circular structure found near the center of the wearing surface of the permanent incisors.

FLOATING TEETH   The periodic rasping of rough or irregular edges of a horse's teeth is known as floating. This is a detail of horse care that should be attended to regularly (about twice a year) to ensure a smooth grinding surface in the horse's mouth. It also prevents the animal from developing sores or cuts in his mouth from a sharp tooth or "hook" and thereby cause him to go "off his feed" or obtain only minimal benefit from consumed food (as a result of inadequate chewing). A horse with sharp teeth will constantly mouth the bit, because it bothers him to set it in one place, a further reason for keeping well up on the condition of a horse's teeth.

FULL MOUTH   When a horse has a complete set of permanent incisors, he is said to have a full mouth. This usually occurs at five years of age.

GALVAYNE'S GROOVE   A vertical brownish-yellow groove on a horse's tooth used in determining his age past ten years. Named for the horseman who first pointed it out, the groove begins as a notch on the outside of each upper corner incisor just below the gum. It is first visible at the age of ten and ex-

183

Temporary incisors to 10 days of age: First or central upper and lower temporary incisors appear.

Temporary incisors at 4 to 6 weeks of age: Second or intermediate upper and lower temporary incisors appear.

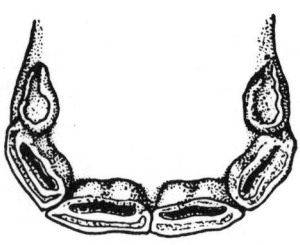

Temporary incisors at 6 to 10 months: Third or corner upper and lower temporary incisors appear.

Temporary incisors at 1 year: Crowns of central temporary incisors show wear.

Temporary incisors at 1½ years: Intermediate temporary incisors show wear.

Temporary incisors at 2 years: All show wear.

Incisors at 4 years: Permanent incisors replace temporary centrals and intermediates; temporary corner incisors remain.

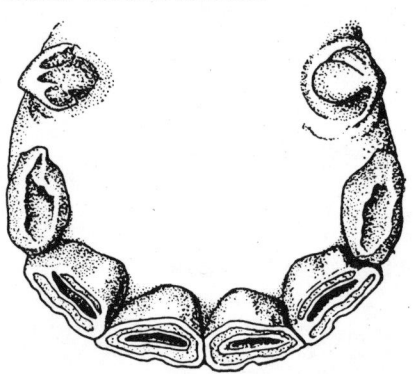

Incisors at 5 years: All permanent; cups in all incisors.

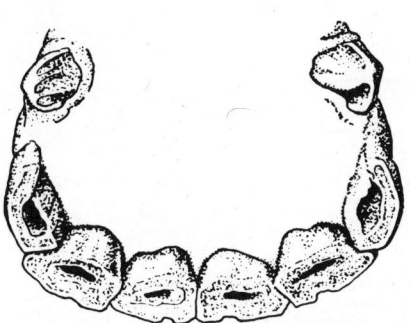

Incisors at 6 years: Cups worn out of lower central incisors.

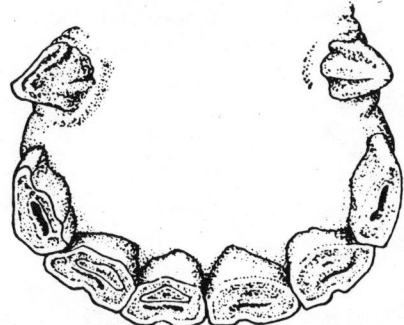

Incisors at 9 years: Cups worn out of upper central incisors; dental star on upper central and intermediate pairs.

Incisors at 7 years: Cups also worn out of lower intermediate incisors.

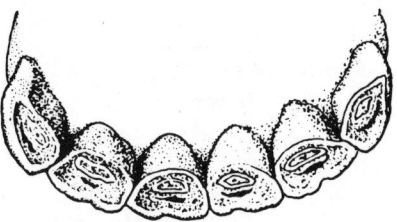

Incisors at 10 years: Cups also worn out of upper intermediate incisors, and dental star is present in all incisors.

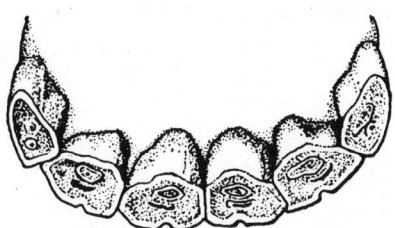

Incisors at 11 or 12 years: Cups worn in all incisors (smooth mouthed), and dental star approaches center of cups.

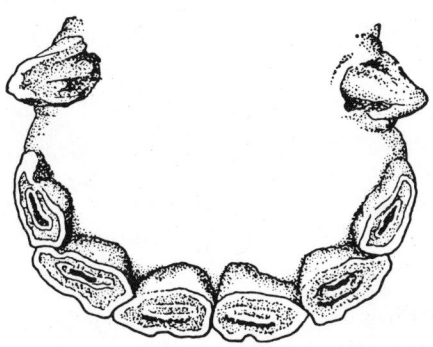

Incisors at 8 years: Cups worn out of all lower incisors, and dental star (dark line in front of cup) appears on lower central and intermediate pairs.

U.S. DEPARTMENT OF AGRICULTURE

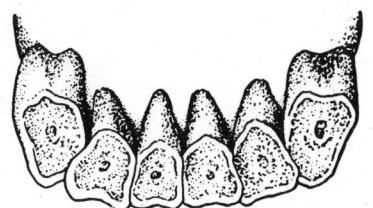

Characteristic shape of lower incisors at 18 years.

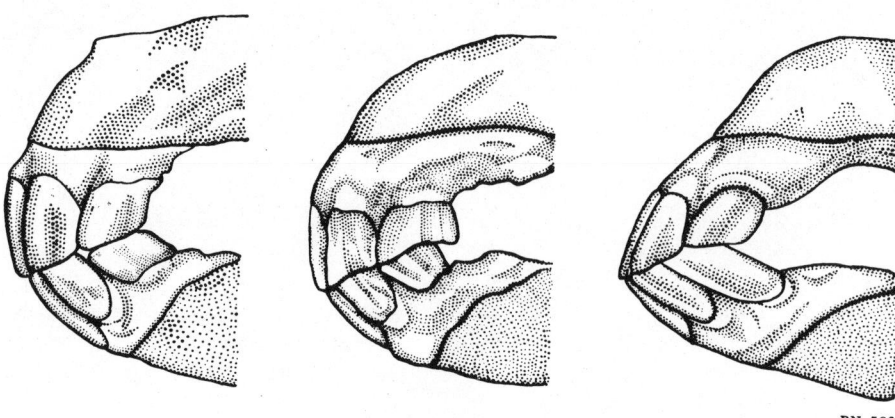

BN–5969

Side view of 5-, 7-, and 20-year-old mouth. Note that as the horse advances in age the teeth change from nearly perpendicular to slanting sharply toward the front.

U.S. DEPARTMENT OF AGRICULTURE

tends the entire length of the tooth at the age of twenty. Thus, at the halfway mark, a horse may be adjudged to be fifteen years old. By the age of twenty-five years, the groove has disappeared from the top half of the tooth and is no longer perceptible at the age of thirty.

SMOOTH MOUTH   As a horse grows older, he gradually loses the cups on the wearing surface of the incisors until he reaches the age of twelve, when they have disappeared completely. The phrase *smooth mouth* refers to the smooth biting surface of the upper and lower incisors after the cups are gone; it is a horseman's way of saying that the horse is more than twelve years of age.

TUSH or CANINE TOOTH   The tushes or canine teeth appear in the gum space between the incisor teeth and the molar teeth on the male horse at five years of age. They are rarely seen on mares; if they should appear, they are usually rudimentary in nature.

WOLF TOOTH   A very small rudimentary premolar, which sometimes appears directly after the dental space (in front of the first molars) of the upper jaw. Many horsemen believe that they interfere with the bit and should be removed.

PETER WINANTS

BREEDING

BARREN MARE   A mare that has been bred and is not in foal is said to be *barren,* as opposed to a mare that has never been bred.

BREEDING HOBBLES   A device used to prevent fractious or difficult mares from kicking the stallion during breeding. It consists of a collar that fits around the mare's neck, much like a martingale strap with a piece extending between her front legs to which a pulley is attached. A length of strong rope passes through this pulley and attaches to specially constructed fittings, which are strapped around her hocks. In this way, the mare can still progress forward in a somewhat limited fashion, but is unable to lash out behind her and injure a valuable stallion. (On some breeding farms, hobbles are used as a matter of course, regardless of the temperament of the mare and simply as a safeguard for the stallion.)

BY and OUT OF   A foal is said to be *by* its sire (father) and *out of* its dam (mother).

BOOK   A stallion's book is the number of mares contracted to be bred to him in one season.

BOOK A MARE   When a mare is contracted to be bred to a particular stallion, she is said to have been *booked* to him.

COLOSTRUM   The mare's first milk, which appears shortly before or just after she gives birth is called *colostrum.* It is particularly high in proteins, nutrients, and antibodies that provide the newborn foal with resistance to infection. For this reason, it is most important that the foal receive this milk. The colostrum is gradually replaced by normal milk within approximately two to four days after the initial nursing.

COVER A MARE, also SERVICE A MARE   When a stallion breeds a mare he is said to *cover* or *service* her.

CROSSBREEDING   Mating two horses of different breeds.

CULTURE A MARE   Most reputable breeding establishments require that a mare be *cultured* and reported *clean* before they will cover her with one of their stallions. This means that the veterinarian has taken a swab from the cervix, sent it to a laboratory for culturing, and that it has come back negative for infection. Testing for infection in this manner serves the dual purpose of preventing the stallion from becoming infected and or passing it on to other mares and eliminating one of the most common deterrents to conception. Furthermore, should an infected mare become pregnant, there is a good chance of her aborting or having a deformed or damaged foal.

FOALED, also DROPPED A FOAL   When a mare gives birth to her young, she is said to have *foaled* or *dropped a foal,* but foals are never *born.* (In a normal birth, the foal is delivered within twenty to forty minutes after labor begins. Failure of the foal to appear within ten minutes after the water breaks indicates a problem.)

FOAL HEAT   From four to thirteen days after foaling, a mare will usually come into a short period of one to three days during which she will accept the stallion and can be bred again. However, breeding on the *foal heat* is something of a gamble and less than 35 percent of the mares covered in that cycle actually conceive. This is because it is not uncommon for a mare to carry a slight infection after foaling, which remains in her system through the foal heat and then disappears naturally before the next heat cycle. Such an infection seldom requires treatment but is often sufficient to prohibit conception.

FOALING PRESENTATIONS   There are only two "normal" presentations of a foal at the time of birth. Any deviation from these two is definitely a problem requiring immediate veterinarian assistance and often a decision of whether to sacrifice the foal (most frequently) or the mare (in some cases). The two normal presentations are: 1) Forefeet first (extended well in front of the body), followed by the nose (which is more or less resting on the outstretched forelegs), then shoulders, barrel, hips and both hind legs extended behind the foal; and 2) The exact reverse of the former presentation, in which the hind legs appear first in an extended position, followed by the rest of the body through to extended front legs, which in most instances is the natural progression. (It is not difficult to ascertain whether a problem is imminent. For example, should the forelegs appear as they should but are not immediately followed by a nose, that's trouble; should a tail appear first, a breech birth is occurring, and chances of saving the foal and/or the mare are poor.)

189

GESTATION PERIOD   The gestation period for a mare is approximately 340 days, although it may vary from approximately 320 to 380 days following breeding.

GET   The progeny or offspring of a stallion is called his *get:* "Handyman's *get* earned $250,000 in 1970."

INBREEDING   Mating two closely related horses, such as mother to son.

IN FOAL, CARRYING A FOAL or WITH FOAL   A pregnant mare is said to be *in foal, carrying a foal,* or *with foal,* but not *pregnant. See also* SETTLE.

IN FOAL TO   Once it has been determined that a mare is definitely in foal, it is then said that she is *in foal to* (name of stallion).

IN HEAT, also IN SEASON   When a mare is in the period of her estrus cycle during which she is receptive to a stallion, she is commonly said to be *in heat* or *in season.* The average cycle for mares is twenty-one days, but individuals vary widely and a cycle of seventeen or thirty days may still be considered within normal limits. The average length of time in which a mare will accept a stallion is six days, but this, too, may vary anywhere from two to eleven days.

JOINT ILL or NAVEL ILL   A bacterial infection believed to progress from contamination of the umbilicus. The foal runs a fever, goes off his feed (in this case does not nurse), is generally lethargic, becomes stiff, and evidences swelling of the joints. Immediate medical treatment is mandatory if any success is to be had. Much can be done toward preventing this disease by treating the umbilical cord with a tincture of strong iodine within a few hours after birth.

LINE-BREEDING   Mating two horses who have the same ancestor repeated several times in their pedigrees (a form of inbreeding).

MAIDEN MARE   One that has never been bred.

METRITIS   A "dirty" mare—that is, one that did not culture "clean" usually is suffering from metritis, a low-grade localized infection that may prevent her from conception. Treatment consists of intrauterine antibiotics.

NURSING   The normal foal should be on its feet and nursing within one to two hours after birth.

OUTCROSSING   Mating two horses of the same breed that are from completely unrelated families.

PALPATION OF A MARE   A rectal examination in which the veterinarian explores the uterus of a mare is called *palpation*. This is the most accurate method of determining pregnancy, as well as the most efficient way in which to determine the exact stage of heat. The latter can be an important factor when working with hard-to-breed mares or ones that have been "barren" for a number of seasons.

PRODUCE   The offspring (sons and daughters) of a mare are called her produce.

SCOURING   *Scouring* is actually a cattle word that is used by horsemen to describe a foal's case of diarrhea, which is usually indicative of the mare's foal heat. Due to certain hormone or chemical changes in her body at this time, the composition of her milk may change slightly, causing the foal to have diarrhea for several days. The term seems to be used almost exclusively with reference to foals; one rarely hears it used with reference to older animals.

SETTLE or CATCH   When a mare is in foal, she is said to have *settled* or *caught*: "We bred Rose, but I don't know if she *settled*." Or "Did Rose *catch* to the first cover?"

SLEEPER FOAL DISEASE   A bacterial disease wherein the foal may be born dead or is extremely weak at birth, unable to rise or nurse effectively, and usually dies within three days.

SLIP A FOAL   When a mare in foal loses her foal for any reason prior to the termination of her pregnancy, she is said to *slip* or *have slipped* her foal.

SPEC A MARE   A veterinarian's examination of the cervix and vagina of a mare with a speculum to determine her breeding soundness and stage of heat.

STAND A STALLION   When someone *stands a stallion*, it means that the horse is being offered to the public for breeding purposes. In most instances there is a fixed charge for this service.

191

(*See* STUD FEE.) The fee varies with individual owners and the performance record of the horse involved. A horse that is standing his first season and has little or no past performance record may do well to stand for a nominal fee (or for free) to encourage mare owners to send their mares to him until he is an established sire, while horses with exceptional racing or performance records may stand for fees in excess of $25,000.

STUD FEE   The amount of money paid to the owner of a stallion for breeding services rendered by that horse. There are countless ways in which a stud fee may be paid, depending upon the terms of the individual stallion contract. Certain conditions are used with enough frequency as to be listed in a word or two (particularly in stallion advertisements). "Guarantee Live Foal" means that should the mare fail to conceive or abort prior to delivery, no money is due. "Return Privilege" implies a chance to breed back to the stallion at no additional cost if the mare is not in foal, but that the money will not be refunded. "No guarantee, no return" (seen only in the contracts of the greatest stallions) means there is no guarantee that the mare will conceive, no chance to return for another breeding if she does not, and no refund of money. "Private Contract" is another common statement seen in place of a stated fee; it can mean anything from a free service to "approved mares" to limited bookings to quality mares for very high fees. Of course there are variations on all of these, and many that are not mentioned here.

TEASER   A stallion that is essential to any good breeding program. With his help, the personnel are able to detect the estrus or heat cycles of the mares to be bred without exposing the breeding stallion to injury from mares unready to be bred or subjecting him to overuse. The principle behind having a teaser at all is simply that if a stallion is worth the time, money, and effort it takes to stand him at stud, then he is valuable enough to warrant protection from unnecessary injury, which could make him worthless. And that no matter how good a teaser is, he still is not worth what the "standing" stallion is.

VIRUS ABORTION—RHINOPNEUMONITIS   A viral respiratory disease that is commonly found at the racetrack, particularly in young horses that evidence only a slight nasal discharge and a possible loss of appetite for a day or two. It is, however, devastating to a breeding operation. The only manifestation of this

192

disease other than the respiratory problems is abortion in the last trimester of gestation. One can expect approximately 75 percent of all in-foal mares to abort on a farm infected by virus abortion. Vaccination is available and highly recommended, for although the mare protects the fetus for approximately the first five months, after that period the fetus becomes susceptible to the virus.

WAX The average mare will begin to *wax* approximately twenty-four to forty-eight hours prior to foaling, although there is a wide range of variance in individual mares. All this means is that small pearllike droplets appear on the ends of the teats, generally indicating that she is producing milk and foaling is imminent.

WINDSUCKING—NUMO-VAGINA Windsucking is a breeding problem and refers to the act of creating numo-vagina. This occurs as a result of poor conformation in the outer genital region as effected by age, tears in the foaling process, and irregularities of the vulva lips. Numo-vagina is the vagina ballooning with air that should not be there; it frequently introduces contaminants causing infection and making conception unlikely, if not impossible. This term is frequently misused interchangeably to describe a cribber.

BREEDS

ACHAL-TEKE   This breed is one of the more representative and interesting of the many breeds found in the Soviet Union. Often found in herds of one stallion per dozen mares, the Achal-Teke is a genuine desert horse capable of surviving without water for extended periods of time. Even its color is usually appropriate for arid terrain: dull dust-colored grey. The Achal-Teke's physical characteristics of long face, thin neck, narrow chest, long legs, and small, very hard hoofs also reflect this breed's desert environment.

ACHEAN   The Achean is an ancient breed of pony from Greece. It is a small but hardy animal associated with the Pindo family.

ALBINO   The Albinos are a very special type of horse that resulted from a breeding mutation. They have absolutely no pigmentation in their coat or eyes and remain very sensitive to bright sunlight. More frequently found are Albinos that are not completely pure, because of their bluish tinted eyes and pink, flesh-colored skin. Most Albinos tracing their line to Morgan-Arabian descent are registered with the American Albino Horse Club. They are of course quite in demand for parades, shows, and circuses.

ALTER   Part of the Andalusian breed family, the Alter is one of two native Portuguese breeds. While not very numerous in its home country, the Alter line was introduced into Brazil to begin the Mangalarga breed, which now is quite extensive in that country.

AMERICAN SADDLE HORSE   The American Saddle Horse originated in the United States in the early 1800s through several generations of selective breeding to provide plantation owners with a comfortable mount on which they could survey their crops and lands in style. The foundation sire of the breed was a Thoroughbred stallion named Denmark (foaled in 1839) that, when bred to the "Stevenson Mare," a colonial pacer, produced his most famous son, Gaines Denmark (foaled in 1851). The Thoroughbred is thought to be responsible for the Saddler's fire and brilliance, while the English amblers are given credit for his gentleness and easy gaits.

The present-day American Saddle Horse generally stands between 15 and 16 hands in height and is considered the "peacock of the horse world." He has a short back, round barrel, flat croup, and good clean legs. His head is well formed with a long gracefully arching neck. His tail carriage is high. Solid colors predominate—usually black, brown, bay, or chestnut with generous white markings on the face and legs.

There are three types of Saddle Horses, all of which excel in the show ring. The Three-Gaited Saddle Horse performs at the walk, which is brisk; the trot, which is moderate and animated; and the canter, which is a highly collected and controlled motion. He is exhibited with a "roached" mane and tail—meaning simply that the mane is completely shaved off and the tail is shaved close at the top along the bone and pulled rather thin below.

The Harness Horse is shown in light harness pulling a lightweight, four-wheeled vehicle. He performs at the walk, which should be animated and graceful, and at the park trot, an animated trot without extreme speed. Emphasis is placed on manners and brilliance in motion. These horses are exhibited with a full mane and tail.

The most outstanding of all Saddlebreds is the Five-Gaited Saddle Horse, which as his name suggests is shown performing five gaits. In addition to the natural gaits—the walk, trot, and canter—the Five-Gaited Saddle Horse executes two man-made ones, namely the slow-gait and the rack. The slow-gait is a true prancing motion in which each foot rises, hesitates in mid-air, and descends in a single separate sequence creating a four-beat, syncopated cadence. The rack is an all out, full-speed-ahead version of the slow-gait; it can be counted on to bring fans to their feet in a thunderous roar of applause. *See also* TENNESSEE WALKING HORSE.

ANDALUSIAN   Originally bred in Spain along the Guadalquivir River and certain parts of Cadiz, Cordoba, and Seville, this ancient Moorish breed of riding and driving horse is characterized by a Roman nose; heavy forelimbs, chest, and shoulders; and luxurious mane and tail. It is also marked by the flashy *Paso de Andadura* gait, which is a special movement somewhere between the walk and trot.

ANGLO-ARAB   One of the numerous light horse breeds now popular throughout Europe. It is used primarily as a riding horse because of its stamina, strong legs, and jumping abilities. The Anglo-Arab finds its origin in a cross of Thoroughbred and Arab bloodlines evolved by the French government. In turn, the Anglo-Arab line has been used to begin many subsidiary breeds, such as the Bigourdan and the Iberique. To meet studbook requirements, an Anglo-Arab must have no less than twenty-five percent Arab blood.

ANGLO-ARGENTINE Another of the light horse breeds evolved in South America by crossing the Argentine native *Criollo* with the Thoroughbred. These nimble equines have found popularity as polo ponies. *See also* CRIOLLO.

ANGLO-NORMAN The Swiss Anglo-Norman breed was established in 1811 as the result of a cross between the Thoroughbred and the Norman line. It is very popular as a general riding horse as well as basic breeding stock for new lines. The Hungarian Large Nonius and Small Nonius, for example, are based upon the Anglo-Norman stock.

ANGLO-NORMAN TROTTER This breed is a cross between the Thoroughbred and the Norfolk Trotter. It is also referred to as the Demi-Sang Trotter. It is used extensively in France as a trotter, although the breed has been crossed, in turn, with the Standardbred to produce a new strain of trotters called the Noram Trotter.

APPALOOSA This strain developed in Oregon from its historical origin in Central Asia by way of Spain. The name comes from the Palouse River in Oregon; in the local jargon of the Nez Percé Indians, the Palouse breed became slurred into the *Apalouse,* then *Apalouser,* then *Apalousie,* and finally the *Appaloosa.* It is characterized by a white croup flecked with small spots of the prevailing body color, which may be any commonly found solid color. The Appaloosa was recognized as a dominant, consistent breed in 1950. To be classed as an Appaloosa, the color pattern combination must fall into six basic categories. These groups are called frost, leopard, marble, snowflake, spotted blanket, and white blanket. Whatever the pattern, however, the horse must have particolored skin and hoofs, and the eye must be encircled with white. Used mostly for pleasure, this breed has a high level of endurance, energy, versatility, and spirit.

ARABIAN The Arabian is the oldest, fully resolved true breed of horse in existence. It is the purest representative of the hot-blooded type, and its breeding prepotency has traditionally been such that Arab blood has provided an unfailing source of stamina and conformational refinement in virtually all subsequent lightweight breeds.

The origins of the Arabian extend far back into antiquity and lead through an intriguing labyrinth of fact and fable. The most consistent factor in the myths surrounding the Arab is that the breed traces its ancestry to five great mares, founders of five original Arabian strains that then branched out into substrains. These five mares—also referred to as the Five Blue Mares, indicating the characteristic blue-black cast of the Arab's skin—are said to have answered the call of Salaman's trumpeter instead of first quenching their thirst after traveling many days through the desert without water. Thus it was that Salaman selected Al Khamseh—the five to breed and produce the five original strains.

Another legend tells how Ishmael received a wild mare as a divine gift from heaven. The story has it that the mare was crippled as a result of being carried in a saddlebag on camelback when just a foal. This mare eventually gave birth to a colt that was named Benat el Ahwaj—"son of the crooked" that is said to have been the foundation sire of the first strain of pure Arabians, the Kuhaylan. Still another story relates the history of Kuhaylan Ajuz, the first of the blue mares. This version tells of a sheikh mounted on his favorite war mare and hotly pursued by the enemy. Sometime during the course of the battle, the mare dropped a filly and then returned to the demands of war. Later, having traveled many miles from that momentary resting place, the sheikh was astounded to find that the day-old foal had followed the mare the entire way through the desert. This filly was given into the care of an old woman and became known as Kuhaylan Ajuz—"the mare of the old woman."

There are still other legends and folktales accounting for the origin of the Arabian, all of which have been refuted at one time or another. However, when examining the Arabian's ancestry, the Hittite invasion of the areas adjacent to Arabia must be taken into account. It is possible that the war mounts of these conquerors drifted into the Arabian peninsula and that by the time of the Scythian, Parthian, and Persian conquests the strain that might have been traced to the Hittite animals had already refined itself into the pure Arabian. This is the prevailing theory among experts; the only alternative is that these horses were already there, profiting from the fertile land and dense foliage of the Arabian peninsula before it became a desert.

The physical appearance of the Arab is virtually the same as it was centuries ago. He is relatively small in size, averaging 15.2 hands at full growth. He is solid and compact because he has a shorter spine and fewer ribs than other horses; this condition enables him to carry excessive weight without tiring. The withers are not overly prominent, and frequently the Arab will

199

appear to be taller at the croup than at the withers. The Arabian neck arches smoothly from the strong shoulders to the juncture of the head, displaying the characteristically large prominent windpipe, which is vital to his superb lung power. The head of the Arab is distinguished from all others by its dished appearance when seen in profile. This concavity is caused by a slight protrusion of the forehead, which is known as the *jibbah* in Arabic and valued by the Bedouins, who contend that the enlargement permits the horse to have a more sizable brainpan and, therefore, greater intelligence. The fragile look of the Arabian's legs is remarkably deceptive. The bone is extremely dense and smooth and much more durable than the more porous bone of seemingly more substantial horses. The legs are also often completely unmarked by the callosities (chestnuts) found along the inner surface of other horses' legs; if they are present, they are so small as to be almost undetectable.

The distinguishing characteristics of the Arab—the absence of chestnuts, the smaller number of vertebrae, and the fact that the teeth of the Arab are smaller and finer than those of any other type of horse or pony—have caused some students of the horse to believe that the Arabian should be classified as a species in his own right—*Equus Arabicus.*

ARDENNES This is an ancient, hardy, cold-blooded or heavy draft horse breed named after the Ardennes mountains. They are derived from crossing mountain ponies with Belgian and French draft horses. While originally a rather small, stubby horse, they are now very strong barrel-chested animals up to 16 hands high. In addition to the Belgium breed are the related French Ardennes and the Swedish Ardennes.

ARIEGE The Ariège is a small pony found in the mountains of the Pyrenees. It is a strong and hardy animal believed descended from the Diluvial horse.

ASSATEAGUE PONY *See* CHINCOTEAGUE PONY.

AUXOIS This breed is one of the many French, heavy, cold-blooded draft horses. It is similar to the Ardennes and possibly derived from the Bourguignon. It is used primarily for heavy agricultural work.

AVELIGNESE This is a warm-blooded horse found in the south Tirol region of northern Italy. It is derived from the Abellinium-Haflinger breed.

BALI   A strong and sturdy horse indigenous to Indonesia. It is believed originally a descendant from Mongolia.

BARB   Its breeding is of the blood of the Barbary region of North Africa. There exists some dispute as to the actual origins of the Barb: possibly a mixture of Arab and Moroccan or Algerian blood, possibly an offshoot of the Arabian, a separate breed entirely, or a descendant of the Libyan lion-hunting horse. Most evidence suggests that the Barb is a slightly larger and coarser cousin of the Arab.

   The Barbary horse resembles the Arab in conformation, but his head is coarser, his tail is set on lower, and he tends towards a goose rump and shows more knee action when in motion. The Barb averages 14 to 14.3 hands in height.

BARRA   A breed of pony native to the Highland Hebrides.

BASUTO PONY   One of the better known ponies of the lower African region, these small extremely hardy ponies are found in Basutoland. They are derived from Persian, Arab, Thoroughbred, and native strains. They are descended from the first horses brought from Java by the Dutch to South Africa in 1653. From these horses evolved the Cape Horse, which, in turn, became the ancestor of the Basuto ponies existing today. During the Boer War these ponies gained a high reputation and later, around 1822, came to Basutoland as a result of Zulu raids. Because of the rocky terrain in this area, they have developed very hard hoofs and are known for their surefootedness.

BATAK   An indigenous pony, infused with Arab stock, found on the Indonesian island of Sumatra.

BEETEWK   A strain of heavy Russian horses produced from a cross of Dutch stallions on native mares in the area around the Beetewk River. Originated by Peter the Great, these horses were later crossed with Orloff trotters from which evolved an animal with characteristic good temperament, beautiful action, and tremendous strength.

BELGIAN, BELGIAN HEAVY DRAFT or BRABANT   The Belgian is a descendant of the ancient Flemish horse and thought to be a strictly European equine carrying no Oriental blood. Despite his "drafty" appearance and the distinction of being the heaviest of the draft-horse breeds (generally tipping the scale upwards of 2,100 pounds), he is not the tallest. He does boast a

201

deeper barrel, wider chest, and more massive hindquarters than any other heavy-horse type. At one time the Belgian was criticized for an overall look of coarseness, but the once-characteristic stubby round hoofs, short neck and round bones have been sufficiently altered in the past thirty years by American breeders so as to produce a decidedly handsome animal. These horses are most usually sorrel, roan, and chestnut, frequently with a flaxen mane and tail, and are often marked with a white blazed face. As a result of their tremendous width, these horses tend to "paddle" when they move, and the same conformation that produces their strength and power prohibits them from moving with the springy elevation marking some of the other breeds. These gentle giants are renowned for their good dispositions and their rather surprising attribute of being "easy keepers," despite their size. They were first imported to the United States in 1866.

BHUTIA   A small breed of pony averaging 13.3 hands and native to the Himalayas.

BITJUG   A Russian breed derived from crossing Trotters with harness horses.

BORNU   This breed is found near Lake Chad in north central Africa. An offspring of the Barb, it is usually greyish-white with black legs.

BOSNIAN PONY   A very ancient pony now found in Yugoslavia but descendant from the Tarpan breed found in Poland.

BOULONNAIS   A very large workhorse with a heavy chest and powerful quarters, but because of an infusion of Arab blood, the Boulonnais is also curiously characterized by a small well-shaped expressive head. It is one of the best and most popular breeds in France.

BOURGUIGNON   An ancient draft horse from the Burgundy region of France.

BRABANT   *See* BELGIAN.

BRETON   One of the more popular French heavy draft horses. Rather compact with a very large head and massive crested neck. The Postier Breton is somewhat larger than its fellow type, the Draft Breton. The latter usually has more stamina, although it is considered a less attractive breed. A third subbreed is the Corlay Breton. These horses have Boulonnais, Percheron, and Ardennes strains in their blood.

BRUMBY   The Brumby breed, or "Brumbies" as they are called, are found in the scrub country of Australia. Although at one time domesticated and believed of imported stock, the Brumbies have "gone wild" and are now considered valueless.

BUDJONNY   A very recent breeding phenomena achieved by crossing the Don horse with the Thoroughbred, the resulting Budjonny is an elegant attractive horse with golden tinted chestnut and bay colors. Their strong legs have enhanced their jumping ability and make this breed popular for steeplechase.

CABALLO CHILENO   Literally meaning *Chilean horse,* this breed is a common domestic horse found in Northern Chile and of obscure origin.

CALABRESE   This breed, named after the Calabria district of southern Italy, is a popular saddle horse. It stands 16 hands high on the average and is very similar to the Salerno breed found near Rome.

CALICO   *See* SPOTTED HORSE.

CAMARGUE PONY   These ponies are ancient, semiwild, extremely hardy scroungers that forage in the rough pasturage of the inhospitable region around Arles in southeastern France. Little is known of their origin, and today they are occasionally domesticated as cow ponies and tourist attractions.

CAMPOLINO   Along with the Criollo and Mangalarga breeds, the Campolino is one of the three principal Brazilian breeds. It is the heaviest of the trio, with a deep chest, and is used most often for draft work, as well as general saddle purposes. Part of the Campolino's heritage includes Andalusian blood.

CAPE HORSE   *See* BASUTO PONY.

CAPPADOCIAN   The Cappadocian horses were rather small animals found originally in Asia. It is believed they were the true ancestors of the Arab line found in the Yemen region of southern Arabia.

203

CARPATHIAN PONY *See* HUZUL.

CARTHUSIAN Generally found in the southern region of Spain, the Carthusian is a common, if indistinguished, breed. It is the poor uncle to the famous Andalusian, Spain's other major breed. The Carthusian is generally of grey color and features good conformation. It is liked particularly for its intelligence and affection.

CHICKASAW While not a true breed, the Chickasaw horse of northern Florida was the best all-purpose horse in Colonial America. Introduced by de Soto during the expedition of 1539, these early horses were smallish—about 13 hands—yet quite strong. They were used for short-distance racing and general transportation. *See* QUARTER HORSE.

CHINCOTEAGUE PONY The origin of this breed is not clearly defined and neither are their physical characteristics. They are found only on the marshy and sandy Assateague and Chincoteague islands off Virginia, presumably abandoned there during the Colonial period. Adapting to their environment, they have developed through constant inbreeding, from a predominantly Arab horse into a scrawny, somewhat stunted horse. Nevertheless, they are far from "wild" and make good family pets. They are frequently referred to as the Assateague Pony. (Their popularity stems from Marguerite Henry's children's book *Misty of Chincoteague.*)

CHINESE PONY A common domestic animal found throughout China as well as in neighboring Mongolia and Korea. While not quite a breed, it is distinct yet similar to the Sandalwood pony of Thailand, the Hocaido pony of Japan, and the Mongolia wild horse. The Chinese pony is nondescript, of all colors and shapes, quite strong, demands little, and is used as a pack animal as well as for racing.

CHOLA The least-known of the three principal Peruvian breeds, the Chola is usually found on Peru's ranches, where it is an excellent cow horse. *See also* COSTENO and MOROCHUCO.

CLEVELAND BAY The Cleveland Bay is a heavy, old-fashioned coach horse. It has a long body with a large head and strong neck. The Cleveland Bay takes his name from the Vale of Cleveland in Yorkshire, England. It is adapted alike for the plough, for heavy draft, and for slow, saddle work. Some individuals make imposing carriage horses, but they have low action and are lacking in quality. Since it could qualify neither as a harness nor saddle horse, it has been bred with Thoroughbred stock. In turn, the best half-breds were interbred or remated with the Thoroughbred to produce excellent medium and heavyweight hunters. They are excellent breeding stock, and their strains are found in the Clydesdales and Vladimirs. Cleveland Bays were first imported to the United States in 1820 as breeding stock, and they produced a variety of utility horses. The Yorkshire Coach Horse is the result of the same breeding as the Cleveland Bay and derives its name from the English county where it was developed.

CLYDESDALE   One of the best-known horses, the Clydesdale stands over more ground than any other draft breed. Its most identifiable features, apart from their massiveness, are the large feather of fine quality hair on their fetlocks and the appealing white markings on the face and usually on all four legs. The legs are superb; straight and directly under the shoulder, they move in a true, straight, and springy manner. This character of legginess is a basic feature of distinction between the Clydesdale and its near relatives the Shire and the Suffolk. With its symmetry, activity, strength, and endurance, the Clydesdale is broken easily to harness and makes an excellent draft horse.

The name Clydesdale is taken from the Clyde River in Scotland, where the breed developed. Its massiveness was a deliberate objective of early breeding. According to history, the importance of size was impressed upon the British by the Roman conquest. Since the earliest history of horses in Britain describes a horse akin to the Scandinavian pony, a royal edict was issued to systematically increase the size of British horses.

The blood of all the British draft horses (including the Shire and the Suffolk as well as the Clydesdale) was derived essentially from Flemish sources. Indeed, as many as a hundred Flemish stallions were imported at one time. In turn, the Clydesdales have in some cases been bred to produce a more massive stock for other purposes. In the United States, for example, ranchers attempted to increase the weight of their horses on the mountain ranges. They have discovered, however, that the gain in weight has reduced the agility and aptitude of their cow horses. When the Clydesdale is crossed with the Shire to produce the British rough-legged draft horse, the resulting animal is considered superior to either of its parents. It is an im-

provement upon the Shire because of the basic quality contributed by the Clydesdale, and it surpasses the Clydesdale in
strength and substance as a result of the Shire connection. The
blend is being established in the United States as a National
breed.

COB The Cob is not a breed but rather a type of riding horse
or pony that stands no higher than 15.2 hands; it has the substance and bone of a heavyweight hunter. The head is small,
and the neck is arched and elegant. The hindquarters are generous and well-rounded; until a law was passed prohibiting it,
the Cob's tail was docked. Because of his size, the Cob has traditionally been a mount for the elderly, since he could be easily
mounted from the ground, and for children who have out-
grown ponies but are still too young to ride a full-sized hunter.
Much like the Thoroughbred, the Cob's gaits are low and
straight, which gives comfort to the rider and makes him an
ideal hacking horse. He also has the advantage of an inherent
jumping ability, making him a useful and versatile riding
horse.

COLORADO RANGER This horse is a spotted horse, distinguished
by its color markings. On a base of white or red roan, its
spots may be either black or brown. A characteristic of this
breed is its long flowing mane and tail, as well as its very
fine silky hair. Its origins have been traced to a cross between
an Arab and a Barb. *See also* SPOTTED HORSE.

COMTOIS A heavy draft horse similar to the Auxois, the Seine
Inferieure, and the Trait du Nord. They are used for heavy
agricultural work as well as carriage horses. Introduced to
southern France by the Burgundians, they are believed to be
derived from German horses.

CONNEMARA PONY The Irish Connemara Pony originally may
have evolved from the Sorraia Pony of Spain, although for hundreds of years Barb and Arab blood has been infused to improve the pony's characteristics. It has a well-shaped body,
hardy constitution, and docile temperament. Between its black
tail and mane, the original color was dun with a dorsal stripe.
Now these ponies may be grey, bay, or dark brown—with or
without white markings. They average between 13 and 14 hands
and are quite well known for their jumping ability.

CORLAY BRETON *See* BRETON.

COSTENO   Also known as the Peruvian Criollo, the Costeno is one of three basic Peruvian breeds. As an excellent saddle horse, it is the preferred of the trio. While noted for its large chest and thin fine hair, it is best known for its smooth easy gait.

COSTONEGA   A very little-known breed that is the heaviest native American draft horse.

CRIOLLO   Introduced to South America in 1535 from Spain, the imported horses roamed wild throughout the Argentine pampas. From there they have spread with little change to Venezuela, Uruguay, and Brazil (where they are called "Crioulo"). The basic Argentine breed of Criollo has a tremendous constitution with great stamina and endurance. All colors are encountered, although the dun shade is preferred. The Brazilian Crioulo is a bit smaller than its Argentinian relative, and it has benefited over time from an infusion of Alter blood.

DALES PONY   The Dales Pony is a very strong pony widely used by sheep herders in the English highlands. *See* FELL PONY.

DARASHOORI, also SHIRAZI   This little-known breed is a descendant of the Arab. They are popular riding horses because of their easy gait and gentle disposition. A distinguishing feature of the breed is its fine glossy coat.

DARTMOOR PONY   The Dartmoor Pony is a smallish pony found in the Devon area of southwestern England. They used to run wild over the famous Moors but are now quite domesticated. It is a strong and popular children's riding pony, with attractive features including a full mane and tail. They are similar to the Exmoor pony.

DEMI-SANG TROTTER   *See* ANGLO-NORMAN TROTTER.

DOLE-GUDBRANDSDALER   The Dole-Gudbrandsdaler is a small strong draft-type horse found in the cold highland valleys of Norway and Sweden. These hardy animals are equally at home in the role of pack horse on the narrow icy mountain trails or as saddle mounts transporting men over long distances. The Dole, as he is sometimes called, is distinguished by his very long mane and tail (which frequently touches the ground) and the profusion of feathers from his legs. Bearing a striking resemblance to the Fell pony, it is believed that both

207

of these strains as well as the Nordheste and the Scottish Highland pony share a common ancestor in an ancient Celtic pony breed. A related horse is the Dole-Trotter, which is bred specifically for racing.

DON   The Don horse is native to the Russian steppes in the regions of the Don River to the Caucasus Mountains. Originally a rather small, tough, and active animal, this breed has been greatly improved from its Mongolian-Kalmuck beginnings by crossings with Oriental, Turkmene, Thoroughbred, Persian, Anglo-Arab, and Karabair blood. Today the horse averages 15.1 to 15.3 hands in height, boasts an excellent shoulder behind a handsome head and neck, and a somewhat rectangular frame based on what appears to be a long strong leg. As a breed the Dons tend to mature late but are exceptionally rugged and renowned for their stamina.

DONGOLA   The Dongola is a horse indigenous to Ethiopia and Eritrea, composed of Barb and Oriental lines.

DRAUGHT BRETON   *See* BRETON.

DULMEN PONY   One of the two native German ponies, the Dulmen is a semiwild pony indigenous to the Meerfelder Bruch.

EAST FRIESIAN   The East Friesian is excellent breeding stock, and its blood is found in many of the better-known breeds, such as the Masuren, Oldenburg, Toric, and Frederiksborg breeds.

EAST PRUSSIAN   This is one of the oldest German horse breeds. It originated from native strains—the Schweiken and the Panje. With the importation of a Thoroughbred stallion from England (Perfectionist), the line expanded and improved considerably. The devastation of the waning days of World War II marked a major threshold in the development of this breed. With the Russian invasion of East Prussia in 1945, the breed became divided into two groups. About a thousand horses escaped westward and are now known as Trakehner horses. Those that remained are now called Masuren horses.

The Trakehner breed, the durable survivors of the long march, has now become a well-bred, light, elegant saddle horse. In addition to its even disposition, the Trakehner is known for its jumping ability.

The Masuren breed remains a heavier long-boned horse. It

is not as fine an animal as its relative the Trakehner, although it shares the characteristic pleasant temperament. It is more frequently used for heavier draft work.

EASTLAND   An easygoing heavy draft horse, the Eastland is related to the North Swedish horse.

EGYPTIAN ARAB   The original and finest Arabs are the Egyptian Arabs, or as they are sometimes called, the "Original Arab." They began as show horses but are now primarily bred for racing. There are two types of Egyptian Arabs, one known as the Kuhaylan type and the other as the Siglavy type. The former is somewhat coarser in comparison to the compact, clean Siglavy. *See* ARABIAN.

EINSIEDLER   This horse, similar to the Freiberger, is bred and used primarily for military purposes. It is equally appropriate for draft and saddle purposes.

ERMLAND   Also known as the Stuhm breed, this little-known line is found in West Prussia.

EXMOOR PONY   Perhaps the best known of England's five native pony breeds, the Exmoor is also the oldest. It is found in the southwest corner of the country, where the cold, windy winters have fostered the distinctive, thick, wiry Exmoor coat. The ponies should not exceed 12.2 hands and are always of a solid color.

FELL PONY   A breed of wild pony native to Cumberland and Westmorland, England. Originally used only as pack animals, these tough little animals are an undemanding saddle mount for both children and adults. The Fell Pony is characterized by great strength and surefootedness. He is deep through the girth, has a short back, good shoulders, a particularly heavy coat, and luxurious feathers on his legs. He is presumed to be descended from an ancient Celtic pony breed, which appears to include the Gudbrandsdaler as well as the Nordheste and the Scottish Highland Pony in the common ancestry.

FINNISH DRAFT   A mixture of local ponies and imported lines have produced the Finnish Draft and its close relative, the Finnish Universal. The Finnish Draft is the heavier and stronger of the two and plays a very important role in Finland's timber and logging industry.

209

FINNISH UNIVERSAL This breed, like the Finnish Draft, is derived from obscure origins. Lighter and speedier than the Draft, the Universal is used much more for pleasure, especially trotting. Recently the Finnish draft and the Finnish Universal have been crossbred to produce an attractive horse retaining the best characteristics of both breeds.

FJORD PONY Introduced into Denmark from Norway at the turn of the century, the Fjord pony has a very long line extending to the Viking period. This is a hearty heritage, and the Fjord pony remains exceptionally strong, sturdy, alert, and surprisingly good tempered. It is also known as the Norwegian Pony or Westland Pony.

FLEMISH HORSE The Flemish horse is the earliest distinct type breed to evolve from European prehistory. It is the granddaddy of all draft horse breeds. It is known as the Great Horse of the Middle Ages after the famous Battle of Tours in 732. The giant black and powerful Flemish horses, carrying knights encased in heavy armour, literally smashed into the invading Muslims on their delicate Arabian horses and preserved Europe from the Arab domination that befell the Iberian peninsula. (For the closest modern relative of the Flemish Horse, *see* BELGIAN.)

FREDERIKSBORG The famous Frederiksborg line may actually be chronologically considered in two periods. From the Middle Ages to World War II, the Royal Frederiksborg blood (produced by combining Neapolitan and Andalusian stock) dominated European breeders. This old Frederiksborg was an excellent show and parade horse and contributed to the Lipizzaner line. The second period has been marked with considerable infusion of Oldenburg, Holstein, and East Friesian blood. The current Frederiksborg is a solid light harness or saddle horse also suitable for light agricultural duties.

FREIBERGER A sound, solid breed of medium height, the Freiberger contains Norman, Breton, and Holstein blood. It is an allover compact animal and is known for its surefootedness.

FRIESIAN The Friesian is a very old, strong, and compact horse. It is distinguished by always being black in color and by its ample mane, tail, and feathers on its legs. In addition to being an elegant show horse, the Friesian is appreciated for its high action trot. According to legend, this high speedy trot was developed because of the muddy, water-covered land typical of Holland. In the last fifty years, the breed has been infused with Oldenburg blood to avert extinction; in turn, the Friesian breed has contributed much to other famous trotter breeds, such as the Russian Orloff, the English Hackney, and the American Saddlebred.

FULANI HORSE A small horse that is bred by the wandering Fulani tribesmen on the borders of the Federal Republic of Cameroon and Nigeria. These tough and hardy equines come in all colors with varying conformation. Their ancestry is not clearly defined, though they do carry some Oriental blood. They are used both as saddle horses and pack animals.

FURIOSO The Furioso is a minor classic breed in eastern Europe. It is an elegant, correct, and composed saddle mount. Averaging about 16 hands in height, the Furioso is a first-class animal that is in considerable demand as breeding stock.

GALICENO This breed, which is quite common in Mexico, only recently (1959) was imported into the Southern United States. Their obscure origin probably includes Iberian blood mixed with local strains. Its features betray these origins: only slightly larger than pony-sized (12 to 13 hands), shallow chest, straight shoulders, and found in any color. But the Galiceno does have a good head with intelligent eyes and is known for its fast natural walk.

GARRANO PONY This pony is one of the earliest identifiable equines. It is also the most common of Portugal's horses, accounting for three quarters of the country's entire horse population. The influence of this breed may be traced to the Spanish Andalusian and to several breeds in Africa and Mexico.

GELDERLAND A little-known breed, the Gelderland is one of Holland's three principal breeds. It is derived frrom early Spanish, Norman, and Norfolk Roadster blood. It is usually chestnut or gray in color with white markings and is easily identifiable by an unusually high tail carriage. As an active horse with a great deal of knee action, the Gelderland has been used for show jumping and as a harness horse.

GERMAN COACH HORSE   The German Coach Horse is directly related to the Flemish Horse and is similar to but lighter than the Belgian. These heavy horses were used to haul Kaiser Wilhelm's *uhlans* into Belgium during World War I.

GOTLAND HORSE   A small tough breed of horses native to the Swedish island of Gotland, where for many years they ran wild. Although they still are found today on the island, they are also bred by mainland farmers.

GRONINGEN   This is the third of the three Dutch breeds, the others being the Gelderland and the Friesian. The Groningen is a heavy powerful horse with a deep barrel and strong back. It is usually black or dark brown. Unlike the Friesian, which when threatened with extinction was rescued by careful management, the Groningen appears to be dying out.

GUZMANES   A minor Spanish breed derived from the Barb stallion named Guzman.

HACKNEY   The Hackney is a breed used primarily as a harness horse and renowned for its high-stepping, brilliant trotting action. The modern Hackney is generally bay, brown, black, or chestnut, usually with some white markings, and stands between 14.3 to 15.2 hands in height. Its head is small and either straight or convex in profile with a small muzzle, large eyes, and small ears. The shoulders of the Hackney are flat and powerful, and his body is compact with short legs and strong hocks, which end in well-shaped feet.

The walk of the Hackney is important and should be brisk and springy. The trot should be lofty and straight, with the foreleg being thrown well forward as well as perpendicular to the ground.

During the past eighty years, the Hackney Pony has evolved from the horse variety and is now regarded as a separate breed. These ponies range in height from 12 to 14 hands and are becoming increasingly popular in the United States as harness ponies for show.

HACKNEY PONY   *See* HACKNEY.

HAFLINGER   A small powerful breed of mountain horse found in the South Tirol area in the Bavarian Alps. These sturdy equines evolved from a cross of German and Austrian

Noroker horses of Oriental stock. It is this Arabian blood which is credited with the fine, handsome head and unusually good temperament of the Haflinger. Their strength and sure-footedness make them particularly well suited to the mountainous terrain, and they are frequently used as pack animals.

HAITI PONY   The Haiti Pony is a common type of pony found on the island of Hispaniola. Through extensive inbreeding, the pony has largely erased its original blood (probably Oriental) and is now rather nondescript.

HANOVERIAN   The Hanoverian is the most important light horse breed in West Germany. It is a strong well-bred saddle horse of considerable size, standing between 16 and 17 hands. Its long history may be traced back to Germany's indigenous ponies, the Dulmen and the Senner. The early Hanoverian contained a healthy input of Neapolitan blood during the fifteenth and sixteenth centuries, which gave it the characteristic of the convex head. Its primary use then was as a carriage horse and farm animal. The modern Hanoverian has received improvements from the Thoroughbred and the Trakehner lines. This new type, with a better head, well-set neck, and good withers, has developed into a ranking saddle horse. Its distinguished action and jumping ability have made the Hanoverian a valuable show jumper, hunter, and *dressage* horse. Hanoverians are very popular as breeding stock, and their blood may be found in the Braunschweig, Mecklenburg, Pommern, and other lines.

HIGHLAND PONY   The Highland Pony is the lesser-known of Scotland's two native pony breeds, the other being the Shetland. Although at one time there were two types of Highland ponies, the older and purer Western Isles type gradually has merged with the Mainland type to produce the modern Highland Pony. He is exceptionally strong and capable of packing considerable weight. Most frequently of dun color, their very long mane and tail are usually silver tinted. The most prominent characteristic of the Highland Pony is its short strong legs under noticeably muscular quarters and loins.

HOKAIDO or HOCAIDO   A common pony breed found in Japan. It is not unlike most Asian ponies, such as the Mongolian or Chinese types.

HOLSTEIN   Dating back to the 14th century, the Holstein is now a relatively rare German horse. Contributions to the line have come from Oriental and Spanish lines and most recently from Cleveland Bay blood. It is noted for its long legs, strong bone (averaging nine-and-a-half inches), and long stride, which have produced its considerable jumping abilities. However, with its Cleveland Bay blood, it is also a heavy horse used for general saddle and farming work.

HUZUL   A descendant of the Tarpan, the Huzul is a mountain pony of great endurance. He is encountered in prominent dun shades with a dark mane and tail. The stock has been improved with the introduction of Arab blood. Since he is often found in the Carpathian region of Poland, he is also known as the Carpathian Pony.

ICELAND PONY   These ponies were brought to the island by the Norse settlers in the late ninth century. Over the years two types of ponies have been developed: draft and riding strains. The draft ponies were used extensively for farming, until the introduction of the American jeep. The riding pony has a distinctive trot (known as the "Tølt") and is widely used for trekking since Icelanders enjoy the popular sport of cross-country camping. Recently imported to the United States, the pony is gaining in popularity.

IRISH HUNTER   A type rather than a breed, the Irish Hunter has been sought after for more than 2000 years. It emerged during the seventeenth century following the introduction of Thoroughbred blood to Ireland. Yet it is larger than the Thoroughbred, standing rarely under 16 hands, has a larger head, longer legs, and, in general, carries more bone. Other characteristics include good if not overly large feet, unusual surefootedness, good shoulders, and powerful quarters. These desirable qualities are believed to reflect the influence of Ireland's limestone terrain. The combination of these features have produced jumpers and hunters of outstanding quality and character. Their spirit, courage, and love of jumping have made the Irish Hunter much in demand for international show jumping competitions.

JAF   This breed is a very attractive, hearty desert horse. Hard and active, the Jaf is known for its desert-bred feet and very tough hoofs. Indeed, in their native areas of Iran, they are never shod.

JAVA PONY   Another of the many domestic pony breeds found in remote pockets of the world, this breed is equally undistinguished, comes in all colors, and has no precise conformation. Nevertheless, they are excellent service animals that perform a sundry of tasks despite the tropical heat of Indonesia.

JOMUD   A direct descendant of the very old Turkoman breed and a relative of the better-known Russian Achal-Teke breed, the Jomud is a wiry desert horse. It is capable of surviving in the hot, waterless desert environment and, in addition, has considerable stamina and endurance.

JUTLAND   The Jutland is a very old horse and is traceable to the twelfth century. It is a heavy, cold-blooded draft horse weighing up to 1,800 pounds and standing up to 15.3 hands. These features reflect the influence of the Suffolk Punch, Cleveland Bay, and Yorkshire Coach blood found in the Jutland. It has rather short legs with feathers, an overall compact body, and is usually chestnut in color, although it was originally black and brown. (For its near relative, *see* SCHLESWIG.)

KABARDIN   An excellent Russian mountain horse, the Kabardin is considered the best of all mountain riding horses. It is known as a surefooted, fearless horse with hard feet and tough tendons. The Kabardin is the product of Turkoman and Arab blood, and, in turn, when crossed with Thoroughbred blood, it is known as the Anglo-Kabardin breed. An unusual attribute of the Kabardin is its sharp sense of direction.

KARABAIT   The Karabait is found in the Georgian Republic in the Soviet Union and is an ancient breed of horse. It is noted for its endurance and is frequently of golden chestnut color, although all colors are encountered. It is believed there are three types of Karabait used respectively as a saddle horse, in harness, and for pack transport. This breed has particularly influenced the development of the Don breed.

KARABAKH   The Karabakh is an elegant racing horse from the Azerbaijan region of the Soviet Union. Its small head and straight face lead a smallish chest between good flat shoulders and strong quarters. Its coat is marked by black points and most frequently dun in color. Recently the Karabakh has been introduced to England.

215

KARACABEY   Although there are several other strains bred in Turkey, the Karacabey is the only horse native to the country. They are raised in seven studs, which are organized by the state and are used as cavalry remounts as well as light draft horses in agricultural work. The average size is between 15.3 and 16.1 hands, with emphasis on stamina and conformation.

KASANSKI PONY   The Kasanski Pony of Kasan province, Soviet Union, is a type of pony of the Viatka breed found in the Balkans. It is marked by a prominent dorsal stripe on a dun, chestnut, or palomino coat, a somewhat plain head, and fairly good conformation.

KATHIAWARI PONY   A breed of pony presumed to be of Arab descent, which is found on the Kathiawar peninsula located in the northwest coast of India (now Pakistan). These ponies may come in all colors, including spotted and indicate their Arabian admixture by the characteristic inward turn of the tips of their ears. They are a particularly hardy strain as are their close relative the Marwari ponies, which are found in the neighboring Marwar province.

KIRGHIZ   The Kirghiz—from the region of that name in the Soviet Union—is a domestic horse at home in mountain areas. The old Kirghiz was used largely as a pack animal, although a new Kirghiz has emerged recently with the infusion of Don or Thoroughbred blood. This breed has proved to be quite a fine saddle horse.

KLADRUBER   An ancient horse traceable back 500 years, the Kladruber nearly became extinct by the time of World War II. This older Kladruber is a massive, big-chested horse that can be up to 19 hands in height. It is similar to the Lipizzaner breed and equally in demand as parade and coach horses. Following the war, the breed was saved by the introduction of Oldenburg, Hanoverian, and Anglo-Norman blood. It is now slightly smaller (only 18 hands!) and generally grey rather than the original black or grey. They still carry their characteristic good shoulders and quarters, high-set tail, and strong clean legs and joints.

KNABSTRUP   The Knabstrup is a principal European spotted horse. It is found mostly in Denmark and was introduced to that area in the early 1800s from Spain. Its characteristics are similar to the Frederiksborg. *See also* SPOTTED HORSE.

KONIK The Konik is the most directly domesticated descendant of the Tarpan. It is found in eastern Poland and has influenced many Polish breeds and Russian horses. The Konik is well-proportioned, although often cow-hocked, and, according to some, rather heavy headed. But its good disposition, long life, and exceptional fertility help account for its wide influence on other breeds. Its usual colors are yellow or grey and blue dun.

KUHAYLAN ARAB A type of Egyptian Arab breed. *See* EGYPTIAN ARAB.

KURDISTAN This Turkish breed is a popular and common agricultural work horse. It is rather thin-necked and flat-chested; these features are more than offset by its good temper, strength, and willingness to work. Recently the Kurdistan has been bred with other heavier horses to produce an animal (known as the Kurdistan Half-Breed) suitable for transport and portage uses.

KUSTANAIR This is a very durable horse with considerable stamina found in the grasslands of the Kazakh Republic, Soviet Union. It has been improved recently with the infusion of Don blood.

LATVIAN *See* LITHUANIAN.

LIBYAN BARB Although descended from the purebred Arab and the Barb, the Libyan Barb has degenerated over the centuries into the common "North African Horse." While neither particularly attractive nor of good conformation, it is redeemed by its formidable constitution and very active character. As a general utility horse, it is used for all purposes including military service and agricultural work.

LIPIZZANER (Also Lippizaner): the zenith of the show horse. For more than two centuries, the Spanish Riding School in Vienna has been maintaining the standard of excellent in the skills of riding achievable by both horse and man. The name of the school reflects the Spanish origin of the Lipizzaner (Conversano and Neapolitano). Capitalizing on this breed's intelligence and sense of memory, they are trained for their performances which are held in Vienna every Sunday during the summer. Since Lipizzaners are known to mature late, their training does not begin until they are four years old, and the initial schooling takes two years. They are thus at least six years old before they even begin to learn their special skills. Even so, the horse specializes in only one or two movements to attain their renowned perfection. The rider, who starts by working in the stables, also will have a course of several years ahead of him before he can make his earliest public appearance. Taking this all into account, it still takes twelve years for a rider to achieve fully qualified *Bereiter* (or Riding Master) status.

While the Lipizzaner may come in several colors, only the ones born black which turn into grey and then white are used by the school. They have large heads perched on substantial, high, convex necks. True to their show-horse use, they are extremely attractive horses, with strong shoulders and legs and thick, luxurious manes and tails. Their late maturity is matched by a long life—some perform as long as thirty years. The breed originated near Trieste in Northern Italy and is now found in Austria and Hungary.

LITHUANIAN   This exceptionally strong harness horse has a large head, long neck, very strong legs, and averages 16.2 hands in height. The Lithuanian is derived from the Zemaituka breed, but to increase its strength and pulling power, it has been reinforced with Finnish Draft Horse, Swedish Ardennes, and Oldenburg blood. These abilities are now considered its most important features, and standards must now be achieved before the stallions are permitted to stand at stud. They are usually found to be bay in color, although occasionally a black or chestnut Lithuanian are encountered. It is a very close relative to the Latvian breed.

LLANERO   Also known as the "Venezuelan Prairie Horse," the Llanero is similar in conformation and heritage to the Criollo of Brazil and Argentina. They are derived from the Barb and and the Andalusian horses introduced into the Western Hemisphere by the Spanish in the sixteenth century. Adaptable to any kind of work, they are numerous and popular throughout Venezuela. The most common colors are dun or yellow with black or dark manes and tails or white and yellow pintos.

LOFOTEN PONY Now extinct, the Lofoten Pony was a descendant of the Tarpan breed.

LOKAI A little-known Russian horse from the mountain region of Tadzhikistan in Central Asia. It is quite similar in conformation to the Kabardin breed.

LUSITANO The Lusitano is one of two native Portuguese breeds. Like the other breed, the Alter, it is similar to the Spanish Andalusian. This breed is a very solid, attractive horse with a delicate head and ears, large eyes, and noticeably large neck. A distinguishing feature is its long wavy tail, which is set lower than on most breeds. It is extremely popular in central and southern Portugal.

MANGALARGA A descendant of the Portuguese Alter breed. It is a relative of the Brazilian Campolino breed.

MARSH TACKY A wild race of indigenous American ponies native to the Carolinas. They are said to have descended from bands of wild Thoroughbreds that roamed the area after the Civil War and in characteristics are slightly more refined than the Chincoteague ponies.

MARWARI *See* KATHIAWARI.

MASUREN *See* EAST PRUSSIAN.

METIS TROTTER This is a new breed of trotters now being developed in Russia. It is achieved by crossing two excellent trotting breeds—the Orloff and the Standardbred. The result has been a fine quality trotting horse for the ever-growing sport of harness racing.

MEXICAN HORSE This is the popular common horse of Mexico. Found in various colors and conformation, it is a remnant of the original horses brought to the New World by Cortés in the sixteenth century.

MINHO *See* GARRANO.

MISSOURI FOX TROTTING HORSE This horse from the Ozarks is perhaps better described as a type rather than a breed. It is known and identified by its specialized "fox trot" gait, which is a broken gait consisting of a brisk walk with the front feet and a trot with the hind feet. The horse bobs his head with each step at this gait, while his feet maintain a steady cadence at a speed from five to ten mph. These horses come in all solid colors and pintos as well. They should be close coupled and compact and should be up to carrying weight. They average between 14 and 16 hands in height and present an overall picture of good conformation.

MORGAN The Morgan is an American breed that originated with a horse named Justin Morgan, foaled in 1793, that was so prepotent his offspring always favored him rather than the mare. This prepotency was carried on from generation to generation, until the horses were recognized as a breed, and Justin Morgan was established as the one foundation sire.

The description of Justin Morgan is perhaps the most adequate representation of the breed: Justin Morgan stood 14 hands high. He was a compact, extraordinarily solid horse, very muscular, with powerful shoulders, thick neck and crest, shapely legs, and well-formed feet. He was bay in color with a thick, heavy mane and tail and long, shaggy fetlocks, which are the only characteristics that time has modified.

The Morgan of today now ranges between 14.1 and 15.1 hands in height with bay, brown, black, and chestnut being the most usual colors. His versatility is evidenced by the variety of classes that may be offered for Morgans at horse shows including: Park Horses; Park Horses in Harness; Parade Horses; English Pleasure Horses; Western Pleasure Horses; Pleasure Driving Horses; Combination Pleasure Horses (ride and drive); Stock Horses; Cutting Horses; and Roadster Horses, in addition to being used in pulling contests. The Morgan is further renowned for his extremely kind nature, and this coupled with his remarkable physical strength, adaptability, and compact size make him a most popular breed.

MOROCHUCO One of the three Peruvian breeds (*see* COSTENO and CHOLA), that developed from the original Spanish horses imported during the sixteenth century, the Morochuco is a small sturdy mountain horse, which has found popularity as an all-purpose agricultural horse.

MUSTANG The Mustang, or the "Spanish Mustang"—mustang is derived from the Spanish word *mesteño*—is a direct descendant of the Spanish horses introduced to the New World by Cortés. They have migrated through Mexico to the United States, where many became Indian ponies (for example, *see* PAWNEE PONY), when they were widely used for the Pony Express, and finally developed into the cow pony. Their blood may be found in the American Quarter Horse. There are very few remaining today, and these are not to be confused with the semiwild horses of Nevada today.

NARRAGANSETT PACER   Named after Narragansett Bay in Rhode Island, these small sorrel-colored horses are distinguished by their predisposition to pacing. Popularized in Cooper's *Last of the Mohicans,* the origin of this breed is obscure. In Colonial times Rhode Island was less puritanical and rigid than the other colonies, which seems to have made horse racing—and the breeding of race horses—more acceptable. Slowly the breed spread throughout the Colonies, and it contributed to the development of the Tennessee Walking Horse.

NEW FOREST PONY   One of the five native English ponies, the New Forest Pony is one of the oldest. It is a slightly larger pony, usually 12 to 14 hands, with drooping, rather narrow quarters, and extremely sure feet. It has a large, Oriental-type head, reflecting the past infusion of Arab blood. Quiet and willing, it makes an excellent riding pony for the teenager or small adult.

NEW ZEALAND PONY   A common undistinguished breed that proliferates in New Zealand. It is at heart a cow pony, of any color or conformation, and possibly originated from the Asian ponies.

NIEDERSACHEN HEAVY DRAFT   This German breed of draft horse, like other heavy horses of the area, is most likely derived from the original Belgian and Ardennes bloodlines. Today it is similar to the Rhineland Heavy Draft in both color and conformation. It is a very heavy, almost square horse, which is noted for its low-slung belly.

NIGERIAN HORSE   Still another of the many common indigenous animals of obscure origin, the Native Nigerian Horse shows traces of Barb blood. It is used as a utilitarian, general-purpose horse.

NORAM TROTTER   *See* ANGLO-NORMAN TROTTER.

NORD HESTUR   *See* NORTH SWEDISH TROTTER.

221

NORIKER   This is an ancient breed traceable to the mountain region of southern Europe, possibly from the area once called Noricum by the Romans. At one time there were two types of Noriker horses, the Oberlander and the Pinzgauer (a heavier spotted type), but the line has been consolidated into one Noriker or "South German Cold-Blood" breed. It is a smallish horse, larger than the Italian Avelignese pony, which has Noriker blood. Used for heavy agricultural work, this breed has a heavy head, broad chest, wide, strong quarters with a low-set tail, and feathers on its legs.

NORMAN HORSE   The Norman, native to the French province of Normandy, is an excellent, well-bred horse. It has been carefully bred for several hundred years and is now a compact, active, and strong horse. While not as numerous as they once were, they are frequently used to improve other breeds, such as the Breton and the Charollais. There are now two types of Normans—the saddle type, which was used widely by the military, and the cob, which is a heavier general-purpose animal used in agriculture.

NORTH AFRICAN HORSE   *See* LIBYAN BARB.

NORTH SWEDISH HORSE   Evolved from ancient Scandinavian ponies (it resembles the Finnish breed) and a relative to the Norwegian Dole, the North Swedish is a cold-blooded horse that has many attributes of a warm-blood. Although it almost died out around the turn of the century, it has enjoyed a comeback and now is very popular. It is noted for its energetic, exceptionally hardy constitution—it is strong, has a long life-span, and may even be immune to many diseases. A deep body and great strength have made the North Swedish Horse very useful in agriculture and in the timber industry.

NORTH SWEDISH TROTTER   Also called the Nord Hestur, this breed is the only cold-blooded trotter in the world. It enjoys the remarkable constitution of its heavier cousin the North Swedish Horse, averages about 15.2 hands in height, and is usually chestnut or brown in color.

NORTHLANDS PONY   This is the least-known of Norway's three native ponies. (*See* FJORD—NORWEGIAN or WESTLAND as it is also called—and DOLE-GUDBRANDSDALER.) It is descended from the basic Tarpan breed and is usually associated with the "Baltic" group of pony breeds. (*See* KONIK.) The Northlands are strong, sturdy ponies, about 13 hands high, with smallish heads and ears. Usually dark colored, they typically have a very full mane and tail.

OBERLANDER   *See* NORIKER.

OLDENBURG   The Oldenburg is a basic German breed found in the northern part of the country. Somewhat heavier than its near relative the Holstein, the Oldenburg has traces of Anglo-Arab and Thoroughbred blood. This breed is a well-bred cavalry and harness horse with a compact muscular body, but rather short legs. It has been widely used to improve other breeds, such as the Friesian, the Frederiksborg, the Lithuanian, the Latvian, and the Masuran.

ORLOV or ORLOFF TROTTER   The popularity of trotting races in the Soviet Union gave rise to the development (by Count Orlov Tschesmensky) of the Orlov Trotter. It is a large horse, rather bony, but of good conformation. Its large head, arched neck, muscular shoulders, and good legs reflect the purpose for which it was bred. Indeed, the Orlov Trotter was considered the standard of Trotter excellence until the development of the American Standardbred. The breed has been improved further, however, by Count Rostopschin; this new type is known as the Orlov-Rostopschin Trotter.

OSAGE HORSE   *See* PAWNEE HORSE.

PAINT HORSE   *See* SPOTTED HORSE.

PAWNEE HORSE   The Pawnee Indian tribe of the plains country of the Arkansas River area (now Nebraska) were the first Indians in the north to use horses. The Pawnee Horse was captured from the Spanish Villaspur expedition (and, in turn, captured by the Osage tribe, hence it is known also as the "Osage Horse"), and for many years this breed represented the purest Spanish blood in the Midwest.

PERCHERON   A breed of heavy draft horse that originated in the LePerche district of France. The Percheron combines extensive muscular development with style and grace. Although he rarely stands less than 16 hands in height and weighs upwards of 1,900 pounds, the Percheron's Arabian blood is evident in his smoothly proportioned body and head, which is finely chiseled and delicate. More than 90 percent of this breed is black or grey in color.

PINTO   The Spanish name for a Paint Horse. It is believed the American Spotted Horse came in large part from Spain. *See* SPOTTED HORSE.

PINZGAUER   *See* NORIKER.

POLISH ARAB   Like the German Arab, this breed is based on the imported Arabian stock that has been modified slightly to adapt to local climatic conditions. As a consequence, it is larger than the original Egyptian Arab, although it retains the classic Arabian features of the face, shoulders, and sloping quarters.

PONY OF THE AMERICAS   The Pony of the Americas is the only domestic American pony that is a specific breed with an official studbook. The breed was founded by Mr. Leslie Broomhower of Mason City, Iowa, by crossing a Shetland stallion on an Appaloosa mare that passed on to the pony strain the Appaloosa color characteristics. Since the Appaloosa is considered a color breed, the Pony of the Americas is essentially a pony with distinctive markings. To qualify for registration, a pony must be neither smaller than 11.2 hands nor taller than 13 hands and must meet the distinguishing markings of the Appaloosa breed—that is, mottled skin, vertical striping on the hoofs, white encircling the eyes, and an acceptable color pattern. *See* APPALOOSA.

POSTIER BRETON   *See* BRETON.

PRZHEVALSKI   The Przhevalski horse of northwestern Mongolia (Gobi) is historically unique as the only true descendant of a wild horse that has not become extinct as a wild species. It represents the so-called steppe horse of Asia; by contrast the European wild horse (the "forest type") and the African (the "desert type") progenitors of domestic breeds have not survived domestication and conscious breeding. Despite attempts to tame this animal, they have never been broken. The name is ascribed to a Russian explorer who first reported on the breed. It is sometimes spelled Przewalski and may be found at some zoos.

QUARTER HORSE   The American Quarter Horse traces his ancestry to Spanish and British horses brought to the New World during the earliest periods of European colonization of North America. His name is derived as a result of his reputation for remarkable speed for the distance of a quarter of a mile and finds its origin in the early colonial sport of "quarter pathing." The English settlers brought with them a deep love of horse racing; despite the thickly forested countryside along most of the Eastern seaboard, they were determined to hold their race meets. The first of these contests were held on the streets of the Colonies, but this soon proved too hazardous for the inhabitants, and the race paths had to be carved out of the bush from a quarter of a mile to 500 yards in length. Since very few Colonists could afford to keep a horse just for racing, the same horses that competed in these quarter meetings also carried their masters on daily rounds, and were frequently hitched to a wagon or plow, and helped round up the small herds of beef and dairy stock to be driven into primitive cow pens used by the early settlers.

The long hours spent in the company of man, and the early experience of working closely with other domestic animals are factors thought to account for the breed's exceptional responsiveness and friendly disposition among human beings and for the uncanny "cow sense," or sharpened instinct, for other animals that has made the Quarter Horse superior at all forms of cattle work. This kindly attitude toward man and other animals, combined with his versatility and adaptability, proved to be saving virtues at a time when the future looked dismal for the Quarter Horse. Developed principally along the Eastern seaboard, the Quarter Horse and short-distance racing were soon displaced by Thoroughbreds and longer running events, which stirred a keener interest in the Atlantic Colonies and inspired the settlers to build oval tracks.

Pushed westward and southward with a poorer class of planters, pioneers, and frontiersmen, the Quarter Horse was able to survive his misfortunes in the East, not only because of the lightning sprints that had earned him fame in short-distance running, but also because of the rugged, stalwart character and instinctive response to other animals—ideal qualities for the long haul to the West and the cattlework to be done there. The Quarter Horse thus found a new home and new audiences to inspire with his electric dashes.

225

Now the particular favorite of Westerners, the Quarter Horse breed lists more registrations than all other breeds combined, and the All American Futurity—the Kentucky Derby of Quarter Racing—held at Ruidosa Downs, New Mexico, has the richest purse in all racing history.

Since the first organization to register and record the Quarter Horse was not founded until 1940 and the studbook was not officially opened until 1941, it has taken a great deal of research to construct an accurate picture of precisely how the breed originated and determine the stallions worthy of credit for a major role in founding the breed. The earliest stock to contribute significantly to the breed was a strain known as the Chickasaw Horse. Animals belonging to this family were closely descended from the Spanish stock brought to Florida and other points slightly to the north. The Chickasaw Indians, quick to learn the value of the horse, bought, traded, and stole horses of Spanish importation.

Because of the strong infusion of Oriental blood among horses of Spanish breeding, the Chickasaw herds retained their quality and are thought to have been excellent mounts. Many mares of this strain are suspected to have been secured by the Colonists and crossed with horses brought from England, thus providing a nucleus for the first native breed of the New World.

The sires ultimately decided to have figured most prominently in the formation of the breed and that, in some cases, founded subfamilies of their own are: Janus, 1752; Peacock, 1764; Mark Anthony, 1767; Babram, 1770; Bacchus, 1778; Celer, 1780; Twigg, 1782; Brimmer, 1787; Printer, 1804; Whip, 1809; and Tiger, 1816.

In conformation the modern Quarter Horse is something of a dichotomy. On the one extreme is the breeder's ideal—a chunky, short, rounded animal with excessively muscular haunches and forequarters. On the other hand, there is the racing ideal that so closely parallels the lean, horizontal build of the Thoroughbred as to make the two nearly indistinguishable. Somewhere between the two lies the rancher's version of the "true" Quarter Horse build. Ultimately, the essence of the Quarter Horse is not so much displayed by his looks but by his happy disposition, his willing adaptability, and all but indomitable spirit.

SHETLAND PONY   Undoubtedly, the Shetland is the most popular of all pony breeds. It originated centuries ago in the

Shetland Islands, off the coast of Scotland. Today's purebred Shetland averages about forty-two inches in height and comes in a wide variety of colors. The American type of Shetland is much more refined than the Island type, which resembles a miniature draft horse. The ponies are equally at home under Western or English tack, are natural jumpers of obstacles within reason, and are ideally suited to work in harness.

SHIRE   From east central England comes the tallest of all breeds, the Shire, the height of which averages 17 hands. The Shire is one of the earliest heavy horse breeds to be developed specifically for agricultural uses. He is rangier than the other draft horse types and has a longer back. His legs have an abundance of feathers; in color, he is most often bay, brown, or black.

SPOTTED HORSE   Spotted horses are not a breed, but rather a type of horse distinguished by their color. Although any combination of colors may be encountered, spotted horses are most often predominately white base with varying patches of color. The spots may be of black or brown arrayed in patterns of four general categories: the blanket pattern, the mottled or marbleized pattern, the snowstorm or snowflake pattern, and the leopard or polka-dot pattern. The well-known Appaloosa and Knabstrup breeds proliferate with small spots resembling ink splatters. Paint or pinto horses have large patches of color, and true paints always have a mane and tail that are the same color as the neck and the rump. There are three classifications of paint coloration: Morocco, Overo, and Tobiano. All spotted horses vary widely in conformation. Their legacy is very old, and spotted horses are found in the earliest graphics of mankind.

STANDARDBRED   A distinctly American breed of harness horse, the Standardbred traces his heritage far back into the American past. Almost as soon as the early settlers established an adequate network of roads and turnpikes, there arose the need for a better type of driving horse than those available. As Colonial roadbuilding improved, thus permitting faster and smoother vehicular traffic, the need for faster harness horses began to grow. Of course the Colonists could not resist a diversion as exciting as racing, particularly one in which just about anyone could participate—provided of course that he had a horse and vehicle of some sort—and so harness racing was born on the dirt roads and byways of the young republic.

The Standardbred is descended from the Thoroughbred Messenger; his great-grandson Hambletonian 10 is considered the foundation sire of the breed. Hambletonian 10, much better known as Rysdyck's Hambletonian, was so unattractive as a colt that his owner/breeder, one Jonas Seeley of Orange County, New York, sold him to William Rysdyck, one of his hired hands. Rysdyck raced Hambletonian for a short time at the fairs and meets in upstate New York but met with little success and soon retired him to stud. Almost immediately, Hambletonian 10 established himself as the greatest sire of harness racers that was ever to be seen. At that time of horses racing over the slow tracks and pulling old-fashioned, high-wheeled sulkies, a two-and-a-half-minute mile was remarkably fast time. In spite of this, no less than forty of Hambletonian's progeny equaled or bettered this mark. In the twenty-four years that he stood at stud, he reached such a large number of the best harness mares that something close to ninety percent of the Standardbreds registered today can be traced to him.

The early developers of the Standardbred as a racing animal were concerned more with performance than pedigree. It was through their method of testing a horse at a mile and qualifying to run only those horses that equaled or surpassed a certain "standard," that the name Standardbred was obtained. Today the standard is two minutes, twenty seconds for the mile. A non-Standardbred horse may compete in Standardbred racing events, providing it is able to qualify, but such instances are rare because of the selective and specific breeding for speed practiced among Standardbred breeders. Standardbreds race either at the trot or the pace (*see* HARNESS RACING SECTION), depending on which gait is best suited to the individual horse.

The characteristics of the Standardbred are generally like the Thoroughbred, with certain modifications resulting from the differences in gait and use. The Standardbred is usually heavier-limbed than the Thoroughbred, with a longer body, shorter legs, and greater endurance. The average height is 15.2 hands.

STUHM *See* ERMLAND.

SUFFOLK PUNCH The smallest of the draft horse breeds, the Suffolk Punch stands between 15.2 and 16.2 hands and weighs about 1,800 pounds. The purebred Suffolk exists in only one color—chestnut—with very few white markings. He is the only heavy horse family to trace back to a single stallion—the "Crisp" horse of Ufford, England, foaled in 1768. Although the Suffolk lacks some of the grandeur and majesty that make some of the other draft breeds seem more imposing, his own qualities of strength, gentleness, willingness to work combined with an appetite making him an "easy keeper" endeared him to people the world over.

TENNESSEE WALKING HORSE The Tennessee Walking Horse, although relatively new with its registry officially organized in 1935, finds its history entwined with that of the American Saddler—long before 1835, when the first settlers brought civilization to the frontier West of the Appalachian Mountains in Kentucky, Tennessee, and Missouri. From these early wilderness outposts arose a refined and gracious culture of vast plantations, elegant mansions, magnolia blossoms, and excellent bourbon whiskey.

Instead of the original mountain folk, a populace of moneyed aristocrats, quite given to the accoutrements accompanying gentility, took their place. In the courtly surroundings favored by this class of landed gentry, it was only fitting that the horseflesh should be equally dashing and stylish—a credit to their owners—and so evolved the need for the American Saddle Horse and his cousin the Tennessee Walking Horse.

Since it was virtually impossible to oversee or inspect a plantation in any way but on horseback, these great landowners required a horse that could carry them tirelessly and comfortably for hours in the saddle while they surveyed their lands, supervised the cultivation of crops, and tended to general plantation business. Speed was not a requisite of these "plantation saddle horses," since the purpose of the tours was the careful and leisurely inspection of the entire estate. Owing to the practice of examining the crops by rows, these horses in Tennessee became nicknamed "turn row" horses. Endurance, however, coupled with a gentle, relaxing ride were of the utmost importance, for it just would not do for a gentleman to return from his rounds aching and exhausted from a day of spine-jarring jolts. It was thus that the Tennesseans wished to produce a horse much like the American Saddler, which would be able to accomplish the rounds of the day with minimal strain on his rider as well as himself and which could, when necessary, make a presentable if not exceptional showing on social occasions.

With this in mind, the Tennessee breeders attempted to upgrade the quality of their stock at the beginning of the nineteenth century through crossings with Thoroughbreds, Arabians, Morgans, Saddlers, and Standardbreds. The resulting offspring of this selective breeding were the foundation stock of the present Tennessee Walking Horse breed.

The original stock with which the breeders began was truly a Colonial hodgepodge, mingling the blood of Canadian and Narragansett pacers with that of the Arabian, Thoroughbred, Morgan, and Standardbred strains. When the Tennessee Walking Horse registry was officially organized, it became evident that the greatest number of horses entered in the first volume were direct descendants of a Standardbred trotter named Black Allan. As a result, he was designated Allan F-1 and became the foundation sire of the breed.

Not only are the history and development of the American Saddler and the Tennessee Walking Horse almost indistinguishable, but also the horses themselves are frequently mistaken for one another when viewed by the uninitiated. On the whole, the Tennessee Walking Horse is an animal of less refinement than his cousin, having a noticeably longer back with a tendency toward a certain coarseness in the appearance of his legs and body and a decidedly lower carriage of his tail. His head, while not actually plain by comparison, does not possess the delicate, finely chiseled hauteur exhibited by the Saddler, and his neck is not flexed to such a bold, disdainful carriage as that of the gaited horse. This is in part because his neck is somewhat shorter than the Saddler, and the entire head carriage is lower.

Tennessee Walking Horses, unlike Saddlebreds, may be found in a whole rainbow of colors including the usual chestnut, brown, bay, grey and black, and then extending into white, varying types of roan, piebald, and skewbald as well as a real Palomino gold.

The running walk for which the breed was named is a definite four-beat rhythm in which each individual hoof ascends and descends at distinct intervals. The unusual gliding motion stems from the fact that the Walker uses his legs only from the point at which they are joined to his body at the barrel—downward, leaving the upper portion of the shoulder as well as the surface area of the back on a constant lateral plane. The effort at maintaining a steady horizontal position of the back causes a constant bobbing of the horse's head, a characteristic shared by all Tennessee Walkers. For showing purposes, the official speed of the running walk is between six and eight mph.

In addition to his exceptionally comfortable running walk, the Tennessee Walker is renowned for having a disposition more desirable than that of any other breed, with the possible exception of the Morgan.

TERSK A Russian breed, the Tersk was evolved between 1921 and 1950 at the Tersk and Stavropol Studs in the northern Caucasus to preserve the old Strelets Horse, which was famous in the early part of the twentieth century. The Strelets breed had been produced from pure-bred Arabians bred to Anglo-Arab mares, and so it was that the Tersk was created.

Tersk horses are very much like purebred Arabians, with the exception that they are larger. Their usual color is light grey. Gentleness and a natural aptitude for *dressage* work coupled with their striking appearance makes the Tersk popular for circus acts. They are also particularly well suited to cross-country riding.

THOROUGHBRED The Thoroughbred is undeniably the fastest of all horse types and is considered by many naturalists to be the swiftest creature in the world. He is able to maintain a speed of 45 mph for distances of a mile or more, whereas animals such as the cheetah may achieve a pace of 70 mph but only at the point of maximum acceleration and lasting for a fleeting instant and a few hundred yards. It leaves the animal exhausted.

The conformation of the Thoroughbred, coupled with the generosity of the individual, makes it physically possible for one particular breed to achieve a speed that will leave any other horse in the dust. In relation to other breeds, the Thoroughbred is extremely tall with an average height of 16.0 hands. His long, slender legs move with low, ground-eating strides, which may cover as many as 25 feet and more in one sequence. To attain this fantastic horizontal reach, his action is free and flexible, propelled in each cycle by the forward thrust of the "drive shaft" (the line from the point of the hip to the hock, which in the Thoroughbred is, as a rule, longer than that of other horses), which is thought to be the crucial source of his running power.

In the pink of racing condition, the Thoroughbred tends to appear thin and gaunt, being noticeably wasp-waisted behind the barrel and tapering to a slim rear girth, which looks even smaller in view of the extreme depth through the heart. It is this huge area, running from the withers to the lower chest just behind the forelegs, that is thought to be responsible for the Thoroughbred's immense stamina and running drive. The fact that the heart itself is larger than that of much bigger animals bears significant relationship to his courageous spirit.

The origins of the Thoroughbred trace back to the seventeenth century in England, where the sports of steeplechasing and fox hunting encouraged the popular demand for horses of greater speed, and the personal interest of Charles II in flat racing further stimulated efforts to develop a superior running horse. Steps in the right direction had already been initiated generations earlier, when the mating of Oriental stock with native horses of cold-blooded origin became an increasingly frequent practice among horsemen.

The product of this breeding was a variety of English hybrid horses sometimes called the English Running Horse, which was taller, longer-legged, and faster than other types of the period. When the best mares of this hybrid strain were mated with top stallions of Eastern blood, the offspring were decidedly faster than either parent or the product of either parent when bred to its own kind. The degree of speed they achieved, however, could be sustained only for relatively short distances for the type still fell far short of the Arab when it came to the quality of endurance.

To invest their running horses with more of this Eastern trait, crossings to Arab blood were continued by English breeders whose ambitions were precisely fulfilled by the three imported Oriental stallions: their progeny became the foundation sires in the Thoroughbred strain. The three imported sires were the Byerly Turk, imported in 1691; the Darley Arabian, imported in 1704; and the Godolphin Arabian—his actual date of entrance into England is unknown. Matchem, foaled in 1748, was a grandson of the Godolphin Arabian; Herod, foaled in 1758, was a great-great-grandson of the Byerly Turk; and Eclipse, foaled in 1864, was a great-great-grandson of the Darley Arabian. Within the century following the birth of these three giants, the Thoroughbred became firmly established as the fastest breed of horse in the world.

TIBETAN HORSE Another of the common nondescript breeds found in many countries. This durable indigenous equine, probably evolved from the Chinese and Mongolian ponies to the East, is indispensable to the Tibetan people.

TRAKEHNER   *See* EAST PRUSSIAN.

VENEZUELAN PRAIRIE HORSE   *See* LLANERO.

WALER   A light horse breed from Australia, the Waler was originally sired by Arabians, Thoroughbreds, or Anglo-Arabs out of the best available local mares. By the beginning of the Twentieth century, the Waler was close to becoming a pure-bred Anglo-Arab, with a preponderance of Thoroughbred blood in many cases.

Walers were used during World War I in India, but quarantine laws did not permit their reentry into Australia, so they were destroyed in the desert by orders of the Australian government.

Australian saddle horses of indeterminate breeding may sometimes now be called Walers, but experts agree that it would be difficult to find any number of Walers up to the standard of 1914.

WELSH MOUNTAIN PONY   The rich green valleys, mountains, and hills of the Principality of Wales have combined to produce one of the most beautiful ponies in the world, the Welsh Mountain Pony. He is marked by a small refined head, a bold eye, and a small alert ear. His way of going is quick and agile with the flexion of knee and hock required of a breed that made its home on rough, steep terrain.

The Welsh Mountain Pony is particularly nimble and sure of foot, with a natural ability for jumping, innate intelligence, soundness of limb, and a tough constitution. In the past, the most frequently encountered colors were bay, brown, black, roan, dun and cream, with an occasional chestnut or grey; however, recently the number of bright chestnuts has decidedly increased.

Because of their outstanding qualities of gentleness, adaptability, and courage, Welsh Mountain Ponies are extremely well suited for children and are just as reliable in harness as they are under saddle.

The Welsh Studbook is divided into two sections. In Section A are registered the Welsh Mountain Ponies, which may not exceed 12 hands. Section B is the registry of the Welsh Pony, which may not exceed 13.2 hands and is essentially a larger, stronger edition of its foundation breed, the Welsh Mountain Pony. The Welsh Pony was originally derived by mating the small Welsh Cob with the Welsh Mountain Pony.

YORKSHIRE COACH HORSE   This animal is bred extensively in Yorkshire from the Cleveland Bay, although the Thorough-bred has taken a place in its development. It is a very large animal, usually bay in color, and characterized by a fine head, lengthy quarters, and high-stepping action. *See* CLEVE-LAND BAY.

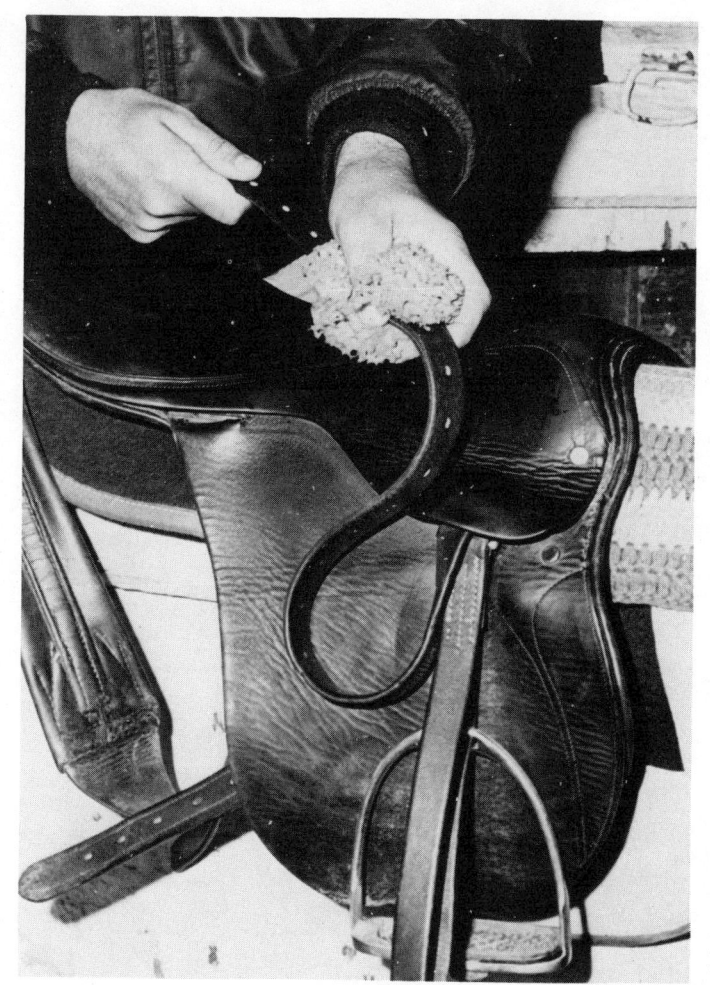

TACK
AND
EQUIPMENT

ANKLE BOOTS   Used on front or hind legs, an ankle boot is a padded leather or felt boot that is strapped around a horse's ankle to protect it.

BAT   A short, flexible whip with a wide flat end, designed to produce more noise than pain.

BAT-WINGS   A type of heavy bullhide chaps characterized by wide, flapping wings and the convenience of snapping on. Because of the ease with which these particular style chaps may be put on and taken off—a cowboy need not remove his spurs to do so—they have become the most popular chaps on the range. (Also known as "buzzard-wings")

BELL BOOTS   A rubber protector for the heels and coronet, bell boots either pull over or buckle around the horse's foot. The name comes from their domelike construction consisting of a tapered neck (which fits around the horse's pastern just above the coronary band) that swells into a definite "bell" and covers the entire hoof.

BIB   A leather protective device designed to keep a horse from tearing his blankets or removing bandages. It may be either flat or curved to conform to the underside of a horse's chin and attaches to the halter rings by means of snaps or straps. Some bibs also have a strap that passes over the horse's nose to help keep it in place.

BIB MARTINGALE   Seen mainly at the racetrack or in the breaking sheds, a bib martingale is simply a running martingale in which the split has been filled in with leather. The purpose of this arrangement is to prevent a horse from "dropping his head and stepping through" or otherwise becoming entangled with the straps.

BILLET STRAPS   The straps on the saddle which buckle into the girth and keep the saddle on the horse.

BIT   Anything that passes through a horse's mouth and is then conducted to the rider's hands by means of reins is considered a bit. The mouthpiece may be made from a number of substances including rubber and vulcanite, various types of metals, and, in a few instances, wood or leather. Although there are literally hundreds of bits in existence, they may be classified

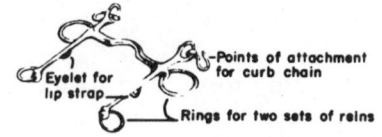

Points of attachment for curb chain

Eyelet for lip strap

Rings for two sets of reins

PELHAM CURB BIT

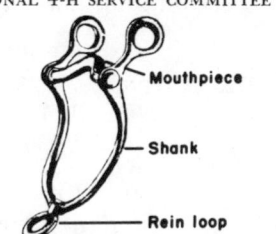

Mouthpiece

Shank

Rein loop

ROPER CURVED CHEEK BIT:
USED ON MANY ROPING HORSES

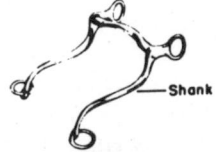

Shank

WALKING HORSE BIT

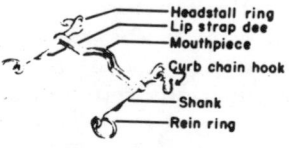

Headstall ring
Lip strap dee
Mouthpiece
Curb chain hook
Shank
Rein ring

WEYMOUTH CURB BIT

SNAFFLE BIT:
THE MOST WIDELY USED

Link
Swivel
Dee

DEE RACE BIT:
OFTEN USED ON THOROUGHBRED

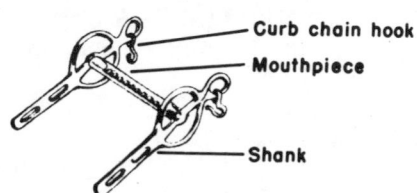

Curb chain hook

Mouthpiece

Shank

LIVERPOOL BIT:
A CURB BIT USED ON HEAVY HARNESS HORSES

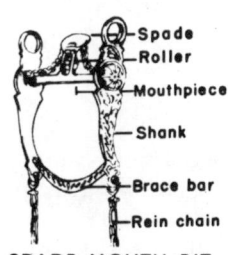

Spade
Roller
Mouthpiece
Shank
Brace bar
Rein chain

SPADE MOUTH BIT:
USED ON MANY STOCK HORSES

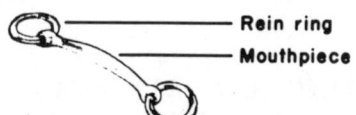

Rein ring
Mouthpiece

BAR BIT: USED ON TROTTING HARNESS HORSES
WHICH CARRY CHECK REINS
AND ARE DRIVEN WITH STRONG HAND

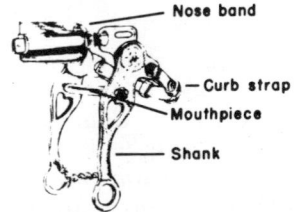

Nose band

Curb strap
Mouthpiece

Shank

HACKAMORE BIT:
USED ON MOST COW PONIES

Rein ring
Mouthpiece
Link

HALF-CHEEK SNAFFLE BIT
USED ON HARNESS RACE HORSES,
ROADSTERS AND FINE HARNESS HORSES

ART WORK COURTESY, DR. M. E. ENSMINGER AND WASHINGTON STATE UNIVERSITY into four major categories—snaffle, curb, pelham, and double —and then subdivided according to similarity or construction and purpose.

BIT BURR   A flat leather piece with short stiff bristles that fits onto the mouthpiece of a bit inside the cheek or ring, touching the side of the horse's mouth at the corners. It is used to discourage disobedience on a horse that persists in bearing out (moving away from) when asked to turn, usually in one particular direction. For example, should a horse continually run to the left to avoid jumping, and all the rider's efforts to pull him to the right (or in front of the obstacle) fail, a bit burr could be used on the left side of the bit. That is, when the right rein is pulled, the bristles push against the left side of the horse's mouth, hopefully dissuading him from running out.

BIT CONVERTER   A leather strap to convert or join the curb and snaffle rings of pelham type bits so that a single rein may be used.

BIT GUARD   A rubber or leather plate that rides the mouthpiece and protects the horse's lips from the cheeks of the bit.

BIT LOOPS   Small leather loops connecting the bridle cheeks with the upper cheekpieces of a full cheek snaffle bit to prevent the bit from turning in the horse's mouth and to accentuate the nutcracker effect of the bit.

BITTING HARNESS or RIG   A harness used for breaking, training, mouthing, exercising, and driving in long reins. The "harness" consists of a body roller with various rings and dees to which reins, overcheck, or just about any combination of straps and lines may be attached. A full "rig" includes the bridle with reins (long or side), overcheck, and crupper.

BLANKET   Essentially a piece of horse "clothing" that covers his body from withers to tail, encompassing his chest, barrel, loins and flank. It usually fastens across the chest (although some types slip over the animal's head to reduce the temptation to chew the buckles) and straps around his barrel with two long pieces called surcingles. Blankets are used for warmth against the cold, but may also be used "in place of" his natural coat before the cold weather has a chance to cause a heavy winter coat to grow, thereby maintaining a finer coat (for show purposes) or delaying or eliminating the necessity of clipping horses expected to work through the cold months.

BLINKER HOOD   A nylon hood that slips over a horse's ears, fastens under his jowls, and extends down his face about halfway between his eyes and his muzzle. Around the edge of the holes cut for his eyes, leather cups of varying shapes are sewn. A "closed cup" for example, would completely cover the eye; a "half-cup" would be open in front but prohibit peripheral vision. "Blinkers," as they are called, are used primarily on racehorses that are distracted by other horses running alongside them, and it is thought that by limiting the animal's vision, he is more apt to concentrate on the business of runing.

BODY ROLLER   A body roller consists of two large padded squares intended to simulate the panels of a saddle and affixed to and held in place on the horse's back by a wide leather surcingle buckled around his girth. It is used to accustom green horses—those just "up from grass"—to the pressure of a saddle to avoid saddle sores resulting from sudden work with saddle and rider.

  The term is also used to denote a leather, canvas, or web strap buckled around the horse's barrel for the purpose of keeping his blanket and sheet in place. These, too, are padded to prevent chafing at the withers.

BOOT HOOKS   A small hooked implement that slips into the straps provided inside the top of knee-high riding boots to help in pulling them on a rider's leg.

BOOT JACK   A device of varied forms to assist in removing riding boots. The most common type of "jack" grips the heel of one boot while being held to the floor with the rider's other foot.

BOSAL   A distortion of the Spanish *bozal* meaning muzzle, a bosal is a leather, rawhide, or sometimes metal piece encircling the horse's face just above the mouth. It may be used in place of a bit as when it becomes a component of a hackamore.

BREAST COLLAR (POLO or BREASTPLATE)   A leather strap, sometimes padded, that crosses the horse's chest and loops

239

around the girth on either side to prevent the saddle from slipping toward the rear. It is held in place by a narrow strap passed over the horse's neck in front of the withers and buckles for easy adjustment.

BREASTPLATE   The purpose of a breastplate is to hold the saddle in place and keep it from sliding toward the rear.

BREASTPLATE (HUNTING)   A breastplate consisting of a yoke and straps attached to "dees" located on either side of the pommel of the saddle to prevent the saddle from slipping back. In addition, either a running or standing martingale attachment may be sewn or buckled onto the ring of the yoke to eliminate the necessity of using a separate martingale on a horse requiring one. This style of breastplate is preferable to the polo variety for use over long periods of time (as when out hunting), since it is less apt to chafe the front edge of the horse's shoulders or chest.

BRIDLE   The piece(s) of leather that hold the bit in the horse's mouth and the reins through which the rider transmits his signals to the horse.

BRIDLE CHAIN   Because the reins on a horse's bridle may get wet when he drinks or may tempt him to chew them while he is tied, some Western riders prefer to have a short piece of chain attached between the bit and the reins: it is called the "bridle chain."

BROWBAND   A piece of leather connecting the two sides of the bridle headstall and passing across the horse's forehead just in front of his ears. As well as preventing the crown piece from slipping backward, it is often used as a decoration or means of identification and is available in many colors, styles, and materials.

CABESTRO   From the Spanish meaning halter, *cabestro* is used by the American cowboy to describe a horsehair rope halter as opposed to one made of leather.

CAN OPENERS   Western slang for spurs.

CANTLE   The back of a saddle.

CAVESSON   The traditional separate noseband that is a component of most English bridles. Consisting of an adjustable band, it buckles around the horse's nose suspended from a crownpiece lying beneath the bridle headstall and threads through both sides of the browband behind the animal's ears. It also has a buckle fastening for easy adjustment. The cavesson's basic use is that of providing a point of attachment for a standing martingale, although it may serve to slightly restrict the opening of the horse's mouth. In the past it was a heavier piece, which was often used to carry reins for training purposes or a tie rope for use in the field.

CHEEK PIECES   The leather straps on a bridle positioned along the horse's cheeks that connect the crown piece and the bit.

CHIFNEY or COLT LEAD   A chifney is used when leading a horse in place of a bridle. When a horse requires more control than is afforded by a halter and it is impractical to bridle the animal as a means of "getting something in his mouth" (such as a bit), the chifney is a good solution. It is a metal device shaped like a half circle joined with a straight bar and equipped with three snaps located as follows: one at each end of the bar and the third equidistant between the two on the curve. The bar fits into the horse's mouth, while the curve encircles his lower jaw. The snaps attach to the halter rings at either side of his mouth and under his chin.

CHINKS   A sort of abbreviated version of chaps resembling a leather apron that is divided in the front and open in back. Chinks are a great deal cooler than conventional chaps and are especially favored by women riders.

COME-ALONG   A slip-type rope halter so constructed that should a horse balk or refuse to follow, it will tighten and then loosen as soon as the horse *comes along.*

COOLER   A large rectangular woolen cover that is thrown over a horse after work while he is cooling off to prevent chill and muscle soreness from drafts and uneven cooling.

CORONA   A Western saddle pad shaped to fit the saddle, with a large colorful roll around the edge.

CRIBBING STRAP   There are many different types of cribbing straps, but all are a device that buckles around the horse's throat to inhibit or prevent him from expanding his neck and thus gulping air. (There are some horses that will crib in spite of any strap or the tightness with which it is adjusted.)

CROWN PIECE   The uppermost part of the bridle that passes over the top of the horse's head behind his ears and buckles into the cheek pieces which attach to the bit. It also contains the throat latch that connects the two sides of the bridle and buckles under the horse's throat, preventing the bridle from thus slipping over his ears and off.

CRUPPER   A piece of round (sometimes padded) leather encircling the dock of the horse's tail leading into one or two straps that connect to: 1) a saddle, to prevent it from slipping forward (mainly used on ponies because of the lack of well-defined withers permitting a saddle to slide); and 2) the harness of a driving rig for the purpose of maintaining the lateral position of the rear portions.

CURB BIT   A curb bit consists of a single-bar mouthpiece of varying shapes (the most common being one with a "port" or arch in the center to discourage the horse from putting his tongue over the bit) to which vertical cheekpieces are attached at either end. The portion of the cheek (as the cheekpieces are called) above the mouthpiece has a ring to which the cheek strap of the bridle is attached, while the part below the mouthpiece has a ring to which the rein attaches. In addition, a hook attaches to the upper ring for the purpose of holding a curb chain, which fits against the horse's lower jaw in the groove of his chin. Another tiny ring is located on the lower cheek to hold the lip strap that helps to keep the curb chain in place.

    The principle of a curb bit is one of leverage as well as direct pressure on the bars of the horse's mouth. When the reins are pulled, the bit turns in the horse's mouth as his lower jaw is pressed between the mouthpiece and the curb chain. The longer the lower portion of the cheek (provided the length of the upper cheek remains the same), the more severe the bit, higher the port, and greater the action on the roof of the mouth and tongue. The overall effect on the horse is one of flexion—that is, bringing his head down and in towards his chest from the poll (or top of his head) and to "give" (or yield) with his lower jaw.

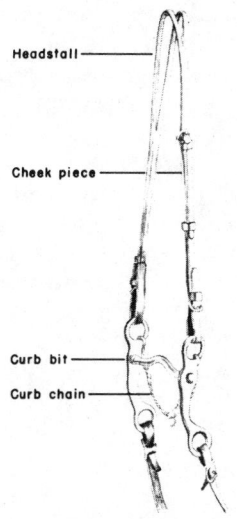

Headstall

Cheek piece

Curb bit

Curb chain

**SPLIT-EARED BRIDLE
WITH CURB BIT**

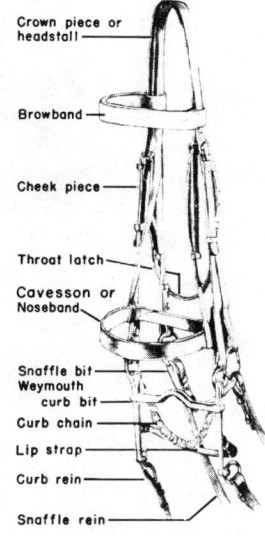

Crown piece or headstall

Browband

Cheek piece

Throat latch

Cavesson or Noseband

Snaffle bit
Weymouth curb bit

Curb chain

Lip strap

Curb rein

Snaffle rein

WEYMOUTH BRIDLE

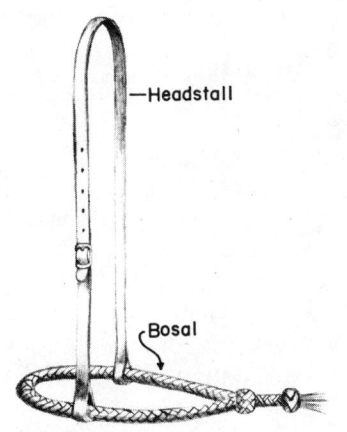

Headstall

Bosal

**BOSAL HACKAMORE:
POPULAR FOR BREAKING HORSES**

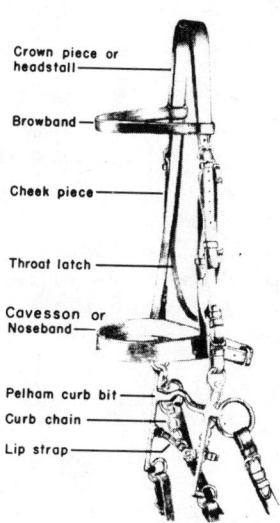

Crown piece or headstall

Browband

Cheek piece

Throat latch

Cavesson or Noseband

Pelham curb bit

Curb chain

Lip strap

PELHAM, DOUBLE-REINED BRIDLE

NATIONAL 4-H SERVICE COMMITTEE

CURB CHAIN   A flat link chain attached to the upper rings of a curb bit. It fits against the chin groove of the horse's lower jaw and helps exert pressure on the bars of his mouth through compression between the mouthpiece and curb chain.

DOUBLE BRIDLE, also FULL BRIDLE   A bridle with a bitting part that is composed of two elements—a curb bit and a bridoon (which is the name applied to a snaffle, when it is used in conjunction with a curb). The two bits fit into the horse's mouth with the snaffle positioned slightly above the curb, so as to fit well into the corners of the mouth, while the curb rests on the bars. The snaffle has the effect of raising the horse's head as it acts on the corners of the lips, while the curb causes flexion at the poll by exerting pressure on the bars, tongue, and groove of the chin. *See* CURB BIT, SNAFFLE BIT.

DRAW REINS   Long leather reins attached to the girth (either between the horse's front legs or beneath the saddle flaps on a line with the horse's mouth when his head is in proper carriage), then threaded through the snaffle rings of the bit (from the inside toward the outside), and into the rider's hands. Draw reins apply the effect of a pulley and tend to pull the bit both back and down. For this reason they may be used effectively to improve the carriage of high headed horses but because of their pulley nature should only be used by educated hands.

DRIVING WHIP   A long whip used while driving a horse in harness; it enables a driver to signal or punish the animal without leaving his seat.

DROPPED NOSEBAND   A noseband that buckles below the bit for the purpose of preventing the horse from opening his mouth to evade the bit or putting his tongue over the mouthpiece.

EAR NET   A meshlike material sewn to fit over a horse's ears and held in place by tying under his jowels. It is used to protect sensitive horses from insect bites.

FIGURE-EIGHT NOSEBAND   A type of dropped noseband made in the shape of a figure of eight. *See* DROPPED NOSEBAND.

GAG BIT   A type of snaffle that is suspended on a pulley—that is to say, the reins pass vertically through the rings, so that when pressure is exerted by pulling on the reins, the bit rises in the horse's mouth.

GALLOPING BOOTS   Felt or leather boots with leather straps and a padded leather panel that protect a horse's front shin, ankle, and tendon from blows from his own feet while galloping.

GIRTH   The leather, canvas, or corded piece that holds the saddle in place on the horse's back by passing underneath his belly and attaching to either side of the saddle.

GIRTH TYPES—*English*   *Balding*   Named for the English polo player who designed it, the balding girth is made of thick leather in a single piece divided into three strips which cross each other near the horse's elbows to narrow the girth at those points and prevent chafing.

Cord   A straight girth made of several pieces of cord that might be cotton or nylon, which is particularly good for thin skinned horses or those that chafe easily.

Elastic End   Straight or shaped leather girth with an elastic inset on one end that ends in two buckles. It is used to allow the horse more freedom of expansion, particularly in the strenuous sports of racing and show jumping. There is a chance of the saddle slipping more easily with an elastic end girth.

Fitzwilliam   Sort of "two girths in one," the Fitzwilliam consists of a narrow piece of leather lying over a wider one (the narrow piece having one buckle at each end while the wider one has two). The three buckle arrangement provides added security and prevents the saddle from slipping.

Humane Girth   The buckles of this girth are fastened by leather straps to a ring attached to the girth, for the purpose of equalizing the stress between the two girth straps.

Lampwick   Like a web girth, but made of very thick soft material.

Lonsdale   A short-bellied girth used on saddles that have long girth straps so as to bring the buckles under the horse and away from the rider's leg.

Overgirth   A strap, most frequently made of leather or web, that goes over the entire saddle (passing on top of the seat) for added safety.

Shaped Girth   A light flexible leather girth shaped so as to be narrow behind the horse's elbows to prevent pinching and is folded and stitched in such a manner as to present only rounded edges.

Three-Fold Leather   A straight leather girth that is folded into three thicknesses for strength and durability. Care must be taken when using this type of girth to place the folded edge facing towards the horse's head and the open edge toward his tail to prevent pinching and chafing.

Tubular Web   A straight web girth woven into a tubular form; it is less likely than the flat style to cut at the edges.

Web   A woven material (cotton, linen, or wool) girth.

White Linen Show Girth   Used on Saddlebred horses for show, it is considered flashy and is lined with rubber to prevent slipping.

GIRTH—WESTERN   The Western girth or "cinch" is actually a shortened form of the Spanish word *cincha* meaning girth. Traditionally these girths are woven of cord made of mohair or horsehair; however, other materials such as cotton, nylon, and rayon are also now used. Whatever material is used, the construction is basically the same, finishing in a ring at either end to take the tie strap (latigo) of the saddle. These rings are available in several styles such as:

1.   plain round ring for ordinary tie strap;
2.   round ring with a buckle tongue added for use with tie strings with buckle holes;
3.   round ring with center bar for buckle tongue to avoid having tongue slip from tie strap due to an ordinary ring being pulled out of shape as a result of heavy roping.

GROOMING   The act of cleaning a horse from head to hoof and nose to tail is called *grooming*. The necessary tools include:

Body Brush   A soft brush used after the dandy brush to remove any remaining dust, "polish" or "put a shine on" the horse's coat, and to brush the hair into place.

Curry Comb   Step one of the grooming process begins with the curry comb. It is a metal or hard rubber grooming tool used in a circular motion on the horse's body (never on his face or legs) to loosen dirt and hair before brushing.

Dandy Brush   A stiff brush used after the curry comb to lift up dirt and hair and stimulate the skin.

Hoof Pick   A metal hook which is used to remove such foreign matter as dirt, manure, stones from a horse's foot.

Mane Comb   A short large-tooth comb for use on a horse's mane and tail. It is usually made of metal or plastic without any sharp edges that might break or tear the hair.

Pulling Comb   Horse's manes are "pulled," not cut, and a pulling comb saves wear and tear on the "puller's" fingers. It is much smaller than a regular mane comb and has more teeth, which are only half as long as those on other combs. The mane is combed flat, a few hairs separated for pulling, and then these are wrapped around the comb, which is pulled with a swift jerk. The mane should be combed flat after each "pull" to see how it lays, and to ensure an even line. (Manes can be pulled without a comb but rarely without causing blisters and more than one paperlike cut.)

Rub Rag   A linen or terry cloth towel that is wiped over the horse's body after grooming with curry and brushes as a sort of finishing touch. Rub rags are also useful for rubbing dry the sweat marks from a saddle.

Sponge and Pail of Water   A damp or wet sponge is a necessity for good grooming. The horse's face and lower legs should be wiped clean daily, as well as the area underneath the dock of his tail and along the tail bone. (A gelding's sheath and mare's udder should be washed from time to time with a mild soap and warm water.)

Sweat Scraper   Scrapers are used to squeeze sweat or excess water after a bath from a horse's coat, thus enabling him to dry more quickly. They are available in two types—1) the two-hand variety consisting of a flexible piece of brass fitted with leather handles at each end, which is bent into a half-circle and drawn across the horse's body; 2) the one-hand style, which leaves the other hand free to hold the horse, is simply a channeled piece of metal used in the same way.

HACKAMORE or JAQUIMA   A bitless bridle that is a sort of halter-type device with a rolled leather noseband and reins fitting under the horse's chin instead of a lead rope. (When the noseband is made of wire (cable), the device is called a bosal.) As the reins are pulled, pressure is exerted on the soft part of the horse's nose, cutting off his wind. Greater leverage may be added to this piece by using a "hackamore bit" (which does not pass through the horse's mouth), consisting of a metal device with two long shanks to which the reins are attached.

HALTER   A leather, nylon, or rope device that is used on a horse's head to control or lead him from the ground. It fits around the animal's nose and over the top of his head behind his ears. In addition, it may have a T-shaped piece running under the jowls (like a throat latch) and down to the noseband and attaching beneath the chin.

247

HEAD BUMPER   A protective covering that attaches to the crown piece of a halter and fits over the horse's ears to prevent head injuries during shipping in a van or trailer.

HEADSTALL   The leather bridle straps, exclusive of the bit and reins.

HOBBLES   A pair of leather cuffs attached to each other by a short swivel chain; the cuffs are buckled around the horse's forelegs just above the pastern joints. Hobbles are used to permit a horse a certain amount of freedom to graze but ensure that he will not go too far by limiting him to a slow walk.

HOCK BOOTS   A leather boot that is buckled around a horse's hock to prevent injuries such as capped hocks during shipping or, in the case of a horse that chronically kicks his hind legs, injuring himself against the sides of his stall.

HOOD, FULL HOODS and JOWL HOODS   Made of cotton duck and frequently lined with wool, full hoods (covering the horse's head and neck, with eye and ear holes cut to fit) and jowl hoods (covering the top of the head and jowl area) are used mainly on Saddlebred horses to keep their heads and necks warm, thus preventing the undue thickening of these areas; a build-up of fatty tissue can result from exposure to cold. A full hood also serves to help keep the coat clean.

LIP STRAP   A strap that attaches to the shank of a curb or pelham-type bit to keep the curb chain in place and prevent it from being detached from the bridle.

LONGE LINE or LUNGE LINE   A long (about 30 feet or more) canvas, nylon, or sometimes leather strap or rein with a snap on one end that attaches to the horse's halter, cavesson, bridle, and the like; it is used in breaking and schooling methods as well as for exercising a horse by moving him in a circle around the trainer who remains stationary at the center point.

LONGE WHIP or LUNGE WHIP   A long whip with an equally long lash that is used to direct a horse while longeing.

MARTINGALE   A leather device designed to restrict the upward motion of the horse's head as well as to bring his chin in for the purpose of allowing the effective use of the bit. All martingales should be fitted with a small red rubber "stop," which holds the neck strap to the rest of the martingale to make sure that the slack remains above (or in front of) the neck strap and cannot hang in a loop through which the animal might become entangled with his legs. (Horses have been known to "jump" through a martingale while negotiating an obstacle or simply "put a leg through" one while galloping, with serious injuries resulting from the subsequent falls.) There are three types:

Standing Martingale   A simple adjustable strap connecting the girth and underside of the horse's cavesson, which is held in place by the neckstrap encircling the horse's neck just in front of the withers.

Running Martingale   An adjustable strap that loops around the girth and then forks into two pieces, each of which ends in a metal ring through which the reins are threaded. Like the standing martingale, it is held in place by means of a neckstrap. When using a running martingale, it is necessary to equip your reins with rein stops (small leather pieces affixed to the reins that prevent the rings of the martingale from slipping up too far toward the horse's head and getting caught on the hook-in studs of the bridle).

Irish Martingale   Not a martingale in the sense of the other two types but simply a pair of rings attached to each other by means of a small leather strap. The reins are threaded through the rings to prevent them from being flipped over the horse's head so that both wind up on the same side of his neck, as might be the case if he were to stumble badly, shy suddenly, or unexpectedly throw his head around for any reason.

MECATE   From the Spanish, a mecate is a horsehair rope that may be used as reins on a hackamore or as a lead or tie rope. The longstanding use of hair ropes for this purpose has resulted in the term being used to denote *any* hair rope, particularly in view of the fact that they are too light and too easily kinked to be used as a lariat, so there is no confusion as to what is meant.

MUZZLE   A leather headstall with a wire mesh muzzle which fits around and covers the horse's mouth and nose. It is used to prevent him from: 1) biting at bandages or blankets; 2) eating his bedding; 3) biting other horses in confined quarters (as when shipping); and 4) in rare cases biting people, if the animal is particularly prone to do so.

249

PELHAM BIT   Shaped like a curb bit, the pelham combines in a single piece certain qualities of both the snaffle and the curb. In addition to the mouth and cheek pieces of a curb, the pelham has a large ring at each end of the mouthpiece to which the "snaffle" rein attaches (the curb rein being fastened in the usual curb bit position). The severity of a pelham depends upon the length of the lower cheek piece (shank) in relation to the length of the upper cheek, as well as on the tautness with which the curb chain is adjusted. Pelham mouthpieces vary greatly and may be found either with or without ports and made of metal or hard or soft rubber; the shank may range anywhere from short short (Tom Thumb) to extremely long.

POLO BOOTS   Heavy felt protective boots extending from just below the knee to cover the ankle and rectangular in shape. Four or five straps are sewn to the middle of the boot to buckle around the horse's shin and keep the boot in place while polo is played. For added protection, some styles are leather covered.

POMMEL   The front of the saddle.

POMMEL PAD   A small woven "rug" fitting underneath the pommel of the saddle to protect the horse's withers from chafing.

PORT   The curved or arched center part of the mouthpiece of a bit, designed to discourage the horse from putting his tongue over the bit and, in some instances, exert pressure on the roof of the mouth.

RATTLERS, WOODEN   Assorted-size wooden balls that are strung on a leather strap and fastened around a horse's pastern. Rattlers are used on Saddlebreds to increase their leg action and to prevent them from interfering.

REINS   Leather straps (occasionally of other material), which attach to the bit and are held by the rider as a means of transmitting commands and signals to the horse. They come in many widths and styles (such as plaited or laced to prevent slippage) or with special devices (such as rubber handholds often used in racing and show jumping to offer the best possible grip, particularly in wet weather or on a sweating horse) and may be closed (traditional English style) or open (traditional Western style) at the held end. The reins on Western bridles are left open (or "split"), so that if the rider dismounts or is thrown from his horse, the loose ends of the reins will fall to the ground. Since most Western horses are taught to ground tie, they are expected to stay in one place; however, should the horse attempt to stray, he will step on the trailing reins, jerk himself in the mouth, and hopefully decide to remain.

REIN STOPS *See* RUNNING MARTINGALE under MARTINGALE.

ROWELS The toothed wheels on spurs.

SADDLE A saddle is essentially a seat for a person on horseback. It may be of Western or English style, with a deep or shallow seat, large or small in size, light or heavy in weight, and equipped, altered, or fitted with just about any variation or modification for which a rider may wish to ask. However, in spite of the many variables, all saddles do share a few things in common.

The foundation of all saddles is the *tree,* which is usually made of wood (or in some cases of fiber glass); it is constructed in the basic shape of the saddle. This bare frame is then stuffed and covered with leather.

The *stirrup-leather bars* (attached to the tree and from which the stirrup leathers are suspended) are always drawn through whatever panels, skirts, and flaps might be placed over them. Some type of girth attachment device is provided, be it girth straps of the English type with holes for the buckles, or the Western *latigo* or *cinch straps,* which tie around the rings of a Western girth.

English saddles fall into three basic categories. SHOW SADDLES—The extremely flat saddle, which features a cutback pommel, straight vertical flaps, and a tendency to thrust the rider back towards the cantle, is designed to show off the horse's forehand. It is used exclusively in Saddlebred and Gaited horse classes.

HACKING (or FLAT) SADDLES—This type features a slightly deeper seat than the show saddle; it is cut a little toward the forward seat and still used for all-around riding on Thoroughbred-type horses.

FORWARD SEAT (or JUMPING) SADDLES—Originating

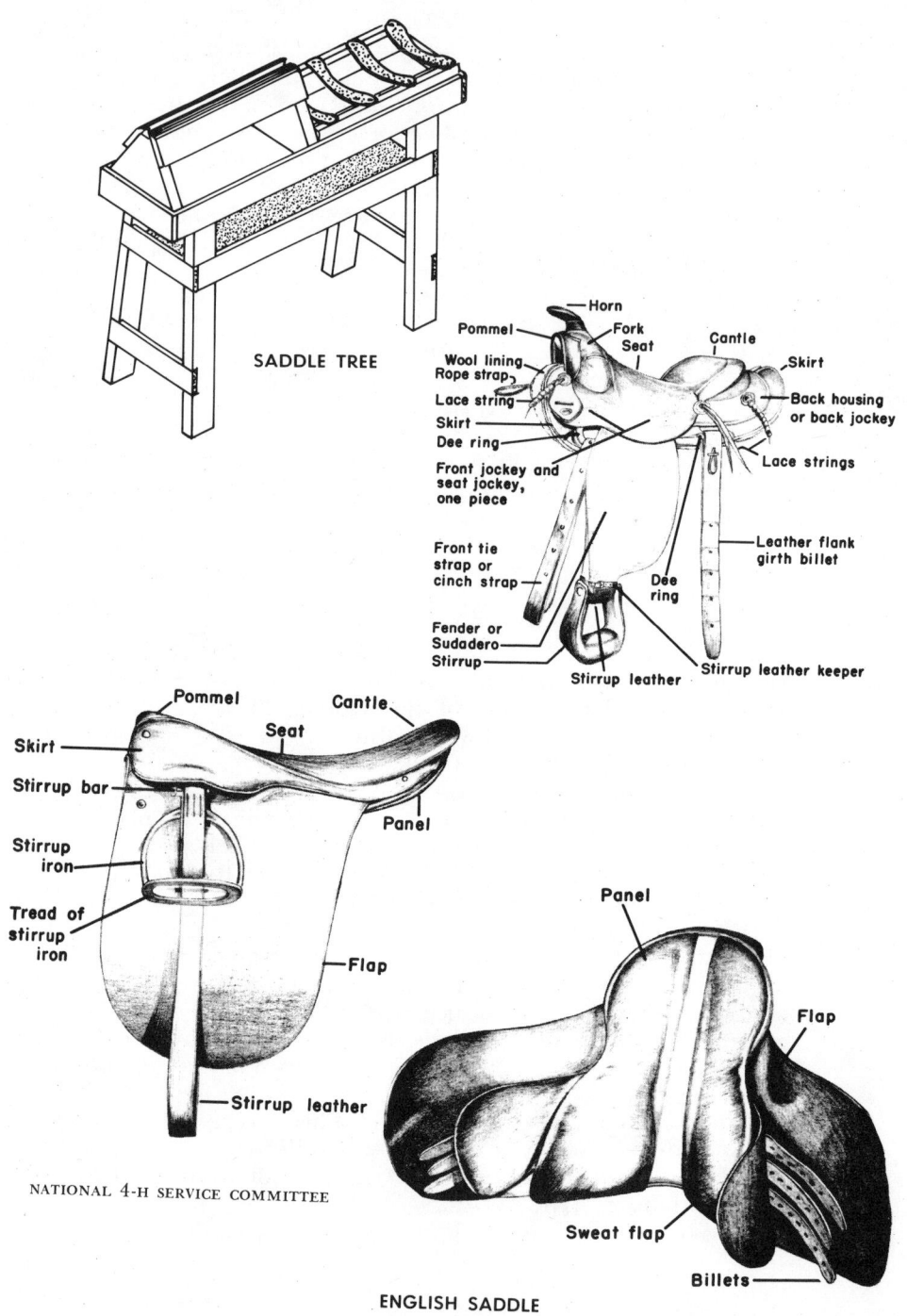

SADDLE TREE

Horn

Pommel

Fork
Seat

Cantle

Skirt

Wool lining
Rope strap

Lace string

Skirt

Dee ring

Front jockey and
seat jockey,
one piece

Back housing
or back jockey

Lace strings

Front tie
strap or
cinch strap

Leather flank
girth billet

Dee
ring

Fender or
Sudadero

Stirrup

Stirrup leather keeper

Stirrup leather

Pommel

Cantle

Skirt

Seat

Stirrup bar

Stirrup
iron

Panel

Tread of
stirrup
iron

Flap

Panel

Flap

Stirrup leather

NATIONAL 4-H SERVICE COMMITTEE

Sweat flap

Billets

ENGLISH SADDLE

in Italy, the forward seat saddles are distinguished by the definite forward cut of the flaps and the use of padded knee rolls. The cantle is rather high behind a pommel, which is frequently cut back; the seat tends to be quite deep. Many adaptations of this type of saddle have been created both in the United States and Europe; in recent years it has become the most popular style of hunting, jumping and cross-country riding saddle.

Western saddles are much heavier and generally larger than English saddles. They feature a deep and somewhat sloping seat flanked by a high cantle and high pommel with a horn to which a lariat might be attached (when holding roped cattle and horses). *Sudaderos* is the name of the extremely wide sweat flaps, while *rosaderos* (or fenders) are the vertical wide leather shields sewn to the back of the stirrup leathers. The entire saddle may be hand tooled and decorated with silver ornaments.

SADDLE BLANKET   A blanket, most often of wool, placed between the saddle and the horse's back to:

1.   Protect the panels of the saddle from wear and sweat;
2.   Protect the horse's back from the movement of the saddle;
3.   Absorb sweat to help keep the horse's back dry.

SADDLE PAD   A pad that is cut to fit the shape of a saddle and used for the same purposes as a saddle blanket. Saddle pads are available in a number of materials such as felt, sheepswool, quilted cloth and synthetic fleece; the major differences between them are ease with which they can be kept clean (for a dirty pad can do more harm than no pad at all) and price.

SEWN IN   When the parts of a bridle are *sewn in*, it means that all attachments—that is, bit-to-cheek pieces, reins-to-bit—are stitched and cannot thus be changed or removed, as opposed to the hook-in stud fastenings (or old-fashioned buckles), which permit experimentation with bits, and the like.

SHANK OF A BIT   The part of the cheekpiece of a bit extending below the mouthpiece. On bits that employ a curb chain, the longer the shank (in proportion to the length of the upper cheek), the greater the amount of pressure (through leverage) that can be exerted on the horse's lower jaw.

253

SHEET   A lightweight blanket generally made of cotton, which is used to keep a horse's coat clean and for warmth in cool weather before a heavier blanket is required.

SHOE BOIL BOOT   A cylindrical, heavily padded, donut-shaped boot that is strapped around a horse's pastern; it prevents him from placing pressure on the point of his elbow with his hoof when lying down with his foot folded beneath him.

SIDE REINS   Adjustable leather straps (sometimes with an elastic inset), which loop around the girth and snap onto the bit. They are used in pairs (one on either side of the horse) as a training device to aid in "setting" a horse's head in proper carriage.

SNAFFLE BIT   The simplest form of a snaffle bit consists of a straight bar with large rings at either end to which the cheek-pieces of the bridle and its single rein attach. Its most popular type is the *jointed snaffle,* which is a two-part mouthpiece joined in the center so the bit can "fold" in two. Multiple variations of the snaffle exist in a wide range of styles such as twisted, wire, full or half-cheek, dee ring, and egg butt; however, the principle remains basically the same. All snaffles are designed to act on the corners of the horse's lips, while a jointed snaffle has the additional feature of exerting a sort of squeezing pressure on the tongue as well.

SPLIT-EAR BRIDLE, also ONE-EAR or SHAPED-EAR   A popular type of Western bridle consisting simply of a bit supported by a headstall that is split to fit over one ear.

SPURS   A valuable tool to the rider with sufficient control of his leg to use them properly, spurs can, on the other hand, be a dangerous and harmful instrument for one that does not. Spurs are available in many sizes and shapes, dull and sharp, with and without rowels. In normal circumstances, there is no need for using a sharp spur (even rowels can be dull), but the selection of spurs is a matter of individual taste.

STIRRUP   Stirrups come in many varied shapes and sizes, but all are designed with one purpose in mind: to provide a point of purchase for the rider's feet. English stirrups are made of metal, frequently have a pitted (or roughened) surface (or tread) to help the rider maintain his foothold and are found in two basic styles—straight and offset.

Straight irons, as the name implies, have the hole that is cut for the stirrup strap located in the center of the top, so that the branches extending to the tread on either side are equal and the iron hangs squarely.

Offset irons have the hole for the stirrup strap positioned off to one side, resulting in one branch being longer than the other to encourage the rider to cock his ankle inward and, so the theory goes, tighten his leg. Rubber *stirrup pads* are available; they snap into place in the tread to prevent the rider's foot from slipping.

Western stirrups are most frequently constructed of wood, although plastic and metal are also used. Better quality stirrups are covered with rawhide or metal or a combination of rawhide or leather over metal. This is primarily to prevent the horse from being irritated by splinters, although it may also be done for decoration. Some stirrups are fitted with leather hoods (*tapaderos*), which cover the front portion of the stirrup to protect the rider's foot when riding through rough country.

STIRRUP LEATHER or STRAP   This is the leather strap that attaches the stirrup to the saddle tree. Like stirrups, leathers are available in multiple types, weights, and widths and are usually a matter of individual preference.

SWEAT SCRAPER   Available in two types, sweat scrapers are used to remove sweat after work or excess water after a bath from the horse's coat to permit him to dry more quickly. The first type requires two hands and consists of a flexible piece of brass fitted with leather handles at each end, which is bent into a half-circle and drawn across the horse's body. The second style requires only one hand (leaving the other one free to hold the horse) and consists of a single channeled piece of metal that is scraped across the horse's coat in the same way.

TACK   The word *tack* is actually a shortened form of the word *tackle,* which in this case is used to mean equipment.

TAIL SET   An elaborate device consisting of several leather straps used to train and maintain the elevated, folded tail carriage of the American Saddlebred show horse.

TONGUE TIE   A small leather or rubber device that encircles the horse's tongue, is pulled snug, and then fastened under his chin. Used for short periods of time—that is, during a race or a jumping round in a show—on horses that insist in putting their tongue over the bit.

WEIGHT PAD   In many types of competition, horses are required to carry a certain amount of weight; if a rider is too light to meet the requirements, additional weight must be added. This is usually accomplished by means of a weight pad, which is a sort of saddle pad equipped with front and back pockets to accommodate strips of lead and hold them without shifting.

BALLING GUN   An instrument used to give a horse a pill or large capsule (bolus); it consists of a metal chamber and plunger that is placed toward the back of the horse's mouth. The plunger is then depressed, ejecting the pill into the animal's throat.

DOSE SYRINGE   A metal instrument used to administer liquid medicine. It is used by drawing liquid into the chamber and expelling it through the tubelike end into the horse's throat via a plunger.

HOOF TESTER   Large pinchers without a cutting edge but with a spherical surface that makes it possible to bring about a very localized pressure upon the sole or wall of the hoof to determine the location, and possibly the nature, of a lameness.

ICE BOOTS   A high canvas or rubber boot that can be filled with ice to cool an injured leg(s). Ice boots extend well above the knee, zip up the side, and are reinforced with leather on the bottom so that the horse's foot will not tear through. They are generally used on two legs at a time since they are kept in place by a single suspender, which passes over the horse's withers, and forks to attach in two spots on the top edge of the boot.

NECK CRADLE   The most popular style of cradle consists of wooden rods strung together (with alternate wooden beads to keep them separated) with a buckle fastening at the top and bottom of either end. This ladderlike device is buckled around the horse's neck with the rods extending from beneath his jaw to a few inches above the front of his chest. With this arrangement, the animal is able to extend his head downward to eat but cannot bend it towards his body, thus possibly preventing him from gnawing on sores, tearing off bandages, or ripping his blanket and/or sheet.

TWITCH   Available in three types, a twitch is used to distract a horse's attention when he might otherwise put up an argument (as when being clipped or treated by the veterinarian). The device consists of a wooden shaft to which a piece of rope or chain is attached on one end. The horse's upper lip is drawn through the loop that is then twisted and held snug by the handle with as much force as is necessary to prevent the animal from jumping about. This procedure usually requires two people—one to hold the twitch and one to do the work—so the fairly recent addition of a "one-man" twitch, which screws on the lip much like a nutcracker, is a particularly useful convenience.

APPENDIX

ORGANIZATIONS OF INTEREST TO HORSEMEN

American Association of Equine Practitioners
Route #5
14 Hillcrest Circle
Golden, Colorado 80401

American Buckskin Registry Association, Inc.
P.O. Box 1125
Anderson, California 96007

American Hackney Horse Society
527 Madison Avenue
New York City 10022

American Horse Council, Inc.
1776 K Street N.W.
Washington, D.C. 20006

American Horse Shows Association
527 Madison Avenue
New York City 10022

American Morgan Horse Association
P.O. Box 265
Hamilton, New York 13346

American Paint Horse Association
P.O. Box 12487
Fort Worth, Texas 76116

American Suffolk Horse Association
P.O. Box 421
Olympia, Washington 98501

American Quarter Horse Association
P.O. Box 200
Amarillo, Texas 79105

Appendix

American Saddle Horse Breeders Association, Inc.
929 South Fourth Street
Louisville, Kentucky 40203

Appaloosa Horse Club, Inc.
P.O. Box 640
Moscow, Idaho 83843

Eastern States Dressage Association
P.O. Box 13
Readington, New Jersey 08870

Empire State Horseman's Association
Pound Ridge, New York 10576
Executive Vice President: Mr. J. A. Vanorio

Green Mountain Horse Association
South Woodstock, Vermont 05071

Half-Arab & Anglo-Arab Registries
224 East Olive Avenue
Burbank, California 91503

Horse Protection Association
3316 N Street N.W.
Washington, D.C. 20007

International Arabian Horse Association
224 East Olive Avenue
Burbank, California 91503

International Lippizaner Horse Club
1345 Moffat Avenue
Verdun, Quebec, Canada

The Jockey Club
300 Park Avenue
New York City 10022

The Jockey Club
Data Processing Division (all performance & breeding records, etc.)
P.O. Box 7186
Lexington, Kentucky 40505

260

The Morgan Horse Club, Inc.
P.O. Box 2157
Bishop's Corner Branch
West Hartford, Connecticut 06117

National Appaloosa Pony, Inc.
P.O. Box 297
Rochester, Indiana 46975

National Cutting Horse Association
P.O. Box 12155
4704 Benbrook Highway
Fort Worth, Texas 76116

National Quarter Horse Registry, Inc.
Raywood, Texas 77582

National Steeplechase & Hunt Association
P.O. Box 308
Elmont, New York 11003

National Tennessee Walking Horse Committee
115 Depot Street
Shelbyville, Tennessee 37160

National Trailriders Association, Inc.
2402 North 27th Street
Phoenix, Arizona 85008

The Palomino Horse Association
P.O. Box 446
Reseda, California 91335

The Pinto Horse Association of America, Inc.
P.O. Box 3984
San Diego, California 92103

The Pony of the Americas Club, Inc.
P.O. Box 1447
Mason City, Iowa 50401

The Professional Horseman's Association
R.D. 1–P.O. Box 22
Sewickley, Pennsylvania 15143
Secretary: Mrs. H. B. Black

Appendix

The Quarter Horse Racing Guild
801 South Anaheim Boulevard
Anaheim, California 92805

The Rodeo Cowboys Association, Inc.
320 Boston Building
Denver, Colorado 80202

The Tennessee Walking Horse Breeders Association of America
P.O. Box 286
Lewisburg, Tennessee 37091

The Thoroughbred Racing Association of the United States, Inc.
220 East 42d Street
New York City 10017

United States Combined Training Association
50 Congress Street
Boston, Massachusetts 02109
Attention: Mr. Neil R. Ayer

United States Equestrian Team, Inc.
Gladstone, New Jersey 07934

United States Polo Association
250 Park Avenue
New York City 10017

United States Pony Clubs, Inc.
Pleasant Street
Dover, Massachusetts 02030
Secretary: Mrs. John A. Reidy

United States Trotting Association
750 Michigan Avenue
Columbus, Ohio 43215

The Welsh Pony Society of America
202 North Church Street
West Chester, Pennsylvania 19380
Secretary: Mrs. L. F. Gehret